Social Work Research in Practice

Heather D'Cruz and Martyn Jones

Social Work Research in Practice

Ethical and Political Contexts

2nd Edition

Los Angeles | London | New Delhi
Singapore | Washington DC

Los Angeles | London | New Delhi
Singapore | Washington DC

SAGE Publications Ltd
1 Oliver's Yard
55 City Road
London EC1Y 1SP

SAGE Publications Inc.
2455 Teller Road
Thousand Oaks, California 91320

SAGE Publications India Pvt Ltd
B 1/I 1 Mohan Cooperative Industrial Area
Mathura Road
New Delhi 110 044

SAGE Publications Asia-Pacific Pte Ltd
3 Church Street
#10-04 Samsung Hub
Singapore 049483

Editor: Alice Oven
Assistant editor: Emma Milman
Production editor: Katie Forsythe
Copyeditor: Sarah Bury
Proofreader: Sarah Cooke
Indexer: Judith Lavender
Marketing manager: Tamara Navaratnam
Cover design: Lisa Harper
Typeset by: C&M Digitals (P) Ltd, Chennai, India
Printed by CPI Group (UK) Ltd, Croydon, CR0 4YY

Library of Congress Control Number: 2012956001

British Library Cataloguing in Publication data

A catalogue record for this book is available from
the British Library

ISBN 978-1-4462-0078-0
ISBN 978-1-4462-0079-7 (pbk)

In Memoriam
Daphne Monica D'Cruz (née Doggett) (1931–2007)
James Joseph D'Cruz (1927–2012)

To
Penny, Ben and Hannah

Contents

About the Authors

Dr Heather D'Cruz was employed in Australian public sector organizations (1979–1996) and as an academic at various Australian universities (1996–2009). More recently, she was an Adjunct Research Associate, Centre for Human Rights Education, Curtin University, Western Australia (2010–2012). Heather's research interests are in child and family policy and practice, and identity, diversity and inclusivity. She is the author of *Constructing Meanings and Identities in Child Protection Practice* (2004, Tertiary Press, Australia). She is also a co-editor (with Struan Jacobs and Adrian Schoo) of *Knowledge-in-Practice in the Caring Professions: Multi-disciplinary Perspectives* (2009, Ashgate, UK), and (with Margaret Kumar and Niranjala Weerakkody) of *Where are you From? Voices in Transition* (2010, Common Ground Publishers, Altona, Australia). She was an invited Visiting Leverhulme Fellow (2007–2008), sponsored by the University of Salford, UK.

Associate Professor Martyn Jones is Associate Dean (Human Services) in the School of Global, Urban and Social Studies at RMIT University, Melbourne, Australia. He was employed previously in social work education at Deakin University, Australia and at Exeter University in the UK. Martyn has had a long-term interest in the relation between research and practice in social work, and the potential benefits for marginalized populations. His current academic pursuits include the changing contexts of human service practice, and models of collaborative knowledge exchange.

Acknowledgements

The original book published in 2004 was based on print study materials (*Social Work Practice Research A: Study Guide and Reader*, © Deakin University). This new edition is substantially different in content, although the overall theme of the ethical and political dimensions of social work research remains constant. We would like to acknowledge Deakin University for their encouragement and interest in this new edition. We would also like to thank colleagues in Australia and overseas who have provided constructive feedback and encouragement of our ideas over the years. We would like to thank our students, without whom many of the developments in this text would not have emerged in our quest to make research interesting, engaging and practical. We extend special thanks to Struan Jacobs for his unstinting help and willingness to wade through lengthy drafts of some chapters and offer scholarly advice. We are appreciative of the support and encouragement from our editors at Sage, London, especially Emma Milman, who has been with us throughout the process. Finally, we are grateful to have survived this marathon, through family bereavements, significant health crises, and the multiple demands of academia in the twenty-first century. Completion would not have been possible without the affirming presence of family, friends, and companions.

Heather D'Cruz and Martyn Jones

October 2013

Preface

This book is an update of the book that was first published in 2004. Based on both formal and unsolicited feedback we have received over the years, we have kept to the structure and themes from the first book, the overarching theme being that of addressing different ways of knowing, and the associated ethical and political issues for social work research. However, we have updated the examples (case studies and most activities) and revised the content in line with current issues for the social work profession and for social work research. In particular, we have included new material on indigenous peoples' knowledge, related to colonisation by settlement and by globalization. We have also included new material on research with children as participants.

While we have updated most of the references, we have also kept key sources that may be 'old', but are foundational and classically helpful. We have included recent publications in the Further Reading at the end of each chapter, and a dedicated website for some chapters with additional links to useful materials. We would also recommend the references that we cite as useful sources for you to read.

In overview, this book has never been, nor is it now, a book on the technicalities of how to do research. There are many excellent and substantial texts that are about methods, and we refer to them. While our book provides an overview of each stage of the research process and is organized accordingly, its focus is on the ethical and political issues that need to be considered when engaging in research and, in particular, how these relate to different ways of knowing. Chapter 1 sets the scene and restates our aims in relation to social work research as a method in social work to address professional concerns. Chapter 2 gets you started by looking at deciding on research questions and their relevance for social work. Chapters 5 to 8 are about managing different ways of knowing across design and methods (including conceptual frameworks, data generation and analysis, and disseminating research outcomes). Chapters 3 and 4 provide the conceptual basis for this.

Our approach is to provide a conceptual framework and set of principles for practising social work research ethically with an emancipatory ethos. Because each research project is particular in its conceptual approach, aims, design, and context, we cannot provide you with 'solutions' to many of the ethical and political issues that arise due to different ways of knowing. We do offer a number of 'Activities', which include case studies and examples to illustrate some of these issues and to draw your attention to them, and to familiarize you with how to think them through, supported by the content in each chapter. Our intention is to introduce an approach to research that is about *how to think*, not what to think.

This new edition is timely. Over the past decade there has been growing attention to both the practice–research relationship in social work and questions of power and ethics in knowledge-making, shaped greatly by the onward march of neo-liberalism. The sense of moral mission that imbues social work, together with the profession's concern to ensure its practitioners are appropriately knowledgeable, does indeed place social work at the meeting point of complex, contemporary puzzles concerning the nature and purpose of professional practice. We need to learn how to be thoughtful about this and to beware of easy answers and off-the-shelf recipes. By appreciating the ethics and politics of constructing and deploying different 'ways of knowing', we are more likely to remain vigilant about the contribution that our professional practice makes to the social values we proclaim.

Research can be done competently or incompetently, but we hope to show how it involves so much more than the acquisition of research skills. Herein lie the risks of gauging the quality of professional practice through checklists of 'capabilities' or 'standards'. However carefully constructed, these descriptors tend to reduce complex professional achievements to rather formulaic prose, along the lines of recognising the contribution of research to inform practice. We believe that the learning this text encourages will assist you as a graduating or experienced social worker to perform the research-related aspects of the Professional Capabilities Framework developed by the Social Work Reform Board and applying in England, or the Practice Standards as defined by the Australian Association of Social Workers, or your equivalent elsewhere. Whilst aware of the expectations for 'good professional practice' in research as communicated in such frameworks, we have not designed this book explicitly around them. Nevertheless, by the time you reach the end of the book, you will have a much better appreciation of what lies behind these research-related capabilities and standards, and the kind of thinking that needs to be brought to them.

We hope you will enjoy engaging with the challenges that this book represents. Our interest in and commitment to research is long lived. We have seen how the past decade has opened up more doors for research to find its place in social work. How it does so into the future will in great measure depend on the ethical and political positioning of its practitioners. We trust that you will find the new edition as helpful as the first in grappling with the conceptual and moral questions that are at the heart of social work research.

Heather D'Cruz and Martyn Jones
2013

Additional Online Material

The web page for this book has a number of extra resources for readers to refer to. These include case studies, weblinks, and lists of further reading resources. Look out for the weblink icon in the text to see where additional material is available.

 Visit www.sagepub.co.uk/dcruzjones to find the extra material.

1

Research, Social Work and Professional Practice

Introduction

For the new edition of this book, we have slightly changed the book's title to *Social Work Research in Practice: Ethical and Political Contexts.* We believe that by adding 'in practice' to the title, we more clearly reflect our view that social work research is another social work method or approach, in addition to the more well-known case, group, and community work that are seen by some people as 'real' social work.

Our book is intended as a practical guide to negotiating the ethical and political issues associated with different ways of knowing in social work research. We aim to show that social work research, like all social work practice, has to recognize the importance of ethical and political contexts that influence practice. We show how social work research, along with other practice approaches, can realize the emancipatory goals and objectives of social work. We look at how research can improve practice. We take the approach that practice as direct service to clients may inform important research questions about the effectiveness and appropriateness of policies that shape social work practice and service delivery. Our approach shows how to practice research in anti-oppressive ways, so we do not have a separate chapter on anti-oppressive research.

However, in addition to changing the title of our book to better emphasize our interest in the emancipatory aims of social work achieved through research, in this new edition we also include important developments in the social work that have emerged since 2004 when the first edition of our book was published. These developments include:

- participatory research practice that involves service users, including a specific application as child-centred research
- evidence-based practice that emerged in health and medicine and is now a commonly used concept in social work, and associated debates that incorporate different ways of knowing
- multidisciplinary professional practice that usually involves different ways of knowing, and approaches to 'evidence' as legitimate knowledge, with implications for research

Fundamentally, these additional dimensions consider what knowledge-for-practice is, how it may be generated, what is considered to be legitimate ways of knowing and generating such knowledge for practice: all of these issues underlie research as an approach to social work practice (D'Cruz, 2009: 70–73). We aim to show how social work research is an important way of contributing to social work theory and knowledge. Finally, we hope that, as a result of reading this book, you will start to appreciate and understand social work research and even become passionate about it!

Challenges in teaching, learning and doing research

The aims of this book and the approach taken are a way of addressing some of the fears and misconceptions that may exist among many social work students and also practitioners with regard to research. The general aversion to social work research is almost a standing joke, coming from knowledge of our own student days, much shared knowledge by social work educators, and our own experiences of teaching social work research. Such attitudes have not changed over the years, with familiar descriptions given by many social work educators of students 'bad-mouthing' research (Epstein, 1987: 1) and students and practitioners having 'a phobia' (Marlow, 2011: 2) about research. These attitudes are based on much misinformation, for example, that research is only about 'numbers' or that it is 'cold and impersonal'. For some social workers and students, research is simply 'an added complication to their everyday working lives' (Gibbs and Stirling, 2010: 441).

Aside from the aversion that some social work students and practitioners have to learning and doing social work research, we have also noticed that the processes of learning and doing research pose particular challenges. Social workers are familiar with the mantra of 'applying theory to practice', and there is a considerable literature that investigates the connections between knowledge-for-practice and knowledge-in-practice in social work as well as other 'helping professions', such as nursing, medicine, and psychiatry (D'Cruz, Jacobs and Schoo, 2009a; Greenberg, 2009; Hardy and Smith, 2008; Higgs et al., 2004; Holmes, 2009).

We believe that learning and doing in research is challenging for social workers who tend to work inductively – from the specific and practical back to the theory in their actual practice (Healy, 2000: 145–147). Social work research therefore represents the application of abstract and general concepts ('theory') in specific research projects ('practice') in a way that differs from what is easier and more familiar for most social workers. For research as a practice method, you must first know and understand the different dimensions of research, why they are important, related concepts, and how and when to apply concepts in your own research. This is what applying theory to practice means – without losing sight of the necessity for questioning when formal theories do not adequately apply to practice. This means that even if one learns the prescribed ways of doing research and the concepts described in research texts, quite often one's own research challenges some of these received ideas because of the special and particular circumstances of the chosen project. For example, you may want to collaborate doing research with people with disabilities – which may require you to develop appropriate methodologies to achieve this (see Stevenson, 2010) – by drawing on what is already known and modifying it with the guidance of expert advisers, which includes the group of research participants (Pitts and Smith, 2007).

We teach research to social work students because we believe that social work practice is more likely to be effective when social workers are able to draw on and evaluate previous research. We hope to encourage and assist social workers to conduct their own research to answer those questions arising in their practice that cannot be answered by the existing literature. By the end of this chapter, we hope that you will recognize the importance of research for social work practice. By the end of the book, you should be able to read and critique the social work research literature and develop your ideas about how you might answer the questions that arise for you in your professional practice. There is potential for social work research to evaluate the effectiveness and appropriateness of this or that policy in addressing the problems that particular groups may experience, such as (un)employment, income support, child welfare and health, asylum seekers and refugees, aged care, disability support services (Fawcett et al., 2010: 143–158). Here are some examples of research conducted by social workers:

- 'Understanding resilience in South Australian farm families' (Greenhill et al., 2009)
- 'Conceptualising the mental health of rural women: A social work and health promotion perspective' (Harvey, 2009)
- 'Perspectives of young people in care about their school-to-work transition' (Tilbury et al., 2009)

- '"You've got to be a saint to be a social worker". The (mis)operation of fitness to practise processes for students already registered onto English social work training programmes' (McLaughlin, 2010)
- 'Women with cognitive impairment and unplanned or unwanted pregnancy: A 2-year audit of women contacting the Pregnancy Advisory Service' (Burgen, 2010)
- 'Life story work and social work practice: A case study with ex-prisoners labelled as having an intellectual disability' (Ellem and Wilson, 2010)
- 'Using vignettes to evaluate the outcomes of student learning: Data from the evaluation of the new social work degree in England' (MacIntyre et al., 2011)

Apart from informing practice and policy change as an immediate concern, research also contributes to social work theory and knowledge-for-practice (Adams et al., 2005; Lyons and Taylor, 2004; Powell et al., 2004), in a complex relationship.

Depending on the aims of the research and the methods used, you can investigate structural patterns of distribution of resources, rewards, opportunities, and burdens, for example, gender pay equity or comparing the health and wellbeing indicators for indigenous (First Nations) peoples and non-indigenous people in the community. You can also investigate the situated patterns of such structural distributions: whether and how individuals within such identity categories as 'women', 'men', 'indigenous', 'non-indigenous' experience such inequalities in their daily lives; how they may explain their experiences; how their experiences may differ from or be the same as the structural patterns; and how they may resist, subvert, and otherwise transform situated patterns of privilege and inequality. In short, research can allow us to appreciate structural patterns of human experience and also contribute to understanding the diversity of human experiences, with the approaches being complementary rather than oppositional (Hurley, 2007). However, to achieve appropriate recognition from decision makers, we must make sure that our research is of high quality and is intellectually rigorous.

What is research?

In our experience, many social work students (and practitioners) reject research because of particular images they have of research and researchers. Before reading any further, you may like to spend a few minutes on the exercise below. This exercise is intended to exorcise any demons associated with the word 'research' and explore ways of engaging with what you might enjoy about it.

Exercise: Exorcising the demons and becoming enchanted with research

1 Write the word 'research' on a piece of paper. Underneath it write down all the 'scary thoughts' that come to mind when you think about 'doing research'. Now write down any positive thoughts you may also have in a separate list.

2 Next, think about how you will approach the following task. You think you may be eligible for some welfare, education or housing benefits (for example, social security, money to assist you to study, rent assistance) provided by the government or private organizations. How will you go about finding out about what is available and whether or not you are eligible to receive these benefits? Write down the steps you will take.

3 Now think about another process you used to find out more about something you had limited knowledge of previously. Write down what you did to find out about it.

4 Look at the headings or descriptions you have given to the processes of enquiry in these two examples. (Remember, we are looking at what you did – that is, the *process*, not the specific *content*, of the enquiry. The aim is to be able to see some equivalence between the steps we take to solve problems of limited knowledge as everyday practices and those linked with the more formal processes called 'research'.)

5 Do you see any ways in which you can translate the headings you gave to your processes of enquiry into the more formal language of social research? You may be familiar with some of these formal concepts already. Alternatively, you may want to browse through the later chapters in this book where these concepts appear. Don't worry if these connections are not immediately apparent. They will become clearer as you engage with and reflect on what we discuss in later chapters. We also encourage you to discuss your ideas with peers and friends.

6 Now write down the word 'enquiry' and the positive and negative meanings associated with it. How might the word 'enquiry' be related to the word 'research'? How might you 'control the demons' (if you have any) and maximize the positive meanings associated with the word 'research'?

7 Keep these thoughts as a starting point against which to review your engagement with this subject as you read and use this book.

We have used this exercise to introduce you to some of the processes we already use to live in daily life. 'We are surrounded by research', for example, to raise children, reduce crime, improve public health, and evaluate public policies (Neuman, 2006: 1). We want to show you that research does not have to be anxiety-provoking, involving complicated statistics, computers, or large amounts of resources. However, at the same time, research does require us to be systematic and thoughtful; to be able to think critically; to be reflective on what we know, how we know, and why we want to know; and to be prepared to change our minds if research outcomes offer new insights. Just because 'authority', 'tradition', 'common sense', or 'personal experience' have previously informed us (Neuman, 2006: 2–7), it does not mean that we have trustworthy information. This book adds to these dimensions, the ethical and political complexities associated with different ways of knowing that involve competing claims for what is 'trustworthy' knowledge.

The connections between social work research, practice and theory

While the activity you have done and the related discussion suggest that research is 'seeking knowledge for a purpose', we want to extend this to incorporate the ethical and political dimensions that are essential to social work research. In recent years, social work research has become an important part of social work qualifying degrees and continuing professional education for practitioners (Australian Association of Social Workers (AASW), 2003, 2012; Humphries, 2008: 2; International Association of Schools of Social Work (IASSW), 2001; The College of Social Work (TCSW) (England), 2012). This development is partly a response to government and organizational demands for 'evidence', as 'useful and relevant knowledge' (Humphries, 2008: 2) to support policy development and to inform professional practice (Fawcett et al., 2010: 145–153). It is also a recognition by the social work profession internationally that research is an important method of generating knowledge-for-practice as 'evidence' of 'what works' (Smith, 2009: 37–53), as well as developing theories for practice (IASSW, 2001; Powell et al., 2004). Therefore, the idea of 'research-mindedness' (Everitt, 2008; Humphries, 2008; Institute for Research and Innovation in Social Services (IRISS), 2011–12) has become a key competency for all social workers and is supported by resources such as those on the IRISS (2011–12) website.

However, Humphries (2008: 3) goes on to raise the debates also associated with being research-minded, including what is 'knowledge'; what is research and in whose interests it is conducted; the hierarchy of knowledge; instrumental versus political knowledge; and extends this to include ethics and justice as a set of principles:

- participatory/developmental model of social work, as opposed to a social control model;
- anti-oppressive values;
- striving towards a genuine partnership between practitioners and those who [sic] they serve (Humphries, 2008: 3–4, citing Campling's foreword to Everitt et al., 1992: vii).

You might notice that these valued principles for social work research are not at all different from those informing other areas of social work practice; for example, where social work researchers advocate 'empowerment' of clients as a purpose of research (Marlow, 2011: 21–22; McLaughlin, 2012; Smith, 2009), consistent with anti-oppressive practice.

As applied to social work research, these principles mean that clients are not treated as objects or exploited for their experiential knowledge, particularly when they are often vulnerable and relatively powerless. Instead, these principles validate different ways of 'knowing', which are shared and made explicit as much as possible in the interaction between 'researcher' and 'informant', also referred to as 'participant' to better reflect the espoused collaborative nature of the research process. Subjectivity, as personal experience and worldviews, is also valued and understood as being integral to knowledge gained in the research process. Taken together, you might begin to see some validity to our earlier claim that social work research is another method that can help achieve social work's emancipatory objectives.

Professionalism and research in social work

The human services professions have been subject to many contemporary contextual changes. These include changing welfare regimes, new systems of public management, transformations in communications and information technologies, the impacts of globalization and internationalization, the influence of new social movements and post-colonialism, and so on (O'Connor et al., 2008). Consequently, they are confronted with sustaining a viable professionalism both in respect of the clientele they claim to serve and their organizational locations.

As well as understanding research to be a crucial component in the practice of social work, whether that is in direct service provision or policy development, it can also be seen to be significant when it comes to the question of professionalism. In many respects, controversies that surround claims of professionalism on the part of social work are played out in the way research is or isn't held to be relevant and necessary. Of course, these controversies are very much concerned with the place of knowledge and power in professions. As such, they also point to the need to examine the ethical and political dimensions of research and explore the implications for different kinds of professionalism to which social work might lay claim.

For some, the link between research and professionalism in social work has been very clear, particularly in contemporary contexts where managerialism and control may silence criticism of organizational and policy influences on

practice and the effectiveness of interventions. The introduction of performance management strategies within the public services generally, for example,
now requires compliance with predetermined standards. These standards will
have variously to do with criteria such as efficiency, quality and effectiveness.
The production of such standards may or may not have been informed by studies that have sought to evaluate programmes and performance. Professionalism
in this context could then well become associated with the appropriation of
research to generate standards by means of the systematic evaluation of a given
programme or performance. Professional behaviour would then be monitored
for compliance with these standards, such that research knowledge has become
part of the organizational governance system, for example, as Plath (2012)
describes in a case study of how organizations use 'evidence' to guide policy
and practice.

Additionally, there are increasing expectations for multidisciplinary and inter-
professional practice including research (D'Cruz, Jacobs and Schoo, 2009a), to
improve services to clients through different perspectives on multifaceted and
multicausal problems (e.g. Atwal and Caldwell, 2006; Corner, 2003; Miller,
2009; National Committee for the Prevention of Elder Abuse, n.d.; Salmon,
1994; van Norman, 1998; Woolnough, Arkell with Tobias, 2010). Although
there are clear benefits for multidisciplinary approaches to professional
knowledge-for and -in practice, there are also tensions associated with different ways of knowing in professional teams (D'Cruz et al., 2009b; Holmes,
2009: 63–65; Lawn and Battersby, 2009; Sheean and Cameron, 2009; Smith
et al., 2009). It is important to contextualize the contribution of research as it
occurs in each of these respects.

The growth of interest in evidence-based practice within human services
is a further example of the way in which professional, organizational and
policy agendas can combine to develop a strategic direction for research and
practice that supposedly meets a number of needs (Smith, 2009: 17–34). For
some, evidence-based practice represents an overdue 'coming of age' for the
social work profession, one in which it can legitimate its place not so much
by exhorting social values (or ideologies) but by the irrefutable evidence of
its effectiveness and utility (Sheldon, 1998, 2000, 2001). For others, evidence-
based practice is an unavoidable and not unattractive pathway to gaining
credibility for the profession with key stakeholders and a necessary development in sustaining and promoting its contribution (see Sheldon and Chilvers,
2000). A fit has also been noted between the liberal individualism that under-
pins both contemporary public policy and those professional activities most
amenable to being evaluated on 'hard evidence' (Howe, 1997; Humphries,
2008: 4–6). Fundamentally, debates about evidence-based practice relate to
what social work knowledge-for-practice is, and includes questions about

what is knowledge, what constitutes evidence, and how we may best derive such evidence for professional knowledge (Butler and Pugh, 2004; Dominelli, 2005; Fawcett et al., 2010: 143–147; McLaughlin, 2007; Smith, 2009: 49–53; Webb, 2001). What is increasingly important is that social workers should make connections between 'the academy' and 'the field', formal theory and research, and practice-generated theories and practice-based research, which includes service users' perspectives, as bases for social work knowledge-for-practice (D'Cruz, 2009: 69–73).

The effective pursuit of equality is seen as dependent on a properly informed analysis prior to action. While social values and goals still drive the professional agenda, research enters as a vital part of the professional repertoire in directing efforts towards these ends. Moreover, the reference points that can come from research are construed as important in sustaining purposeful action that might otherwise become diverted or misplaced (Humphries, 2008; McLaughlin, 2012; Shaw, 2005; Smith, 2009).

The research-minded practitioner asks questions such as:

- Does it work?
- Does it achieve what was intended?
- Is it worthwhile?
- Is it worth the resources, money and time?
- Is it 'good'?
- Is it 'bad'?
- Is it 'good enough'? (Everitt, 2008: 26)

Research as an antidote to the 'taken-for-granted' is a common theme in discussions of its contribution to professionalism. Whether it is preparedness to 'think the unthinkable' or show 'uncommon common sense', research is presented as a safeguard against practice becoming a matter of routine, or proceeding on the basis of unexamined assumptions (Humphries, 2008: 4–6; Rubin and Babbie, 2007: 3–20).

If we consider research in terms of its capacity to invigorate and inform professional behaviour, then we might begin to list some of the ways in which this could become manifest. Here are some examples of the contributions of research in this respect, which are to:

- add to the sum of our knowledge
- address a specific issue of concern
- find out what our clients think of our services
- ascertain social needs in a particular area
- develop a submission
- influence policymakers
- organize people

- translate individual needs into a social voice
- give vulnerable, hidden and unheard people a voice
- change the ways in which things are done
- evaluate and improve services
- develop and test new interventions (Everitt, 2008; Fawcett et al., 2010: 145–158; Marlow, 2011; Smith, 2009)

Running through these ideas about research and professionalism is the assumption that knowledge generated as a result of research can challenge existing practices and policies and help keep the profession up to date by continually improving its services for the public good. The suggestion, then, is that professionalism, and the survival of a professional group, is dependent at least to some degree on being responsive to new and changing situations, and is innovative in the form and nature of the expertise it claims to offer.

Processes for generating and managing knowledge within the organizational and policy spheres of public services are significant for understanding the emerging relationships between professionalism and research (Jones, 2004; Powell et al., 2004). Of course, new technologies are texturing these processes in particular ways and becoming part of the emerging politics and ethics of knowledge and research. Meanwhile, concurrent contextual changes are substantively affecting definitions and purposes of professionalism with regard to its relationship with service clientele. When hierarchical models of professional expertise are aligned with colonizing patterns of Western society, new versions of professionalism are required if the credibility of the human services within an anti-colonialist context is to be sustained (Ife, 2001). This, too, has immediate consequences for understanding research politics and ethics, if research is to remain a constituent and vibrant feature of the new professionalism. An appreciation of diverse paradigms (ways of knowing) and methodologies (ways of building knowledge) can assist the contribution of research to the kinds of critically aware professionalism required to meet the array of contemporary challenges for social work.

Critical thinking, reflexivity and research

Research, it has been suggested, involves 'thinking systematically'. As we undertake research, we engage with an array of information that arises from our interaction with books, journals, files, databases, participants, colleagues, agencies, and so on. The orderly generation and processing of information demands of us an intellectual discipline that extends our everyday capacities for doing just that. An important aspect of this intellectual discipline concerns critical thinking.

There are several traditions of critical thinking in Western societies, all of which have implications for the conduct of social work research and practice. Perhaps the most dominant has been that associated with philosophical branches of argumentation and reasoning:

> Critical reasoning is centrally concerned with giving reasons for one's beliefs and actions, analysing and evaluating one's own and other people's reasoning, devising and constructing better reasoning. Common to these activities are certain discrete skills, for example, recognizing reasons and conclusions, recognizing unstated assumptions, drawing conclusions, appraising evidence and evaluating statements, judging whether conclusions are warranted; and underlying all of these skills is the ability to use language with clarity and discrimination. (Thomson, 1996: 2)

This variety of critical thinking has found its place in social work research as a result of attempts to introduce the tenets of 'scientific reasoning' into the ways practitioners might appraise knowledge in everyday practice. Neuman (2006: 2–7) discusses how reasoning might be improved by learning how to spot common fallacies and ways of knowing, as 'alternatives to research' that are common to our daily lives. These alternatives, which exert significant influence on the beliefs we hold strongly include 'authority' and 'tradition' (parents, teachers and experts), 'common sense', 'media myths', and 'personal experience'. While such approaches to everyday knowledge may be a personal choice, for social work practice they may not offer sound knowledge about the effectiveness of particular interventions, or the harm that may be an unanticipated consequence, while aiming to solve perceived problems. Some examples include the negative outcomes associated with the placement of children in foster care, even if for their protection (Erera, 2002: 46–47), or the additional stress caused to children in investigations for 'sexual abuse' (Davis, 2005). Similarly, the attention to 'confounders' (Gibbs, 1991) is seen to provide a safeguard against drawing dubious conclusions about the relationship between interventions and outcomes by highlighting flaws in causal reasoning (see also Neuman, 2006: 63–69). Logical thinking and formal scientific method become the way to advance the state of knowledge in practice, although we have a broader view of 'science' as systematic, disinterested, open-minded, honest, and critical thinking (Marlow, 2011: 6–7) rather than experimental, laboratory-based research.

The added dimension now current within critical thinking concerns the place of critical reflection and reflexivity. In attending to processes of thinking, critical reflection is also concerned with 'the thinker' but locates subjectivities particularly within socio-political contexts. There is still very much a hunt for assumptions, but now it is to do with how they shape the way we construct problems, needs, issues and so on, and a critical appraisal of what those assumptions might tell us about the contexts and histories of which we are a part (Grbich, 2007: 17–18).

While such explorations take us into personal, experiential realms, they imply the capacity to become not just more self-aware, but socially self-aware (Fook, 1999). Within this approach, our contributions to knowledge-building via research would be seen as embedded within the everyday construction of sets of beliefs and practices ('discourses'), where claims to legitimacy have to do with the subtle and not so subtle exercise of power. Here, the concept of reflexivity assists in sustaining a sense of agency (a capacity to act purposefully) within this complicated process of knowledge construction.

Reflexivity works with the idea that knowledge 'is made rather than revealed' (Taylor and White, 2000: 199). In practising reflexively, we become directly concerned with 'the constructedness of all claims, including our own' (Hall, 1997: 250, cited in Taylor and White, 2000: 199). Such a view accentuates rather than dilutes our responsibilities as knowledge makers. It requires us to consider how power is exercised in the knowledge-making processes in which we engage. Furthermore, locating ourselves within these operations of power is seen as an intensely moral action. Reflexivity suggests that we cannot find refuge from moral responsibility by following principles of good research practice. The principles are not inviolate, but sustained by the success of the discourses in which they are embedded and are there to be continually scrutinized. Meanwhile, research practice necessitates the interpretation and reconstruction of principles amid competing imperatives, occurring within complicated and contradictory social contexts that more often than not render simple rule-following redundant.

This kind of approach to research can make life difficult. It is a cautionary antidote to the false certainties sometimes evident in research textbooks that seem to imply we can learn how to do research by learning a new set of techniques. Of course, the plethora of techniques that have become part of research tradition within Western societies are there to be learned and their associated skills acquired. Yet, research cannot be spared the debates that have entered into the examination of social practices. Inasmuch as we conceive research as being a social practice concerned explicitly with the generation of knowledge, we will have to contend with difficult questions concerning the political and ethical dimensions of our knowledge making.

Social work research as a social practice

If we were to make social work research itself the subject of research enquiry, what are some of the questions we might pose? We might find ourselves asking some of the following, for example:

- Who carries out research?
- Who decides what is to be researched?
- Where do the resources (time and money) for research come from?
- What permissions are obtained in order for research to proceed?
- What in practice do researchers do?
- Who reads reports of research?
- What influence does research have?
- Who benefits from research?

By asking questions such as these, we are led to enquiries concerning the social organization, political economy and professionalization of research, and the sociology of research knowledge, and so on. In other words, we can view social work research as a social practice. How we understand it as a social practice will depend very much on the perspectives we employ.

Viewing research through a liberal lens, for instance, we might understand the social role of the researcher as that of an independent investigator who follows certain codes of conduct and professionally endorsed techniques to produce new knowledge. This knowledge is then put at the disposal of others (policymakers, practitioners, industries, communities) to act on or not, as they see fit. Viewing research through a radical lens, we might construe the researcher as being a social actor whose activities are party to the reproduction and/or transformation of existing social relationships of exclusion or inclusion, domination or oppression. Both processes and outcomes of knowledge production are then considered contributors to social change, and actions weighed accordingly.

As a social practice, we would expect networks to form among like-minded researchers and movements to develop that advocate for their preferred approach to research. It has been commonplace to refer to the 'paradigm wars' that have beset social research in recent decades (Denzin and Lincoln, 2011: 1, 15 (note 2)). The emergence of evidence-based practice in social welfare has triggered another site of antagonism. User movements have been pursuing the agenda of empowerment in social work research (Beresford, 2000; Braye et al., 2008). Indigenous groups have increasingly promoted consciousness of the colonial history of research, with implications for not only greater cultural sensitivity but also a fundamental rethink of the tenets and methodologies of Western research practices (Smith, 1999, 2005).

In some respects, this suggests that social work research is beset by a series of dilemmas and the erstwhile researcher has to determine where they stand on a number of political and ethical issues before they can proceed. In a cogent critique of 'critical' social research, Hammersley (1995) has warned of the pitfalls of conflating the pursuit of political goals with the activity of research and, particularly, questions the philosophical presuppositions of those who seek to change oppressive social structures by means of research praxis.

Similarly, Rubin and Babbie (2007: 50–53, 2008: 90–94), writing specifically about social work research and the place of politics and values, comment on how politics and ethics intersect and also differ in social (work) research.

> Although ethics and politics are often closely intertwined, the ethics of social work research deals more with the methods employed, whereas political issues are more concerned with the practical costs and use of research. (Rubin and Babbie, 2007: 50)

Writing in the US context, they discuss three case studies (Coleman, 1966; Herrnstein and Murray, 1994; Jensen, 1969), aiming to show how 'nowhere have social research and politics been more controversially intertwined than in the area of race relations' (Rubin and Babbie, 2007: 51–52, 2008: 92–93). Rubin and Babbie imply that such studies should be critiqued solely according to 'scientific, methodological grounds', not political ones (2007: 52, 2008: 93); although we ask whether methodologies can be seen as neutral of their assumptions and therefore the questions that are asked and how they are researched. We ask whether researchers can claim innocence due to claims of neutrality and whether it is possible to investigate social phenomena dispassionately as we do not want to censor alternative or uncomfortable views.

In accentuating social work research as a political and ethical practice, this book presents a rather different way forward. We shall be echoing the sentiments expressed by Fook (2000, 2002), who has argued for an open, inclusive and flexible approach to social work research. Our approach tries to take cognizance of the complicated, changing and uncertain contexts with (and within) which research occurs. Admitting diversity into our practices creates greater possibilities for effective and responsive research.

As Fook (2000: 2) puts it:

> A rigid, or even loose, commitment to one type of perspective, be it positivist, qualitative or deconstructive, does not seem to provide the flexibility of thinking needed to work in changing circumstances.

Yet, as Fook also points out, this could lead to the idea that anything goes and, consequently, she defines a crucial issue: 'can we develop an approach which allows us openness, but also builds upon and uses established methods of working?' (2000: 2). As we shall try to show, inclusivity in research is not the same as a 'free for all' or even an eclectic outlook. Rather, it sees all perspectives and methods as a product of time and place and lacking intrinsic properties that could determine whether or not they are right and appropriate in isolation from the contexts of their application. Embedding themselves and their research practices within emerging and contingent contexts, the critical researcher adopting an inclusive approach will understand knowledge and skills in research as resources to be 'used in a meaningful yet flexible way to suit the situation at hand' (Fook, 2000: 2). Such judgements of suitability will engage the researcher in political and ethical, as well as technical, considerations, but in none of these domains can the researcher rely on pre-existing sets of principles or rules to tell them what is to be done.

The organization of the book

This chapter has explored conceptions held of social work research and suggested an alternative framing as social enquiry. It has introduced the relevance of research to social work and suggested how it is integral to the historic missions of the profession.

The book follows sequentially the major stages of the research process. The eight chapters emanate from the following key questions.

- What is the relevance of research to social work?
- What do I want to know more about?
- How might I answer my research question?
- How do I make sense of my data so that I can answer my research question?
- How do I pull all this together and communicate it to others?

This first chapter has also outlined the political and ethical dimensions of social work research and developed these by considering research as a social practice concerned with knowledge making. Chapter 2 determines a focus for research and a research question(s) as this represents the beginning of the process. Chapter 3 examines how knowledge involves different ways of knowing, as perspectives on and assumptions about the world, with particular practical, ethical and political implications. Evidence-based practice is a particular example of such debates, as different ways of knowing encapsulating assumptions about what constitutes legitimate knowledge and how one generates such knowledge for professional practice.

Chapters 4, 5, 6 and 7 look at the matter of answering research questions. This starts with a consideration of methodology, in Chapter 4, as the ways in which we might go about making knowledge. Chapter 5 discusses the more practical task of creating an appropriate plan or design for pursuing research question(s). Additionally, we look at ethical practice in social work research, particularly in regard to participatory and child-centred approaches. Chapter 6 examines specific methods for collecting and generating data. We show how methods used and the type of data generated are affected by the degree of structure introduced by the researcher. Chapter 7 addresses the sense making in research. In drawing links with the theoretical and methodological considerations considered earlier, this approach to analysis aims to ensure proper integrity of the research. The final chapter discusses how research is reported and disseminated. It assumes that this is not a neutral exercise, but that communication needs to pay due regard to the perspectives and positions from which reports are, for example, read and written. The book concludes with a last look at research as social practice and the challenges of being a critical and inclusive researcher. Throughout, we show that conceptualizing and conducting research involves political and ethical considerations.

Putting it all together

Social work research is both simpler and more complicated than is sometimes imagined. Considered as an informal process of social enquiry, it is not so far removed from what we find ourselves doing every day when faced with a novel question or situation. If we think of social work as an occupation that is, by and large, dealing with the novel, then we can see how its practitioners find themselves engaging in processes of enquiry as an integral part of their work. In that sense, research is familiar territory, already part of our professional and personal worlds, even if we haven't labelled it as such.

The complexities of research arise as we formalize our processes of enquiry. We have available to us a rich resource about the doing of research that offers us more rigorous and systematic ways of building knowledge. However, we need to remain conscious that the knowledge we generate by using these more formal approaches represents particular ways of knowing. Opening the doors of research means accessing discourses that have a certain currency in securing legitimacy for claims to knowledge and truth. In the chapters to come, we shall be introducing accumulated bodies of teaching concerned with building knowledge by means of research practices. Beyond this, however, we shall be presenting research as a social practice, politically and ethically laden, which carries a special responsibility for those who choose to pursue it. We shall, therefore, be extending the idea of a critical researcher, presenting this as someone who is able to draw flexibly and inclusively on a range of research practices according to their appreciation of the situation in hand and the social dimensions of their knowledge making.

Further reading

Everitt, A. (2008) 'Social work research and evaluation: the research-minded practitioner', *Locus SOCI@L*, 1: 24–31.

Fawcett, B., Goodwin, S., Meagher, G. and Phillips, R. (2010) *Social Policy for Social Change*, South Yarra, Victoria: Palgrave Macmillan (Chapter 8).

Humphries, B. (2008) *Social Work Research for Social Justice*, Basingstoke, Hampshire: Palgrave Macmillan (Chapter 1).

Kayrooz, C. and Trevitt, C. (2005) *Research in Organizations and Communities: Tales from the Real World*, Crow's Nest, NSW: Allen & Unwin (Chapter 1).

McLaughlin, H. (2012) *Understanding Social Work Research* (2nd edition), London: Sage (Chapter 1).

2

The Research Question

Introduction

In this chapter, we shall be:

1 Examining the nature of question setting in social work research and attending to the relevance of social contexts in this process.
2 Looking at different kinds of research question, the role that questions play in research, and the various facets of formulating questions.
3 Considering what is involved in conducting a literature review and in reading research critically.
4 Commenting on the implications for research-minded practice.

The impetus for research

Reduced to its most simple, research is about answering questions. Of course, research goes about producing answers in particular ways, ways that are persuasive and credible to research communities and the populations they serve. Yet, this is perhaps a peculiar manifestation of a rather fundamental form of enquiry: generating information to throw light on pressing questions.

There are many ways in which research questions might arise. In social work practice research, it is often the needs or issues that confront us in the course of our work which prompt ideas for research. Then, some personal experience of ours may come into play to give us a special interest. So our imagination might be caught, for example, by any one or more of the following, suggested by Wadsworth (2011: 26–27):

- People are disagreeing strongly about some course of action, program or issue.
- Something is crying out as a known problem to be solved.

- There's a threat to something we want to keep and we need to be able to say what we've observed that is evidence of its value.
- We just have a feeling that something's not as good as it could be.
- We collect a lot of statistics and wonder whether they could tell us more.
- Everyone else is looking at such and such and I thought it might be worth looking at too.
- I desperately need some information to reach a particular decision.
- Complaints have been received about the way we work.
- Something's working so well we'd like to know why!
- There's a possibility of being able to try something new but we don't know what would be best.

You might like to pause here and spend a few minutes on an exercise that invites you to consider what prompts your own ideas for research topics.

Exercise: Prompts for research

- Have you had any ideas about topics or issues that you think should be researched?
- What prompted these ideas?
- Can you identify with any of the prompts listed by Wadsworth?
- What other prompts would you add to this list?

Sometimes, the image of the researcher is of a dispassionate enquirer who can examine a topic with requisite neutrality. While open-mindedness is undoubtedly a desirable quality to bring to any piece of research, Alston and Bowles (2012: 34) are convinced that personal interest is also vital:

> Whatever the path by which you become involved, it is critical that *you* are interested in the topic. Research requires much time and effort. Unless you are curious and interested in the area you are about to research, there is little point in devoting your valuable time and energy (and those of other people) to it. (Original emphasis)

Clearly, our personal interests will to some degree reflect our biographies and identities. If we are to see variety and breadth in the areas that become the subject of social work research, then we need to consider, among other things, what diversity exists among social work researchers. Marlow (2011: 46) has suggested that 'in the past most social work research was conducted by a fairly homogenous group'. While there may now be greater diversity among researchers as regards gender and ethnicity, for example, she points out that most researchers are likely to be of a certain socio-economic status, warning of the strong possibility of research continuing to be conducted by well-educated, middle-class people on less educated, poorer people. We need to be vigilant, then, of the diversity of interests and passions that shape the directions of research.

We shall be examining a range of factors that contribute to the generation of research questions that translate into research endeavour. However, the crucial point remains that research is a time-consuming activity that commonly occurs over months, if not years. A sense of commitment to and enthusiasm for the subject of enquiry is invaluable in maintaining sufficient momentum to ensure satisfactory completion, particularly during those phases when the research process feels arduous, if not impossible. Evidently, at such moments, researching jointly with others who share that commitment and enthusiasm can prove crucial.

Research questions for social work

Social work occurs in many places, involving a range of people and communities, addressing a mix of issues and needs, utilizing a cascade of theories and methods. Inevitably, questions for research reflect this spread of interests and the 'received wisdoms' (Rojek et al., 1988) through which they are construed. Looking for commonalities across these varied interests is a daunting task. One approach is to locate unifying themes not so much in the content areas addressed by social work research but in the broader missions of the profession. Witkin (1995: 427) has put it this way:

> Social work has always struggled with its research identity. Unlike related disciplines such as psychology, sociology and psychiatry, social work has no unique subject matter or methodology. ... What the social work profession does have is a unique commitment to a contextual understanding of people, an explicit value base that emphasizes human rights and human dignity, a commitment to serving marginalized and oppressed people, and a mission to foster a more just society.

While this statement might provide a useful framework when considering the focus and conduct of social work research, it still doesn't tell us too much about the kinds of questions that are posed. In his discussion of designing social research, Blaikie (2009: 17) proposes that all research questions 'can be reduced to three main types: "what", "how" and "why" questions'. In a similar vein, other commentators (Dodd and Epstein, 2012; Marlow, 2011) suggest that social work research is generally oriented around one (or more)

of three strategies: exploratory, descriptive or explanatory. As the name suggests, exploratory research aims to generate knowledge about a relatively
under-researched or newly emerging subject; descriptive research to illuminate the features and extent of the subject; and explanatory research to
develop explanations of a subject. Chapter 5 will consider the implications of
these different types of research question and research strategy for designing
research.

Taking as an example the use of the World Wide Web in forming self-help
groups, if we were to find out that little research had been done on this topic
to date, then we might formulate an exploratory question to help define and
map its main features. Descriptive questions would lead to a more detailed
understanding of perhaps the extent of web-based self-help groups, who uses
them, what for, and how they run. Explanatory questions would start to investigate the impact of self-help groups on those who subscribe, and offer ways
of making sense of their success or otherwise.

An *exploratory* study of 'lesbian battering' in the United States (Renzetti,
1992) included researching the experience of being assaulted, the frequency
and occurrence of this, and the services provided to those involved. In a
study which set out to *describe* the social work role in relation to people in
the Grampians, Scotland, who had a diagnosis of personality disorder, Irvine
(1995: 125) pursued four subsidiary questions:

1 How do these clients arrive at the social work department?
2 What problems do these clients experience?
3 What kinds of work are social workers doing with these clients?
4 How are they doing it?

'In what ways does agency work contribute to positive family change?' was
the key research question in an *evaluative* New Zealand study of the effectiveness of social services interventions in supporting families (Sanders and
Munford, 2003: 153).

According to Marlow, there are two prime areas where these kinds of questions surface in generalist social work. One is in conducting 'needs assessments' and the other is in regard to 'evaluations', either practice or programme
evaluations (2011: 39–43). Needs assessments are likely to be exploratory or
descriptive, assessing the incidence of a particular social issue, for example, or
the extent of certain needs. Evaluations are likely to be descriptive or explanatory. They can be evaluating either the process (looking at the experience of
a service) or the outcome (looking at effectiveness) of a particular piece of
practice or of a programme of work.

While these are evidently two significant areas for research in social work,
they do not represent by any means all types of question that can or might

be posed. The very notion of 'needs assessment' as a category for ordering research is not uncontroversial and immediately raises the issue of how and by whom needs are identified (Packham, 2000). Moreover, in times when the profession and practice of social work is in transformation, much research effort might well focus upon the development of new concepts and models relevant to evolving contexts and tasks (Pease and Fook, 1999). On a somewhat contrasting note, there can also be an emphasis upon questions which seek to ensure the utility value of research (Patton, 1997).

Shifting ideas as to how social work might define and progress its sense of mission will clearly alter the way the contribution of research is viewed, and the kinds of questions that then fall within its remit. For McLaughlin, it is imperative that researchers who embrace an anti-oppressive commitment consider whether the research question driving their research is one that will empower or further oppress particular groups (McLaughlin, 2012: 89). Pease (2010: 104) examines how the transformative agenda of critical research requires social work researchers to 'take sides and embrace the values of promoting social justice and human rights'. From these perspectives, which are aligned to the position adopted in this book, the way we construct the research question will not simply clarify the purpose of our research, it will highlight the political and ethical significance of that purpose.

The role of research questions

When we think about question setting for social work research, we do perhaps immediately concentrate upon the role questions play in orienting us to certain areas of knowledge. In this sense, attending to our research question(s) focuses our attention on the substantive content area, or topic, of our enquiry. Shaw and Norton (2007) elaborate on this through their investigation of the kinds of social work research carried out through UK universities. Their study suggests that topics can generally be classified along two dimensions: the population that comprises the primary research focus (for example, service-user groupings or professional communities) and the primary issue or problem of the research (for example, understanding issues related to risk or to poverty, or assessing the value of interdisciplinary approaches).

We can also think about the role played by 'the question' in terms of its place in the processes and structure of our research activity. Blaikie (2009: 17) is in no doubt that 'research questions constitute the most important element of any research design'. Translating an interesting topic into a researchable question (O'Leary, 2004) is one of the key challenges for the beginning researcher, but it is crucial in laying the foundations for what follows. In a formal sense, research questions are seen as central for these reasons:

- They organise the project, and give it direction and coherence.
- They delimit the project, showing its boundaries.
- They keep the researcher focussed during the project.
- They provide a framework for writing up the project.
- They point to the data that will be needed. (Punch, 1998: 38)

Most people who have attempted even a modest social research project would be able to identify with the experience of 'getting lost on the way' (Punch, 1998: 38). There are many complications and compelling distractions that arise. The research question can provide a relatively constant reference point to help plan and navigate the course.

That said, the impression could be that the researcher determines a question at the outset and sticks rigidly to it no matter what they come across *en route*. Here we encounter the issue over how 'tight' or 'loose' an approach to research is being adopted (Miles and Huberman, 1994: 16). The issue has been presented in this way:

> The central comparison is between research which is pre-specified (or pre-planned, or prefigured, or predetermined) on the one hand, and research which is unfolding (or emerging, or open-ended) on the other. … At [one] end of the continuum, specific research questions are set up in advance to guide the study. It is quite clear, in advance, what questions the study is trying to answer. At the [other] end, only general questions are set up in advance. The argument is that, until some empirical work is carried out, it is not possible (or, if possible, not sensible) to identify specific research questions. They will only become clear as the research unfolds, and as a specific focus for the work is developed. (Punch, 1998: 23, 24)

We shall be looking further into the structuring of research when we consider research design. Generally, however, explanatory research would tend to be found towards the 'tight' end of the continuum and exploratory research more towards the 'loose' end – with descriptive research frequently moving between the two.

Explanatory studies, being informed largely by paradigms associated with 'scientific method', aim for specificity of the research question at the outset. Pursuing this in linear fashion through a controlled series of procedures produces reliable and valid results, according to the underlying (positivist) paradigm. By contrast, exploratory studies require openness to what is encountered in the empirical world. In more cyclical fashion, questions are reformulated as the process advances and as new understandings emerge through ongoing interpretation and analysis. In the next chapter, we shall be examining different paradigms in detail and seeing how their varying approaches to ways of knowing have contrasting implications for the way research should proceed.

We have been considering the role and timing of research questions largely in terms of how we conceptualize their place in the research process and structure. In so doing, we have concentrated upon the researcher as the key person behind the research question. Clearly, this is only a part of the picture and shortly we shall be recognizing the relevance of other key players (or 'stakeholders'). Nevertheless, by acknowledging the central place that research questions assume, we can begin to anticipate the significance of addressing who does and who does not become involved in formulating them.

Question setting

The research question (which may indeed have sub-questions attached) tells us – and anyone who may ask – what the research is trying to find out. Sometimes, people will know of a specific question they wish to investigate. Just as often, the erstwhile researcher will simply be conscious of a general area in which they wish to conduct their research (for example, migration, youth suicide, system abuse). Usually, wherever one starts, the process of question setting is characterized by a movement between the general and the specific. Through this iterative process of going back and forth, we steadily make progress in clarifying just what our research will and will not be trying to find out – though often it may feel as though we are going around in circles and getting nowhere! While ultimately it is important to gain sufficient specificity to focus the research, it is also necessary to be able to locate specific questions within their broader field of enquiry, since this will assist in connecting the study to relevant literature and to current knowledge and ways of thinking.

You might like to undertake an activity at this point (adapted from Punch, 1998) for developing a research question, reflecting on the process and outcome. You will probably notice even now how developing questions takes time. However, given the important role played by a well-formulated question, this is undoubtedly time well spent.

Exercise: Initial steps in developing a research question

- Identify a subject area for social work research that is of interest to you
- Generate a list of possible questions for research concerning this subject area
- Try to disentangle different questions from one another, and put them into some kind of order
- Attempt to develop a focus for a viable research project, drawing boundaries around what will and will not be included

Now that you have developed a possible question(s) for research, you might like to try checking the words and phrases you have used for their clarity. If a question is to provide a reference point for the researcher, and others involved in the research, then its meaning needs to be as unambiguous and precise as possible. It is important that you have (working) definitions for the terms you have used in the question so that there is as little doubt as possible about what is meant by them. Indeed, this exercise is very much a part of developing a question and becoming clear what it is the research will be aiming to find out, and what will be outside its scope.

So far, we have been considering how our own knowledge and thinking about the research area will assist us in exploring relevant possibilities for enquiry. Shortly, we shall be looking at how, in reviewing the literature, we draw other sources of existing knowledge into the process. In addition to a literature review, consultation and collaboration with others (fellow research-ers or practitioners, prospective research participants, community or agency representatives, and so on) extends the sources of knowledge and range of perspectives that may contribute to the question-setting process. This process can sometimes be formalized to good effect through establishing an advisory/steering group, critical reference group, or management group at the earliest stages of the project's inception. The involvement of participants and intended beneficiaries of the research in shaping its focus has become a key principle of 'research that creates change' (Munford and Sanders, 2003). As McLaughlin (2012: 148) puts it, 'the advantage of user-controlled research is that it is more likely to address questions that are pertinent to service users'.

The scope of the project will also be shaped and limited by another set of rather more material and practical concerns (O'Leary, 2004). Whether one is applying for funding for the project or working with resources (includ-ing time) committed from elsewhere, question setting commonly involves 'bringing the project down to size' (Punch, 1998: 37). Feasibility, then, is a further factor in the equation (Smith and Pitts, 2007: 18–19), with the guiding principle: 'it is better to do a smaller project thoroughly than a larger project superficially' (Punch, 1998: 37).

Feasibility is one of four criteria to be met in question setting (Williams, Tutty and Grinnell, 1995, as adapted by Alston and Bowles, 2012). The other three criteria ask us to consider whether the topic is relevant, researchable and ethical. *Relevance* refers to the credibility the research would need to have in addressing the concerns of the profession and the social work and human ser-vices sector generally. The question also needs to be *researchable* in the sense of being a question that has the potential to be answered through the generation of research knowledge. Not all questions are of this nature. Questions which concern moral judgement (phrased, for example, as what 'should' be the case) are posing an issue that cannot be answered by research *per se*.

Lastly, a research question needs to be *ethical*. Here, we can think in terms of ethical codes that prescribe such principles as respect for persons, beneficence and justice (NHMRC (National Health and Medical Research Council) et al., 2007) but also in terms of broader ethical considerations that acknowledge the cultural and political dimensions of knowledge making (Smith, 1999). These considerations emphasize the importance of relationships between researchers and participants as fostering ethical conduct throughout the process, taking us beyond regulatory approaches espoused by ethics committees and codes (Smith and Pitts, 2007: 3–39). We shall be discussing the nature of these ethical aspects when looking at ways of designing research.

The criteria for question setting once again underline how research occurs in a social context that has to be taken into account if one wishes to see potential topics for enquiry progress from ideas to actions. They highlight too how the formation of a research project, while driven by what one hopes is a well-formulated question(s), is inescapably bound up with the political processes of gaining financial, organizational and ethical approval to proceed. Working effectively as part of this social context is integral to question setting.

There are three key elements to critical research practice in this respect: reflexivity, participation and negotiation. These minimize possibilities for de-contextualizing our research while enhancing its relevance and relational standing (Grbich, 2007: 18). *Reflexivity* allows us to appreciate how we are positioned in relation to the research through a variety of 'frames' that account for personal worldviews; experiences associated with identities such as gender or age; professional theories/knowledge; and the researcher's interpretations of the situations and events within the research process (McLachlan and Reid, 1994, cited in Grbich, 2007: 17–19). Enhancing *participation* in setting the agenda for research can begin to unsettle an exercise of power which would otherwise perpetuate oppressive practices. Skilful *negotiation* of research foci with gatekeepers (of funding, permissions and strategic objectives) can create possibilities for research into sensitive and high-risk topics of great social benefit, although it is also the case that gatekeepers can control how, or even whether, the research is approved or funded (Hillier, Johnson and Traustadóttir, 2007: 88–89; Hillier, Mitchell and Mallett, 2007: 115–117; Smith and Pitts, 2007: 19–20).

In developing research questions, then, we find ourselves at the interface between a process of conceptual sifting and the exercise of social practices. The accommodation we might reach between the two can vary and be perceived very differently. Policy moves towards increased collaborative research with industry can be viewed as compromising intellectual freedom or as increasing opportunity to 'make a difference'. Perhaps the crucial issues are more to do with who is involved in setting questions for research, and who are the likely beneficiaries.

The factors involved in question setting are depicted in Figure 2.1. One component yet to be fully addressed concerns the important step of reviewing the literature.

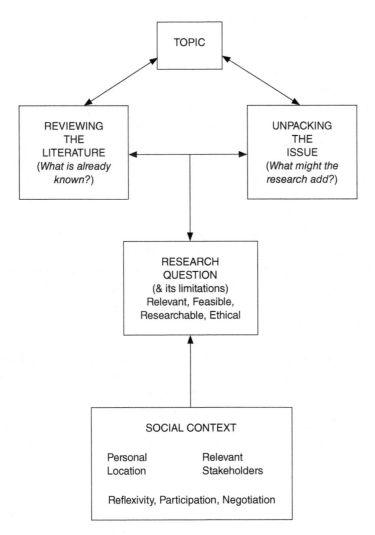

FIGURE 2.1 Factors in question setting

Reviewing the literature

We have seen how the matter of question setting involves moving between the general and specific in order to determine a researchable focus within the field of enquiry. While one might think of developing a question(s) as being essentially concerned with clarifying what the research is trying to find out, the process of reviewing the literature could be seen to represent an attempt to ascertain what is already known about the subject. If the traditional view of undertaking research is to add to our knowledge, then we can understand how the literature review is perceived as crucial in mapping out existing knowledge.

But it is important to understand from the outset that existing knowledge will be partial, incomplete and questionable in a variety of ways. As well as looking for 'gaps' in the literature, the ways in which existing knowledge has been generated may be open to critique from many vantage points. Furthermore, we need to remain mindful that existing literature may reflect, for example, dominant issues in national contexts where research is conducted, or a 'publication bias' in terms of what is deemed worthy, or a shaping through existing literature reviews of what is acceptable knowledge and thus a valid research direction (Smith and Pitts, 2007: 17–18). Consequently, undertaking a 'review' of the literature involves much more than becoming acquainted with existing knowledge. As we shall explain, it requires a critical engagement with the literature and the ways in which it has been constituted.

According to Royse (1999: 23), 'the necessity of immersing yourself in the literature cannot be emphasized strongly enough. Research builds upon the accumulated efforts of all those labouring to expand our knowledge'. Though, as Punch (1998: 43) indicates:

> It is a matter of judgment at what point to concentrate on the literature. Factors involved in this judgment include the style of the research, the overall research strategy, what the objectives of the proposed study are, the nature of the substantive problem and how much is known about it, how well developed the literature in the area is, and how closely this study wants to follow the directions established by that literature. A further important factor is the knowledge that the researcher already has, especially when the research topic comes from practice or experience.

A common place to look when exploring existing knowledge on a particular area of interest is at the articles to be found in well-regarded journals. These will have been subject to a quality control process of peer review and so have some credence within their field. Authored books, edited texts and conference papers by acknowledged experts in the subject also provide starting places in understanding the topic and its surrounding issues and debates. However, to mimimize 'publication bias' and the silencing of challenges to received knowledge from 'experts', in social work research other important sources to consult may include 'grey literature' (Jesson, Matheson and Lacey, 2011: 54–56; Smith and Pitts, 2007: 18), for example: policy documents, practice guidelines, narratives by users and carers, and agency digests of studies in their areas of programme delivery (Orme and Shemmings, 2010).

You may like to pause and think about searching beyond 'the literature' as outlined in the accompanying activity.

Exercise: Searching beyond 'the literature'

It is common to concentrate on 'the literature' as the main source of existing knowledge to review when generating possibilities for the potential research area. For any research enquiry, there may well be other sources it would be sensible and desirable to consult as well.

Returning to the research questions you developed earlier, consider what sources, in addition to the literature, you would wish to consult in formulating these questions. Why would you want to do this?

The growth of internet usage is of course profoundly influencing the availability of information. Online access connects us with an ever-expanding range of providers and virtual learning communities. Moreover, in social work research relevant knowledge is likely to be found within professional and user communities. As suggested previously, this affects the way we think about consulting and collaborating in order to shape our research focus. It may turn us towards less traditional approaches to engaging with current knowledge, such as those we find in participatory models of research (Martin, 1994; McLaughlin, 2012; Pitts and Smith, 2007).

The notion of 'reviewing the literature' is in many respects, therefore, in danger of becoming an out-dated, rather narrow and not always appropriate means of engaging critically with current knowledge relevant to the substance of our social work research. Despite this, it remains a standard procedure and provides one important means by which the researcher can define and justify their project. Marlow (2011: 53) has suggested that the literature review assists by:

- Connecting the research question to theory
- Identifying previous research
- Giving direction to the project

A literature search goes hand in hand with a literature review. When we search the literature, there are a number of approaches we can take. These vary from 'browsing the library shelves' or the World Wide Web (generally, a time-consuming and not the most efficient or effective approach) to using bibliographic databases and information gateways. Scanning recent editions of specialist journals can provide a good place to begin. We might even be fortunate enough to find an article that surveys the literature on our topic. Locating relevant theses can similarly accelerate the process through their often comprehensive literature reviews and bibliographies. Government organizations may well have their own catalogues and gateways. However, it is the electronic databases that are increasingly providing the most efficient way of conducting a systematic search of the literature.

Bell (1993: 41–49) highlights a few key steps in planning a literature search:

1 Select the topic
2 Define the terminology
3 Define parameters (language, geography, time period, type of material, sector)
4 List possible search terms
5 Select sources (library catalogues, computer searching, bibliographies in books, journals and articles, abstracts, or theses)

As Royse (1999: 20) suggests, searching databases may result in one of two common problems: '(1) not finding any (or enough) literature on your topic; and (2) finding too much'. Figure 2.2 depicts a few tips Royse (1999) offers in this respect. The matter of little existing literature on a topic might, of course, also mean it is an area that has received scant attention to date. In this instance, it is often useful to look for parallel studies that may offer beginning, analogous frameworks for consideration (Smith and Pitts, 2007: 17–18). Librarians at university libraries are very helpful in assisting with literature searches. In our experience, they are well read and have a broad understanding of the range of topics of interest to researchers. If you can explain what you are interested in, and what you have done already to conduct your search, they can provide other keywords and ways of searching of which you may not be aware.

Having accessed material, we become involved in a critical analysis of it. This does entail being able to summarize accurately, but reviewing implies much more. It 'places the current research in its historical and theoretical context' (Marlow, 2011: 58) but it also examines all aspects of previous knowledge making relevant to the topic and research question. Some 'gaps' will be explicit in the reported studies, in a statement concerning acknowledged limitations of a project or concerning proposed areas for future research. However, the 'gaps' will also be a consequence of inbuilt factors that are frequently left implicit: for example, the perspectives through which a research question has been framed; the methodologies that have informed how the research has been conducted; or the extent to which participants have been involved in shaping the research. Box 2.1 offers some prompts that may help you to read the literature in a purposeful and scholarly way and to engage critically with

Tips when database searching returns too few 'hits':

- Substitute synonyms (for example, try adolescent instead of teenager).
- Think categorically (for example, 'parenting styles', 'disciplinary techniques').
- Go further than the most recent three years (for example, five or seven years).
- Check your spelling.
- Use fewer words ('parenting' rather than 'parental disciplinary styles').
- Look in a different database.
- Try variations of the key words ('juvenile delinquent' and 'juvenile delinquency').

Tips when database searching returns too many 'hits':

- Add key words (for example, 'suspensions high school' not 'suspensions').
- Skim the most current titles to determine if there are other keywords that may eliminate some of the citations that do not interest you.
- Limit the search by language, year or type of publication.
- Skim the titles and/or abstracts for those articles that are themselves reviews of the literature on your topic.

FIGURE 2.2   Tips for database searching

Source: Adapted from Royse (1999: 21)

it. Ensuing chapters in this book will prepare you to conduct critical appraisals using prompts of this kind, and generally to develop your 'research literacy'.

It should be apparent that a literature review is very different from an annotated bibliography. The latter comprises a list of texts (mostly books and articles), usually presented alphabetically or under headings, with notes against each separate text. It can provide a useful resource that documents materials and indicates in summary fashion their key features. However, the critical engagement with literature that occurs in a review results in the material being organized in a different form: for example, according to the main themes or controversies that have arisen.

Box 2.1   Prompts for reading research critically

- Reflect on your *positioning*

Why am I interested in this topic/area? What do I see as its relevance and potential contribution to social work?

- Consider the *context*

When and where were the texts written? When and where has the research been carried out?

(Continued)

(Continued)

- Examine the *processes of knowledge making*

How are the concepts and ideas being defined? What is the theoretical basis of the studies? Who has been involved in setting the research question? What methods have been used to generate data? How trustworthy are they? Who have been the research participants? How robust are the analyses? Do the conclusions follow from the analyses and arguments?

- Summarize the *themes*

What contributions do these studies make to the knowledge area? What recommendations do they make for further study? What are their acknowledged limitations? In what other ways are they limited or contestable? Have there been any dominant perspectives in this field of study? To what extent have those with an interest in the area been consistently included or excluded?

- Identify your *contribution*

What are the 'gaps' in this field of study? How will your study build on what has gone before? Will you bring new perspectives to the topic, or different methodologies, or other participants? What will be the benefits of your contribution, and to whom?

There is a certain art in writing literature reviews that for most only comes with practice. Royse et al. (2001: 378–379) offer this advice:

- Make sure that the early major or classical studies in the field are included.
- Do not, however, focus so much on the earlier studies that the review of the literature is 'light' on current studies.
- Make minimal use of direct quotations from other sources and, by all means, avoid incorporating long passages from original sources.
- Try to provide a balanced presentation; acknowledge theories or explanations even if you do not subscribe to them.
- Construct the literature review so that the reader can easily follow your organisational scheme and will come away knowing the breadth of the prior research, the gaps in the literature, and the purpose of your proposal or research initiative. Distinguish for the reader the uniqueness of your study or describe how it is similar to others.

Perhaps one of the most helpful ways to learn the art is to consult a range of literature reviews written by others, to analyse the styles and structures used, and to consider how well you think they incorporate the above features. The literature review is commonly situated at the beginning of a research report, and will influence the credibility with which the research is viewed. Credibility is likely to be heightened when the process of reviewing the literature has indeed been formative in developing the focus for the research. The writing of it will reflect the clarity of thinking that has helped finally define the research focus and question after the considerable time and effort that has been devoted to this early stage in the overall research process.

The research-minded practitioner

Having the capacity to read research critically – to be 'research literate' – is one crucial aspect of becoming a research-minded practitioner. Since Everitt et al.'s (1992) formative work on the practical connections between political and ethical issues relating to knowledge and its relevance to 'doing social work research', there has been a growing acknowledgement of the importance of research-minded practice (Everitt et al., 1992: 51–68; Everitt, 2008). Significant advances have occurred in recognizing the place of the 'practitioner researcher' as a key contributor to social work knowledge-for-practice (Gould, 2004; Healy, 2000: 145–147), complementing the 'academic research' associated with university-based researchers (Lyons and Taylor, 2004).

A research-minded practitioner would work in a participatory way with multiple informants, including service users (Beresford, 2000; Braye et al., 2008; Millar et al., 2008; Pitts and Smith, 2007), drawing on a range of perspectives. Engaged intimately with clients and communities, they need to be aware of the ethical and political assumptions they bring to knowing about social issues and knowing how to practice. Research-minded practice focuses attention on the place and nature of knowledge in practice, but it goes beyond this to question how knowledge is produced, who is involved in producing it, and who benefits from it. According to Everitt et al., the practitioner has a responsibility 'to understand knowledge and its construction and to develop and share this knowledge with those with whom they work' (1992: 55). For them, an appreciation of the ethics and power of knowledge production is fundamental to emancipatory practice.

A research-minded practitioner, then, works from a spirit of enquiry, thinking like a researcher in all aspects of social work practice (Everitt, 2008). From this standpoint, knowledge production is intrinsic to both practice and research – and therefore, as we shall explore throughout this book, the capacity to be reflective (Fook, 1996, 1999) and reflexive (Taylor and White, 2000) is a core ingredient for the research-minded practitioner. The aim is to foster an ethical relationship with clients and communities that does not objectify them or their experiences, but at the same time is informed by sound, theoretical analysis (Everitt, 2008; Pitts and Smith, 2007). The implication is that research is as much a part of social work practice as is casework and community work. It is a vital strategy for achieving positive social change. Ultimately, research-minded practitioners are likely to be excellent social workers.

Putting it all together

This chapter has surveyed various facets in determining a focus for research through the setting of questions for enquiry. This is a crucial phase in the research process. It shapes what follows, reflects a diverse range of interests and includes assumptions both about worthwhile areas for enquiry and ways new knowledge can be generated about them. In making research knowledge, one of the crucial questions concerns who is setting the research agenda.

The processes involved in developing research questions incorporate the intellectual ones of locating new projects in the history of previous studies; the practical ones of scoping an initiative that will be properly resourced; and the interactional ones of engaging with key stakeholders (both gatekeepers and participants). All three dimensions face us with distinctive political and ethical considerations. In facing these issues, it is suggested that the critical researcher will need to exercise reflexivity, participation and negotiation. Through developing these kinds of capabilities, and appreciating their place in the production of knowledge, research-mindedness becomes an integral part of social work practice — and one which can be put to the service of emancipatory goals. This requires an awareness of the assumptions behind different ways of knowing and in the next chapter we shall be looking more closely at this and just how crucial it is for what takes place in research.

Further reading

Dodd, S. J. and Epstein, I. (2012) *Practice-based Research in Social Work: A Guide for Reluctant Researchers*, London: Routledge (Chapter 2).

Jesson, J. K., with Matheson, L. and Lacey, F. M. (2011) *Doing Your Literature Review: Traditional and Systematic Techniques*, London: Sage (Reading skills: pp. 46–57; From making notes to writing: pp. 58–69).

Marlow, C.R. (2011) *Research Methods for Generalist Social Work* (5th edition), Belmont, CA: Brooks/Cole (Chapter 3).

Orme, J. and Shemmings, D. (2010) *Developing Research-based Social Work Practice*, Basingstoke, Hampshire: Palgrave Macmillan (Chapter 4).

3

Different Ways of Knowing and their Relevance for Research

Introduction

In this chapter, we shall be:

1 Exploring how some ways of knowing and theorizing social problems and human experience become dominant and legitimated, with alternative perspectives becoming marginalized, considered as subversive or wrong.
2 Considering the ethical and political implications of different ways of knowing for social work research.
3 Looking at different ways of knowing ('paradigms') and how these differences may form the basis of conflicts between a range of interested parties, about 'truth' and valid knowledge, particularly in relation to social issues, that may influence how well or easily we can bring about social change.
4 Considering whether and how we can accommodate differences between interested individuals and groups in social work research, including the extent to which paradigm differences are 'incommensurable' at a level of social work research as practice.

Paradigms

Different ways of knowing are represented by the concept of *paradigms*, first proposed by Kuhn (1970), whose history of the natural sciences discussed how scientists engage in debates about the phenomena that they study in their research (Bryman, 2008: 605). Different beliefs about phenomena being investigated inform the positions that scientists take in debates, which then influence the investigative techniques and theories that are developed.

Bryman (2008: 605), drawing on Kuhn, defines 'paradigms' as:

> a cluster of beliefs and dictates which for scientists in a particular discipline influence what should be studied, how research should be done, ... how results should be interpreted ...

Social work researcher, Marlow (2011: 8), says that:

> Paradigms function as maps, directing us to the problems that are important to address, the theories that are acceptable, and the procedures needed to solve the problems. ... Paradigms reflect changing values, countering the idea that a fixed reality exists out there to be objectively observed.

While there is some agreement about the definition of paradigm as 'intellectual resources', some scholars seem to apply the concept more narrowly to research strategies or designs (for example Blaikie, 2000: 85–127, 256–262) or to 'methods of inquiry' (for example Neuman and Kreuger, 2003: 70–96). Kuhn's definition of paradigm, and his account of their importance, was formed in relation to the natural sciences. The ideas associated with it are also seen as important for the social sciences. While many texts still focus on 'how to do research' as stages and methods, many others now also refer to paradigm differences, and social work and sociological theories about social problems and their influences on how research problems are identified and investigated, for example, Babbie (2007), Neuman and Kreuger (2003) and Sarantakos (2005).

A fundamental feature of paradigms is the recognition that all researchers are part of communities of knowledge, whether associated with professions or disciplines or wider social, cultural and political communities. Hence, research never happens in a vacuum (see, for example, Feyerabend, 1975; Jacobs, 2002a, 2002b; Potter, 1996: 17–41). Instead, it is a social process, and new research is located within previous research, interlinked theories and assumptions and related debates, discussed in published journal articles and textbooks, in print and electronic media, and organizational policies and procedures. However, being part of knowledge communities does not mean that all members necessarily agree about theories and explanations about social phenomena. Debate is as important as agreement in advancing knowledge. What is important is the recognition that knowledge is socially constructed within political relations between participants in any community, which may include clients, funding bodies, organizational managers, team members from other professions, politicians, media (Best, 2004). This means that differences in perspectives involve power struggles over what is legitimate knowledge (and what is not), who is a knowledgeable person (and who is not), and the consequences of these struggles for members of communities (Hurley, 2007). The different ways of knowing within these wider relationships can generate struggles about the research being undertaken and may have to be resolved by negotiation, compromise, and even coercion and subversion ('dirty tricks') if the stakes are high enough. 'Evidence-based practice', and associated debates, is an example of different ways of knowing in a wide community of interest.

Evidence-based practice

The idea of evidence-based practice emerged from medical research, particularly in relation to therapeutic and pharmacological interventions and their efficacy in treatment of diseases (Greenberg, 2009). The most stringent procedures for establishing cause–effect connections between disease/illness, treatment/ intervention and cure/efficacy consists in randomized controlled trials (RCT) which are experiments under laboratory conditions. This form of research is accepted as 'the gold standard', whereby claims for knowledge to be applied in practice are the outcomes of scientific experimentation that is seen to provide clear answers for complex medical and health problems. However, Greenberg (2009: 31–32) points out that the idea of evidence is disputed within the medical community, as value judgements are applied to hierarchies of evidence without regard for the quality of the research designs generating such evidence.

The trend to evidence-based practice has had some consequences for social work research and practice. The language of 'evidence' has now colonized the social sciences and social work through demands for answers or solutions to complex social problems, such as child maltreatment or mental illness (Aarons and Palinkas, 2007; Palinkas et al., 2008; Rapp et al., 2010; Shlonsky and Wagner, 2005). The acceptance of scientific laboratory-generated knowledge as the most reliable way to generate 'evidence' of 'what works' (Dominelli, 2005: 233; Humphries, 2008: 4–6) tends to dismiss other ways of generating knowledge through research and through practice wisdom (or experience), regarding them as untrustworthy and of lesser value (Greenberg, 2009: 31–32). Our intention is to show that social science and social work as disciplines are not averse to attending to social problems and their resolution. We hope to show that knowledge is a complex area, and that social problems are multifaceted and multidimensional, as are ways of knowing through research to address them. Fundamentally, by exploring the idea of paradigms as different ways of knowing, we are asking: What is evidence? How do we accept what is evidence and what is not? And who decides?

While social work scholars argue that it is essential to build links and draw on multidisciplinary perspectives in developing effective interventions (O'Connor et al., 2008; Plath, 2012; Shaw, 2007: 662–663), debates about what constitutes 'evidence' can characterize the dynamics in multidisciplinary teams involved in service provision to clients, for example, claims to greater efficacy associated with how knowledge-for-practice is generated, and perceptions that some ways of knowing are superior to others (D'Cruz et al., 2009a: 3–4, 2009b: 245–249; Hutchinson and Bucknall, 2009). These dynamics in practice teams are also intrinsic to research from which most professional knowledge-for-practice is generated, although what constitutes 'research' is part of these debates about valid knowledge (D'Cruz, 2009: 69–73; Greenberg, 2009: 31–32; Hutchinson and Bucknall, 2009; Klein, 2007).

Social work research encourages us to consider how different ways of knowing are embedded in ethical and political complexities of society, and how this knowledge is achieved, with particular consequences for vulnerable groups in the society. Social work deals with problems that are fraught with debates about moral questions about the 'good society' – what is normal, acceptable, right and reasonable, how this should be achieved, and the associated political struggles (Fawcett et al., 2010; Naples, 2007: 557–559; Schiele, 2011).

Being aware of different ways of knowing is fundamental to understanding why and how any social research – particularly social work research – has political and ethical dimensions that cannot be separated from a discussion of techniques or research methods (Pitts and Smith, 2007).

The politics and ethics of different ways of knowing

Unless social workers appreciate that professional knowledge also confers the power to exclude other ways of knowing, we risk practising in oppressive ways by disallowing our clients' voices in naming their experiences and proposing appropriate solutions to their problems. This may seem most obvious if we are engaged in providing services directly to clients – for example, via case, group or community work. While social work research seeks to generate knowledge, it should be with the awareness of the ethical and political dimensions of how 'knowledge' is generated and interpreted, in supporting social work objectives to achieve social justice and improve the social conditions of individuals, groups and communities.

As you will probably already be aware, participatory and collaborative approaches with adult service users have become important (Beresford, 2000; Braye et al., 2008; Millar et al., 2008) as a way of appreciating 'different ways of knowing' and the 'search for subjugated knowledge' (Hartman, 1990, 1992) embodied in clients as service users and/or as research participants. These approaches are now extended to include children, a group whose knowledge and ways of knowing are continually and consistently excluded by social work professionals (Davis and Hill, 2006; Prout and Tisdall, 2006). While the ideal of participatory and collaborative research (and professional practice) may give professionals some comfort as we try to soften the often harsh edges of professional knowledge/power in practice, we also need to be mindful that these relations cannot be truly egalitarian due to the dominance of professionals and their positioning within institutional power and privilege. Yellow Bird (2008: 278), writing from an indigenous perspective, comments on how the idea of 'empowerment' may mask inequalities between social workers and clients:

> ...'Empowerment', one of the most widely used words in the social work vocabulary, means, 'the ability to make and act upon one's own choices'. To Indigenous Peoples, empowerment is more likely to mean, 'I cannot make choices that are based on my values and beliefs that are in conflict with your values and beliefs and rules and laws. Therefore, my empowerment depends on your generosity, flexibility, and willingness to bend or violate your rules on my behalf'. ...

Wetherell (1994: 306–307) points out:

> Co-research suggests a fantasy of an ideal or utopian communicative scenario where mutuality is perfect, where there is no appropriation of the other person, and where power relations are calibrated to insignificance. The notion of positioning the objects of research as co-researchers also obscures the point that we get to write the articles, we get to write the books, and we (usually) get the royalties from those books, not our 'co-researchers'.

Exercise: Reflecting on the importance of 'many ways of knowing' for social work research

- Why is awareness of 'many ways of knowing' an important consideration in social work research?
- How can social work help 'subjugated knowledge' to be given space in which to be expressed?
- How might 'empowerment' in research, to give voice to subjugated knowledge, be practised in ways that are *not* 'dangerous' and uncritical? (Wendt and Seymour, 2010: abstract)
- Think of examples from your own experience where your point of view or someone else's perspective on an issue may have differed from others. How were different points of view or differences of opinion dealt with? How were different people in the group treated depending on their views of the topic, and the extent of their different views from dominant or preferred views?

The politics and ethics of research: positioning of the self and others

'Positioned subjectivity' (Riessman, 1994a: 133–138) is generally cited as a norm by which a researcher recognizes his or her personal identities and affiliations, and connections to professional knowledge, social and cultural beliefs, and the potential for influencing how the research is conceptualized (Chapman, 2011: 725). However, we do not wish to claim that identities and affiliations, such as gender or ethnicity, determine particular ways of knowing and doing (Butler, 1990: 142).

This is a tension for social work where, as a profession, we are obliged to act so that inequality and oppression are diminished, while at the same time we should be open to questioning the politics and ethics of our participation in the construction of moral claims in a range of social problems, as Wendt and Seymour (2010: 670–682) argue. We cannot assume that our participation as social workers with, and on behalf of, clients is unproblematic and always for the best: for example, in child and family welfare (Campbell, 1988; Corby, 1998: 29–38; Erera, 2002: 46–47; Millei and Lee, 2007; Parton, 1991), elders' care (Black, 2009), mental health (Macfarlane, 2009), and disability services (Johnson, 2009).

The positioned researcher: reflective and reflexive practice

The social work researcher is a practitioner who aims to bring about social change. The importance of both critical reflection (Fook, 1996) and reflexivity (Taylor and White, 2000) in providing ethical and theoretically informed services to clients, for example, in case group and community work, is also essential for social work research (International Association of the Schools of Social Work (IASSW), 2001).

Both *critical reflection* and *reflexivity* are important strategies for social workers to engage with the ethical and political dimensions of practice and research. Schön's (1983) ideas about the importance of 'reflection-on-action' and 'reflection-in-action' for professionals have influenced social work. *Critical reflection* (Fook, 1996) uses critical incidents to examine assumptions informing practice encapsulated by selected incidents, offering opportunities for transformative practice; a process reminiscent of Schön's (1983) reflection-on-action because the reflective process is occurring after the events captured in the critical incidents.

Reflexivity is a concept often used interchangeably with (critical) reflection. In an attempt to tease out the connections and differences between critical reflection and reflexivity, D'Cruz, Gillingham and Melendez (2007) have traced the theoretical origins, aims and methods of both concepts. They found that reflexivity, like critical reflection, involves the ethical and political dimensions of knowledge-in-practice. However, unlike critical reflection that emphasizes reflection-on-action (Schön, 1983), reflexivity tends to emphasize reflection-in-action (Schön, 1983), as a process of reflecting in the moment – 'reflexive monitoring' (Blaikie, 2000: 54–55, citing Giddens, 1984: 5) as events unfold. This includes being critically aware of personal positioning and practice in an immediately responsive way.

Proponents of critical reflection and reflexivity see knowledge as a construction, as participants negotiating an outcome, within a context where it is essential to be aware of the politics of different ways of knowing and the necessity for ethical practice that goes beyond legalistic forms of ethics (Butler and Pugh, 2004; Hurley, 2007; Taylor and White, 2000, 2001). These approaches are controversial within a positivist paradigm, which regards knowledge as objective facts, external to, and independent of, participants involved (Sheldon, 2000, 2001).

To support constructionism and to question positivism are not to deny that there are considerable numbers of people experiencing problems due to unequal distribution of resources, violence, and other manifestations of inequality, for example, poverty, unemployment, homelessness and child maltreatment. It is our obligation as social workers to work for social and distributive justice. However, we have to be mindful of what is defined as a particular social problem and how it is defined, even by social workers as individual practitioners or as a professional group (Best, 2004; Hurley, 2007). Positioning and subjectivity may be suggested in the language that participants use to speak or write about ('represent') social problems. The place of language as a device of knowledge and a device of power (as 'discourse') is important because the descriptive categories and the syntax of representation are not neutral. Language generates simultaneous images of normality and abnormality – the 'dividing practices' that Foucault (1978, 1980) wrote about and that are fundamental to the political and ethical debates associated with different ways of knowing. Critical reflection and reflexivity are practices that assist us to understand the politics by which events or phenomena become social problems, including our positioning and participation as social workers, as we advance arguments to have forms of inequality and oppression recognized as social problems, and presenting policies and suggesting resources to address them.

Being aware of positioning and subjectivity, a researcher should state his or her assumptions and interests in the research and acknowledge the emotional and political aspects of the research process that are often hidden from scrutiny. Instead of treating methodology as a set of neutral techniques that are applied in the same way in every context, the researcher should acknowledge the actual processes – 'how research gets done' – which recognizes that, unlike its representation in textbooks, actual research is not neat and orderly or problem-free. The researcher's awareness of what is actually going on in her or his research will increase the opportunities for flexibility in addressing problems, including the appropriateness of the design and strategies for gaining access to people, places and data (Hurley, 2007; Smith and Pitts, 2007) that may emerge in specific contexts.

Exercise: Exploring my positioning and subjectivity

Write down how your personal positioning (called subjectivity) matters. This includes your experiences, personal values, affiliations, history and biography.
    How might your positioning influence your interests as a social worker? How might you (or do you) perceive particular social problems? How might your positioning influence your attraction to, or empathy for, particular individuals or groups? How might your positioning influence your aversion to, or avoidance of, particular individuals or groups?

Positioning, subjectivity and stakeholders: three case studies

In the previous edition of this book (D'Cruz and Jones, 2004: 34–42), we included three case studies: (1) an inquiry by the Australian Human Rights and Equal Opportunity Commission (1997) into the government's removal of indigenous Australian children into 'white' foster care, known as 'the stolen generations'; (2) Clarence Thomas and Anita Hill – a case study of sexual harassment, gender and race in the USA (1991); and (3) Marietta Higgs and the Cleveland affair – a case study relating to mistaken or correct diagnoses of child sexual abuse in the UK (1987). We have replaced these case studies with three new ones on current issues. However, working from an assumption that 'current' doesn't mean that 'past events' are irrelevant to our learning about different ways of knowing, and the political and ethical issues associated with this, we recommend that you review the earlier case studies so that you can appreciate the issues identified within the history of social work and social policy. The three new case studies we discuss below are: (1) indigenous Australians, their rights and welfare in the twenty-first century; (2) our preoccupation with 'border protection': from whom and why?; (3) who is a child and what is a normal childhood?

Weblink 3.1 Case studies

Exercise: Positioning – myself and others – some reflective questions

In engaging with these case studies, notice how different protagonists are positioned in relation to the topic and how they express different perspectives.

Dolgoff et al. (2005: 104, Figure 6.1), in discussing ethical dilemmas for social work practice, propose some questions that are also useful in reflecting on the ethics and politics of different ways of knowing and their application in social work research: Whose interests are being served? Who benefits? Who defines the problem?

Take special note of the language used and how opposing perspectives are responded to, including how does someone make his or her case plausible, and how do they make opposing views seem less plausible?

Notice your own responses to each item that you read. What are your thoughts on what is being said or claimed? How do you feel when you read the different views and how they are expressed? Why might you have these responses, both cognitive and emotional? For example, do you feel uncomfortable, fearful or angry about some perspectives, and encouraged or happy with other perspectives? Why do you think you have responded in this way? What are your own assumptions about the issues you are investigating? What are the values underpinning your cognitive and emotional responses? Does it matter that the issues in the case studies are specific to particular countries or locations within your own country? As an aspiring or qualified social worker, should we care about what is happening in another country? Why? How might events in another country (or in another place in your own country) be relevant and important for local concerns and issues? How might you connect your responses to the social work professional code of ethics, aims and values, espoused by the International Federation of Social Workers (2010) and by your national code of ethics?

Indigenous Australians, their rights and welfare in the twenty-first century

Ten years after the release of the *Bringing them Home* report by the Australian Human Rights and Equal Opportunity Commission (HREOC) (1997), the Australian government under Prime Minister John Howard 'took over Aboriginal policy' in the Northern Territory of Australia (Fawcett et al., 2010: 176). This intervention is described by Fawcett et al. (2010: 176–187) as a social policy that is 'reactionary entrenchment' rather than 'significant advancement' (pp. 183–187). On 13 February 2008, the Australian government, under a new Prime Minister, Kevin Rudd, made a formal apology to 'the stolen generations', as recommended by the HREOC in their report in 1997 and demanded by the Aboriginal community. However, the new government did not repeal the Northern Territory intervention that was implemented by its predecessor, although some changes were made.

You may like to explore in detail some of the debates and developments relating to indigenous Australians' wellbeing, including the formal apology given to 'the stolen generations' by the (then) Prime Minister, Kevin Rudd, on 13 February 2008.

You may also wish to investigate policies by the Australian Government in regard to socio-economic disadvantage in remote indigenous communities.

You can use the following keywords for your google search:

'the stolen generations in Australia'

'the stolen generations and litigation revisited'

'Northern Territory Intervention Australian Government'

'Australian Government indigenous affairs'

How might these examples be similar to those of indigenous (First Nation) peoples in your own country, if you are not Australian? How might they be different? How might you account for the differences and similarities? Find some examples in your own country, by searching print and electronic media, including news and current affairs programmes. How might you construct research on indigenous people's experiences in your country that might allow cross-national comparisons? What do you think are some of the key ethical issues in doing such research if you are not an indigenous person yourself?

 ## Weblink 3.1a Resources: Indigenous Australians, their rights and welfare in the twenty-first century

Our preoccupation with 'border protection': from whom and why?

Nearly every day in 'rich democracies' (Wilensky, 2002), where many readers of this book will live, there is discussion of the necessity for 'border protection' (or similar language), usually as it pertains to asylum seekers, refugees or so-called 'illegal immigrants'.

You can use the following keywords for your google search:

'Border protection'

'Refugees and asylum seekers'

'Illegal immigrants'

A search on 18 October 2010 of google.com using the keyword 'border protection' generated the following sites.

Weblink 3.1b Resources: Our preoccupation with 'border protection': from whom and why?

From viewing these sites, it may be apparent that the idea of 'border protection' is incorporated into the titles of government organizations in many countries. Is this the case in your country?

What are the roles of these organizations, and are there any similarities and differences between countries? Why do you think this may be? How is 'border protection' justified? What are other points of view about 'border protection' as it refers to human beings? Do you consider that there are any valid points in the different perspectives presented? How are different values involved in different perspectives? What might be some ways of attending to the needs of the human beings caught up in the middle of these policy debates? How might social work research help to give a voice to asylum seekers? For example, see Briskman, Latham and Goddard (2008), who led a 'people's inquiry' into the experiences of asylum seekers in Australian detention centres. Their enquiry focused on the human rights of asylum seekers and was published as *Human Rights Overboard: Seeking Asylum in Australia.*

Who is a child and what is a normal childhood?

Social work practice often involves services to children or on their behalf, either directly (for example, child welfare, child protection, school social work) or indirectly (for example, mental health services for parents, social security for families). But do we realize how much variation is covered under the identity of 'child'? For example, there is a significant age range, being at least from birth to 18 years in most countries, after which, by law in most countries, a 'child' becomes an 'adult'. Additionally, children's experiences vary depending on the context. For example, the time of one's childhood, and place, including urban or rural, wealthy or poor countries, can influence the experiences of what it means to be a child. Also, the variations in children's identities beyond their 'age and stage', such as gender, social class, race, ethnicity, language, disability, sexualities, and so on can also generate diverse 'childhoods', rather than a single experience called 'childhood'.

What the law says: 'child' and 'adult'

For the 'age of majority' in countries throughout the world, find the website: en.wikipedia.org/wiki/Age_of_majority.

What do you notice about the average *age of majority* throughout the world? What is the range of ages for when 'majority' is legally achieved (youngest and oldest)? Are there variations within countries? Does this surprise you? What may be some explanations for why some countries have these variations within? For this, you need to understand a little about how these countries (for example, the USA, Australia, Germany, New Zealand) differ in their political arrangements. Reflect on what the age of majority is in the country where you live. What does it mean to reach the 'age of majority'? What are you allowed to do when you are considered to be an adult? Even if there is a legal age when you are recognized as an adult, are there different activities you are allowed to do before you are recognized legally as an adult? For example, if you want to get a driver's licence or vote or enlist in the armed forces? (See www.unicef.org/rightsite/433_457.htm, accessed 21 March 2013.)

Now find out what the *age of consent* is in different countries and whether this is the same for both heterosexual and homosexual relationships (see www. avert.org/age-of-consent.htm; www.unicef.org/rightsite/433_457.htm).

  Weblink 3.1c Resources: Who is a child and what is a normal childhood?

Other examples: different ways of knowing

You may like to follow a particular issue or current event via the print, electronic media and internet. We listed some examples in the previous edition of this book (D'Cruz and Jones, 2004) and we are not surprised to see that the list has not changed over many years: unemployment/unemployed people, single mothers on welfare payments, attitudes to refugees and asylum seekers, attitudes to Muslims and Arabs since the attack on the World Trade Center in New York on September 11, 2001, and the war on Iraq. Some new issues include terrorism, the global financial crisis and climate change. You may ask what these topics have to do with social work. We are including them because of the consequences for the loss of human rights and civil liberties, justified as 'the war on terrorism'; because of the consequences of global capitalism for poorer nations or for poorer people in our own Western capitalist countries; because of the consequences for becoming so-called 'economic refugees' and 'environmental refugees' as the disparities in wealth and consumption increase with significant effects on some groups in our countries and overseas.

 Weblink 3.1d Other examples: Different ways of knowing

Paradigms: ethical and political considerations

Social work researchers have different views of paradigms. Some, such as Marlow (2011: 14), perceive paradigm differences as 'different approaches to science'. She concludes that:

> ... different understanding including values, intuition, experience, authority, and science ... [and] approaches to science can ... offer advantages in addressing the different types of research questions asked in generalist social work. (Marlow, 2011: 14)

Marlow's position implies that different perspectives are neutral and can be used pragmatically to shape a research agenda, rather than being associated with power, with particular consequences for the research processes and outcomes. In contrast, Everitt (2008) and Humphries (2008) take a political perspective of knowledge (as theory) for social work. They move beyond the pragmatic approach taken by Marlow, who basically sees any approach as justifiable as long as it helps to answer social work research questions. Instead:

> social research [is] not solely ... a range of neutral approaches to the examination of social problems, but [is] a profoundly political exercise, and as having potential to contribute to social change for good or ill. (Humphries, 2008: 1)

To demonstrate how methods and procedures are influenced by positivist, interpretivist and critical approaches, Neuman and Kreuger (2003: 92–94) use an example of researching:

> discrimination and job competition between minority and majority groups in four countries: aborigines in the Australian outback, Asians in western Canada, African Americans in the mid-western United States, and Pakistanis in London. (Neuman and Kreuger, 2003: 92)

While Neuman and Kreuger (2003: 92–94) explain how different paradigms may approach the question differently through *methods* used, they disregard that the different approaches begin from an acceptance that discrimination against minority groups in employment is a possible explanation (values and theory); their interest is to understand patterns of discrimination and how this may occur. On the other hand, if researchers are unwilling to accept that discrimination may be an explanation for joblessness among minority groups, and if they assume that it is caused by individual deficiencies (values and theory), they are likely to approach the research differently, in the questions they ask or don't ask, and how they analyse existing secondary data such as statistics. If interest groups such as social workers, policymakers, and politicians are not ideologically comfortable with the research outcomes, they may adopt the strategy of discrediting the methods as being unsound, or accuse the researchers for being biased. We all do this as we are positioned in particular ways in relation to knowledge about the social world.

In doing research, we argue that 'being pragmatic' involves knowledge of the *political* aspects of the research in question, such that methods that are chosen may be informed as much by political aspects, whereby powerful stakeholders need to be convinced, as by the ethical aspects, where social change is the aim. For example, if you consider that a statistical study may be more convincing for government bureaucrats than a qualitative study, you may combine the two approaches, making sure that the research is methodologically and ethically sound while being mindful of political agendas.

The basic dimensions of paradigms

Fundamental to different ways of knowing (or paradigms) are assumptions about knowledge, related to what 'reality' is, how we know about 'reality' and generate knowledge that is taken as legitimate and true, and what our responsibilities are to others in how we use knowledge. The basic dimensions of paradigms are ethics, ontology, epistemology and methodology. As explained by Denzin and Lincoln (2005c: 183):

> ... *Ethics* asks, 'How will I be as a moral person in the world?' *Epistemology* asks, 'How do I know the world? What is the relationship between the inquirer and the known?' ... *Ontology* raises basic questions about the nature of reality and the nature of the human being in the world. *Methodology* focuses on the best means for acquiring knowledge about the world.

If you are a novice researcher and also relatively new to sociology and social theory, these concepts may be quite daunting. We offer you the concepts so as to encourage you to think critically about our taken-for-granted ways of knowing and being. The most useful advice that we can give is to persevere with the definitions and think them through carefully, looking for ways in which to illustrate the abstract concepts and their meanings in everyday, familiar examples.

Ontology and *epistemology* are connected concepts. Blaikie (1993: 6–7) defines epistemology (theories of knowledge) and the related concept, ontology (theories of being, of what things exist), as follows:

> The root definition of *ontology* is 'the science or study of being'. ... *Ontology* refers to the claims or assumptions that a particular approach to social enquiry makes about the nature of social reality – claims about what exists, what it looks like, what units make it up and how these units interact with each other.

> The root definition of *epistemology* is 'the theory or science of the method or grounds of knowledge'. ... *Epistemology* refers to the claims or assumptions made about the ways in which it is possible to gain knowledge of this reality, whatever it is understood to be; claims about how what exists may be known. An *epistemology* is a theory of knowledge; it presents a view and a justification for what can be regarded as knowledge – what can be known, and what criteria such knowledge must satisfy in order to be called knowledge rather than beliefs. (Original emphasis)

In everyday language, epistemology is a theory of knowledge by which you set out your assumptions about particular problems and what constitutes an appropriate way of knowing about them. Ontology is related to epistemology because how we understand reality will affect what we take to be knowledge of it, and vice versa. Ethical conduct may refer to institutionally regulated ethics protocols, but, more than legalistic and institutional procedures for safeguarding the rights of research participants, ethics includes relationships and power sharing (Hurley, 2007; Smith, 2005: 97–99; Smith and Pitts, 2007; Stanley and Wise, 1993: 203).

Formal paradigms: positivism and emancipatory perspectives

In this section, we make a distinction between positivism and emancipatory perspectives that see research as one way of attending to the needs of silenced and marginalized groups in a society, for example women or indigenous peoples. We also consider children as research subjects and participants in keeping with contemporary developments related to children's participation as citizens in decision making about their lives.

Positivism

Positivism (as an interpretation of 'science' and scientific method') emphasizes explanations that are tested through 'empirical' research of the real world that involves experiments (Manicas, 2007: 8). Table 3.1 summarizes the assumptions made by positivism about ethics, ontology, epistemology, and methodology.

TABLE 3.1　Positivism: its dimensions and assumptions

Dimension	Assumptions
Ethics	• Scientific knowledge and values are separate • Knowledge is an end in itself • How knowledge is used is outside the concern of science • 'Positivists argue for a *value-free science* that is objective … [that includes an expectation] that science is not based on values, opinions, attitudes, or beliefs … [and is] free of personal, political, or religious values.' (Neuman and Kreuger, 2003: 93, Table 4.1)
Ontology	• Social reality involves 'stable, pre-existing patterns or order that can be discovered' (Neuman and Kreuger, 2003: 93, Table 4.1) • Behaviour can be explained in causal, deterministic ways. It has a mechanistic quality
Epistemology	• The reason for research is 'to discover natural laws so people can predict and control events' (Neuman and Kreuger, 2003: 93, Table 4.1) • We know things through our senses and no other way • There is a quest for objectivity to ascertain social facts, with the separation of the knower from the phenomena being experienced
Methodology	• Theories 'as a set of hypotheses' are tested and explanations for human behaviour are generated as 'a logical deductive system of interconnected definitions, axioms and laws' (Neuman and Kreuger, 2003: 93, Table 4.1), as '"regularities" between associated "variables" – "whenever this, then that"' (Manicas, 2007: 8)

Dimension	Assumptions
	• Scientific theories are tested by experiments • 'Good evidence' relies on 'precise observations that other researchers can replicate (Neuman and Kreuger, 2003: 93, Table 4.1)

Sources: Derived from Hekman (2007: 534); Manicas (2007: 7–8); Neuman and Kreuger (2003: 93); Peile, McCouat and Rose-Miller (1995)

 ## Weblink 3.2 A brief description of positivism and its relationship to social sciences and social work research

Emancipatory perspectives

Unlike positivism, emancipatory perspectives, expressed through research, aim to give voice to the experiences of marginalized social groups. Emancipatory perspectives on research include feminist critiques of social science research since the 1960s (Hekman, 2007: 536; Naples, 2007: 547; Stanley and Wise, 1993: 26–44), or indigenous people's perspectives of colonizing practices manifested in knowledge itself: 'they came, they saw, they named, they claimed' (Smith, 1999: 80).

We have included feminist approaches because feminism can be seen to represent at least 50 per cent of any population, with versions of feminism attending to the differences between women – 'liberal', 'radical', 'socialist', 'Black', 'Afrocentric', 'lesbian', 'Latina', 'Marxist', 'postmodern', 'postcolonial' – as based on identity positions and differences between women's experiences (Collins, 2000; Denzin and Ryan, 2007: 588–589; Hekman, 2007: 537–539; Naples, 2007: 548, 555–557; Stanley and Wise, 1993: 189–91).

We have integrated indigenous perspectives under emancipatory approaches in this edition, whereas in the first edition they were discussed separately (D'Cruz and Jones, 2004: 50–54). This revised discussion is not intended to replace what we said previously. Rather, our present discussion reflects an expansion of scholarship in this important area, referring to these developments and incorporating some of our more important points from the first edition. In recent developments, there is significant discussion about the meaning of indigenous perspectives, recognizing that the initial emergence and claims to indigenous knowledge were related to political movements in countries where European colonizers have remained: for example, in Australia, Canada, the USA and New Zealand (Bishop, 2005; Bruyere, 2008; Gray, Coates and Yellow Bird, 2008; Smith, 2005; Weaver, 2008).

Additionally, there is attention to the consequences of globalization as another form of colonization with dominant groups imposing their cultures, languages and values on to communities of difference. One example is where dominant 'Western' and Eurocentric knowledges, for example, social work, teaching or health, have tended to colonize intellectual and professional spaces (Faith, 2008; Hare, 2004; Hart, 2008; Mafile'o, 2008; Nadkarni, 2010; Nimmagadda and Martell, 2008; Osei-Hwedie and Rankopo, 2008; Sin, 2008; Walsh-Tapiata, 2008; Yan and Tsang, 2008; Yellow Bird and Gray, 2008; Yuen-Tsang and Ku, 2008).

While there is a considerable emerging scholarly literature that attends solely to research with children and about children, it is rare to see a 'children's methodology' set out in general research texts, whereas one does see such representations of other social groups, including women or indigenous peoples. We present a section on research with children because children remain the most dispossessed group: they do not vote and they remain dominated by people called adults who claim to represent them and to be able to speak on their behalf. Children are unable to occupy public space in ways that adults do and therefore are generally silenced in regard to what is 'in their best interests' (Lansdown, 2006; Prout and Tisdall, 2006).

 Weblink 3.3 Emancipatory perspectives

Table 3.2 summarizes emancipatory approaches: feminism, indigenous and child-centred dimensions and assumptions.

Readers may want or expect us to cover anti-racism (or 'ethnic theories') (Denzin and Ryan, 2007: 588–589), queer theories (do Mar Castro Varela, Dhawan and Engel, 2011; Giffney and O'Rourke, 2009; Kumashiro, 2004; Morland and Willox, 2005), ageism (Black, 2009; Lui et al., 2011; Quine and Browning, 2007), disabling practices (Hillier, Johnson and Traustadóttir, 2007; Johnson, 2009; Macfarlane, 2009), and the like. We are unable to do this due to space limitations, and for important theoretical reasons. Most of these approaches also rely on emancipatory aims with a focus on specific 'identities', for example, 'people of colour', or gay, lesbian, bisexual and transgendered and transsexual people, or elders, or people with disabilities. We do look at examples of research that has involved people from these groups in emancipatory ways, and refer to sources that represent the views of advocates and researchers from these groups.

TABLE 3.2 Emancipatory approaches: feminism, indigenous and child-centred dimensions and assumptions

	Assumptions: Feminist Perspectives	Assumptions: Indigenous Perspectives	Assumptions: Child-centred Research
Ethics	Equality, trust and mutuality are required that are extended beyond research participants to social life (Hekman, 2007: 536–537; Peile et al., 1995; Stanley and Wise, 1993: 202–203).	'Research is a site of contestation not simply at the level of epistemology or methodology but also in its broadest sense as an organized scholarly activity that is deeply connected to power' (Smith, 2005: 87). 'Mutuality and reciprocity', not 'individualized and contractual' (Ling, 2008: 101–102). Collective or community consent instead of individualized consent (Smith, 2005: 97–99). Relationship-based ethics instead of principalist ethics (Smith 2005: 100–101).	Legal issues related to children's ability to consent based on assumptions about competence (Williamson et al., 2005). Adults (usually parents/ carers, sometimes professionals with legal guardianship) are asked to consent on behalf of children. An 'ethic of care' (Tronto, 1993) and 'ethics of the encounter' (Levinas, cited by Moss, 2006: 190) emphasizes relationships between children and researchers. Researchers need awareness to avoid colonization of children's spaces and ways of knowing by adults.
Ontology	Gender is a central feature of identity and social organization, and its reproduction and organization are political/social/interactional processes located simultaneously in individuals and social structure: the personal is political and the political is personal (Peile et al., 1995). '... no opinion, belief or other construction of events and persons, ... should be taken as a representation of "reality" but rather treated as a motivated construction or version of "reality"' (Stanley and Wise, 1993: 200).	Knowledge is tacit, grounded and emergent in local contexts (Nimmagadda and Martell, 2008: 146–147; Osei-Hwedie and Rankopo, 2008: 203–217; Smith, 2005: 89–90; Yuen-Tsang and Ku, 2008: 186–187), to minimize the imposition of external versions of knowledge and truth, particularly by researchers who may be outsiders to the communities and whose versions of emancipation may also be oppressive due to patronage and the need to 'rescue' the disadvantaged groups. Stories and moral relativism are preferred as opposed to 'ethical universalism' and 'truth' (Smith, 2005: 100–101).	What is true now for a child may not be true later in their lives. There are debates about children's ability to distinguish 'objective truth' from 'fantasies', especially in some practice areas, such as child protection, where legal action requires that children are able to present their experiences without contradictions or ambiguity (Botash et al., 1994; Jones, 1994; Morison and Greene, 1992; Mulder and Vrij, 1996; Myers, 1993).

(Continued)

TABLE 3.2 (Continued)

	Assumptions: Feminist Perspectives	Assumptions: Indigenous Perspectives	Assumptions: Child-centred Research
Epistemology	Feminist ethics the same as feminist epistemology, as ideas related to, and constituted by, an 'epistemic community' (Stanley and Wise, 1993: 200). There is no distinction between ontology, epistemology and ethics, with the terms being interchangeable (Hekman, 2007: 535; Stanley and Wise, 1993: 226).	'... The relationship between culture and ways of helping and knowing draws attention to the epistemological base of social work practice. Local knowledges can only be uncovered through the development of a research paradigm grounded in local world views and ways of knowing' (Ling, 2008: 102).	The purpose of research is to achieve social change, hence the topics chosen and the methods used aim to be responsive to local contexts and to empower children (Balen et al., 2006). The adult-as-researcher's worldview and adult and institutional preoccupations of what is important to research may or may not be what children as participants want to tell us about (Graham and Fitzgerald, 2010a: 134–139).
Methodology	Feminist methodology is not a separate process from ontology, epistemology and ethics, because it acknowledges the processes by which research is involved in the construction of knowledge that is not separate from the researcher or the participants (Hekman, 2007: 535; Naples, 2007: 548). Reflexivity by the researcher is essential methodology to make visible the processes by which knowledge has been conceptualized and constructed by the researcher and participants (Naples, 2007: 548, 557–559;	'Decolonizing methodologies' (Briskman, 2008: 83–93; Smith, 1999: Yellow Bird and Gray, 2008: 59–69;), whereby the relationship between theories, methodologies and knowledge can be transformed into a liberating strategy, rather than maintaining its oppressive practices and consequences (Bishop, 2005; Smith, 1999: 125, 2005: 89–90). Decolonizing research involves the 'divesting of colonial power' (Smith, 1999: 98) and building 'global strategic alliances' with other indigenous and colonized groups (Smith, 1999: 108) in addition to handing over governance to them. Research as praxis may include qualitative approaches, participatory action research,	Participatory and child-centred approaches (Graham and Fitzgerald, 2010a, 2010b; Hörschelmann, and Colls, 2010). 'These discussions of an ethics of care and an ethics of an encounter illustrate the connections between provisions for children and ethical concepts and practices: reflection, situatedness, personal judgement, a relational self, interrupting totalising practices, spaces where children can speak and be heard, surprise and possibility' (Moss, 2006: 191). 'The relational dimension of [children's] participation ... requires information sharing and dialogue ..., based on mutual respect and power sharing.... Professional adults should inform their relationships with children through practicing

Assumptions: Feminist Perspectives	Assumptions: Indigenous Perspectives	Assumptions: Child-centred Research
Reinharz, 1992; Stanley and Wise, 1993: 201–202). Feminist researchers use many different methods for data generation to explore women's experiences (Reinharz, 1992): participatory action research, ethnography, survey research, oral histories, census records, popular culture, and even quantitative methods (Hekman, 2007: 540–541; Naples, 2007: 558).	ethnographic methods, oral histories, focus groups, dialogue, cooperative partnerships (Besserab and Crawford, 2010: 179–193; Ling, 2008: 102; Mertens, 2010: 7; Osei-Hwedie and Rankopo, 2008; Yuen-Tsang and Ku, 2008). However, quantitative methods such as social statistics are beneficial to understand patterns of structural inequality (Smith, 2005: 86–87). Reflexivity is important (Smith, 1999: 137).	"ethics of care" or "ethics of the encounter" (Prout and Tisdall, 2006: 243). In addition to more familiar methods, appropriately modified to suit the participating children, such as interviews and discussion groups (Hill et al., 2006; Hopkins and Hill, 2010: 137; Horton and Kraftl, 2010: 216, 221; Mayall, 2006; Ridge, 2006), ethnographies (Holt, 2010: 204), and participant observation (van Blerk, 2010: 235). Other methods include stories (D'Cruz and Stagnitti, 2009), drawings – for psychodynamic interpretation or simply as complementary to verbal story telling (D'Cruz and Stagnitti, 2009) – or 'compositions' (Robson, 2010: 150–156), play (structured and unstructured), photography, focus groups (Beale, 2010: 190; Grogan, 2010: 43–45; van Blerk, 2010: 235), 'participatory diagramming' (Alexander, 2010: 7; Beale, 2010: 190; Hopkins and Hill, 2010: 139–140). Awareness of researcher's own role in the process, the 'researcher's gaze' (Woodyer, 2008, in Colls and Hörschelmann, 2010: 6–7).

We now ask you to review and compare Tables 3.1 and 3.2 which summarize the differences between positivist and emancipatory approaches. We hope that you are able to see that the main and crucial difference is in how people as research participants are seen (the ethical dimension), which then shapes views of knowledge, how knowledge may be generated, and for what purpose. We develop these ideas further in Chapters 4 and 5 and include some guidelines in Chapter 4 to help researchers to critically reflect on their approach.

You can read about these different perspectives, for example, in Denzin and Lincoln's *Handbook of Qualitative Research* (1994, 2005a); Reason and Bradbury's *The Sage Handbook of Action Research: Participative Inquiry and Practice* (2008a); Denzin, Lincoln and Smith's *Handbook of Critical and Indigenous Methodologies* (2008); and Percy-Smith and Thomas's *A Handbook of Children* *and Young People's Participation: Perspectives from Theory and Practice* (2010). These are excellent resources because they show, in a depth that is beyond the scope of this book, the links between the theoretical and political aspects of ways of knowing with the more practical aspects of research, including methods.

Paradigms and the idea of incommensurability

Paradigms and the idea of their being incommensurable have captured scholarly interest across a range of disciplines over recent years. A search for literature to update this chapter, using keywords 'paradigms' and 'incommensurability', has generated articles in organizational analysis (Hassard and Kelemen, 2002; Tadajewski, 2009), marketing (Tadajewski, 2008), and economics (Tomass, 2001) as well as anthropology, sociology and other social sciences. The debates continue to cover much of the same ground as we discussed in the earlier edition of this book, so we will not significantly alter this content except to update it.

The idea of *incommensurability* has two main strands. The first strand is that the differences between paradigms cannot be reconciled because they are competing (rival) perspectives and 'incompatible worldviews' (Blaikie, 1993: 103; Humphries, 2008: 11). While Humphries (2008: 11–15, citing Gendron, 2001) argues that there can never be convergence between paradigms, due to different ontologies (the nature and essence of things), epistemologies (the study of theories and knowledge), methodologies (systems of methods and rules), and teleologies (ends and purposes), she also recognizes the value of complementarity through mixed methods.

A second strand to the meaning of incommensurability – one that is perhaps less well known but remains an issue – concerns the relationship between 'paradigm' and 'method'. Bryman (1988: 118–126, 2008: 603–606) presents the various arguments for and against the proposition that there is a link between epistemology and method. In the first edition of this book (D'Cruz and Jones, 2004: 55–56), we discussed the claims made by Snizek (1976) and Platt (1986) that a paradigm, defined by assumptions, beliefs, values and related theories about reality, has a 'free floating' relationship to 'methods'.

We do not repeat that argument here, but update it. The arguments made by Snizek (1976) and Platt (1986) are located at a particular time when the idea of paradigms was less broad, relatively uncontested, and did not encompass the approaches discussed in this chapter, for example, feminism and indigenous perspectives. Second, the notion of 'paradigm' is often confused with 'methods', rather than the ethical and political implications of different ways of knowing addressed in this chapter.

Theoretical discussions about relations between paradigms and methods have become more relevant as the sociology of knowledge – informed by feminism, postmodernism, poststructuralism and post-colonialism – has contested the dominant (and previously invisible) positivist, scientific, white-Western-male paradigm, and more recently, the emergence of other identities seeking recognition: gay, lesbian, transgendered and transsexual people, people with disabilities, and children, having further unsettled taken-for-granted perspectives about knowledge and the role of research. Alternative ways of knowing have created a space in which all knowledge is seen as political, the positioning of the knower being essential in its creation with marginal groups given a voice, including to challenge the meanings of 'who is marginal' (Hurley, 2007).

In summary, while there seems to be some agreement that paradigms cannot be reconciled, due to, for example, different ontological assumptions (Blaikie, 2000: 261), there is also agreement about the value of using different paradigms and methods (Blaikie, 2000: 261) for 'complementary' perspectives and 'innovative' designs (Gendron, 2001, in Humphries, 2008: 14; Sheldon, 2001).

The paradigm debate: our position

We have found considerable slippage in how 'paradigms' are defined in scholarly sources that we have consulted in the course of revising this text. We will give a few examples. First is the way in which 'positivism' may be represented as a paradigm in its own right (Hekman, 2007; Humphries, 2008; Manicas, 2007; Naples, 2007), or as an epistemology (Bryman, 2008: 13–15), that is, one of the dimensions of a paradigm. A second example is the way that 'interpretivism' is represented by Bryman (2008: 15–17) and Denzin and Lincoln (2005c: 183) as an opposing epistemology to positivism. In other publications,

Denzin and Ryan (2007: 587, citing Guba, 1990: 17) and Denzin and Lincoln (2005b: 24, Table 1.2) argue that interpretivism is a paradigm in the sense that *all* perspectives or theories (for example, positivism, feminism, queer theory) are frameworks in which researchers 'interpret' the social world. Finally, Blaikie (2000: 85–127, 256–262) identifies four 'research strategies' that he calls 'paradigms', distinguishing them from 'theoreticians' theories' (Blaikie, 2000: 159–161), for example, critical theory, feminist theory, structuralism and post structuralism. Therefore, any discussion about 'incommensurability' has to contend with such slippages between fundamental concepts and what constitutes a paradigm to begin with.

In their sometimes savage debate, proponents of different paradigms are inclined to assume their work is an objective fact, missing the point that all paradigms are theories of knowledge generated by people with their own interests and positions. We agree with Nelson (1990, cited in Hekman, 2007: 543–544) that 'there is no pre-theoretical view of the world', and this gives us some scope for playfulness, along with an awareness of ethical and political social work practice (D'Cruz, Gillingham and Melendez, 2009: 61–85), including research (Blaikie, 1993; Denzin and Lincoln, 1994; Everitt et al., 1992; Fawcett et al., 2010; Feyerabend, 1975; Jacobs, 2002a, 2002b; Stanley and Wise, 1993).

We have continued to argue in this chapter, as we did in the first edition of this book (D'Cruz and Jones, 2004: 56), that methodological stances, as a set of assumptions about social reality and social problems, influence the approach that researchers take, and their framing of research questions, design and analysis. For example, Bryman (2008: 588–589) discusses how a disconnection between paradigm and method may result in a qualitative study using a participant observation method, being open to application from either an objectivist or constructionist perspective. There is nothing emancipatory or post-positivist about qualitative research – if it is used as a method without due consideration being given to the ethical and political dimensions of research process – to research outcomes in relation to knowledge/power, or to the researcher's awareness of positioning in the process. As we argue later in this book, a choice of method may be strategic – to engage with political aspects of research and ensure powerful stakeholders are convinced about the issues (see Jayaratne, 1993). It is well known that powerful stakeholders who disagree with research outcomes may attack the methodology or misappropriate the findings for their own ends (Naples, 2007: 558; Silverman, 1998).

As social workers, we should recognize that we are positioned both politically and ethically in relation to social issues and social problems. We cannot escape our personal or professional assumptions or goals. Nor can we be ignorant of the broader political agenda that permeates all aspects of public and social policy and that is increasingly informed by research. Social workers need ways of progressing such debates in the real world where different ways of knowing need to go beyond intellectual puzzles and polite pluralism of agreeing to disagree. Social workers are obliged to act, to attend to social problems – while being aware of practical consequences of different perspectives, some of which may involve explanations of problems or interventions that may increase oppression and disadvantage – while being aware through reflection-on- and -in-action (critical reflection and reflexivity) of the normative assumptions and intentions underpinning our own actions. To those who deny a link between paradigm and method, we reply that if researchers do not consciously relate their theoretical, political and ethical positionings (paradigm) to a choice of methods, then they are either politically naive or ethically and methodologically unsound.

As we show in later chapters of this book, the selection of design, methodology, data generation and analysis do not proceed by way of random or *ad hoc* decisions (or neutral methods or techniques), but are based on assumptions about reality (ontology) and how this may be known and understood (epistemology). It may be necessary to make pragmatic decisions about methods in order to meet broader political agendas – for example, if key stakeholders are unlikely to be convinced by a wholly qualitative study as they give greater credence to statistical analyses and have particular expectations about what constitutes trustworthy research (Silverman, 1998). At the same time, it is necessary for the researcher to make his or her intellectual and ethical assumptions explicit in justifying the methods as a way of demonstrating methodological rigour. We also emphasize the importance of reflexive and reflective practice in social work research to ensure that both paradigm and method are linked to account for the political and ethical dimensions in achieving social change.

Putting it all together

This chapter has looked at paradigms and their relevance for social work research, theory, policy and practice. The main theme has been the connection between different ways of knowing and the political and ethical issues associated with such differences. The idea of the researcher's subjectivity or positioning has been thoroughly explored as crucial to methodologically and ethically sound social work research. The idea of subjectivity has been extended to acknowledge that all individuals or groups with an interest in the research are positioned in particular ways in relation to it.

We have explored examples of how positioning works in the public domain. We have also shown that positioning of individuals in relation to knowledge is complicated and not confined to single perspectives about the social world and human experiences. A social work researcher must not only be aware of her or his own positioning, but also engage in ways that take account of others' positionings to maximize the effectiveness of research.

Riessman (1994a) shows how ways of knowing as personal positioning address diversity and difference, as well as closing gaps between social work practitioners and researchers and between social workers/researchers and clients. She cites England (1994, in Riessman, 1994a: 138) who says: 'We could begin by returning the human voice to our research, welcoming pluralism in experience, method, and interpretation.' This approach is fundamental to emancipatory research, whereby the emphasis on the respect for research participants and the awareness of the ethical and political consequences of research for subordinated and marginalized groups informs the more practical aspects related to methods.

Further reading

Bryman, A. (2008) *Social Research Methods* (3rd edition), Oxford: Oxford University Press (Chapter 1).

Hekman, S. (2007) 'Feminist methodology', in W. Outhwaite and S. P. Turner (eds), *The Sage Handbook of Social Science Methodology*, Los Angeles and New York: Sage (pp. 534–546).

Klein, J. T. (2007) 'Interdisciplinary approaches in social science research', in W. Outhwaite and S. P. Turner (eds), *The Sage Handbook of Social Science Methodology*, Los Angeles and New York: Sage (pp. 32–49).

Naples, N. A. (2007) 'Feminist methodology and its discontents', in W. Outhwaite and S.P. Turner (eds), *The Sage Handbook of Social Science Methodology*, Los Angeles and New York: Sage (pp. 547–564).

Neuman, W. L. and Kreuger, L. W. (2003) *Social Work Research Methods: Qualitative and Quantitative Applications*, London: Pearson Education (especially Chapter 4).

Potter, J. (1996) *Representing Reality*, London: Sage (Chapter 1).

Useful resource

Trials of Galileo, Compass, ABC TV, Sunday, 9 May 2010, 10.10–11.10 pm (www.abc.net.au/compass/pastepisodes.htm) – watch now, download, read transcript.

4

Methodology

Introduction

So far in this book, we have discussed:

1 How to define a research question taking account of existing knowledge in various forms.
2 The importance and implications of different ways of knowing and how these influence research topics and approaches to enquiry.
3 An awareness of the politics and ethics of knowledge from the start of a research project and, particularly, potential ways in which we may oppress or empower individuals and groups on whose behalf we often claim to undertake research.

In this chapter, we shall be:

1 Differentiating between research techniques as data-gathering and analytical devices (methods) and the intellectual and value positions that inform them (methodology).
2 Examining how these techniques and processes are embedded in dominant values and beliefs about what is the best way to know about social events and experiences (epistemology).
3 Aiming to show why it is important for *all* researchers to explain their methodology when they write about their research. As it is fundamental to ethical, politically aware and trustworthy research, it is important for all researchers to recognize the partiality of all knowledge. In this chapter we ask for reflection on 'how do I know what I know?'

Methodology and methods

Methodology takes account of the social context, philosophical assumptions, ethical principles and political issues associated with doing social research

(Neuman, 2006: 2). We believe we have shown in Chapter 3 the epistemo-logical, ontological, ethical and methodological differences informing the more conventional, positivist paradigm and what we have called emancipa-tory approaches (feminist, indigenous and participatory research with children). We have also shown that methodology includes *methods* – the techniques by which you may investigate and analyse the data you generate (Neuman, 2006: 2).

Methods for data collection and analysis are usually differentiated as either *quantitative* or *qualitative*. We will explore this distinction further in Chapters 6 and 7. However, in this chapter, we want to explore the connection between methodology and methods.

What are quantitative and qualitative methods?

Quantitative methods are those that relate to quantity or number, intensity or frequency. The data sought will be numbers, and will be analysed in ways that allow for mathematical calculations and the generation of statisti-cal rules about the meaning and significance of the results (Bryman, 2008: 21–23, 140–163, 314–338; Denzin and Ryan, 2007: 582). Blaikie (2000: 247–253) summarizes the 'preoccupations of quantitative researchers' as 'measuring concepts', 'establishing causality', 'generalizing', 'replicating' and 'focusing on individuals'.

Quantitative methods involve some form of structured investigation that includes questionnaires or surveys, interviews, observations, content analysis or statistical collections, sometimes involving experimental designs to measure and analyse 'causal relationships between variables, not pro-cesses' (Denzin and Lincoln, 2005b: 7). Structured investigation allows for numerical codes and categories to be generated. The numbers of inform-ants (or 'sources') are usually relatively large to accommodate the rules of ensuring statistical rigour and credibility and analytical techniques to test hypotheses and properly conduct statistical tests of significance, particularly in experimental designs.

While normally associated with positivism and preferred by researchers who seek objectivity and generalizability of research outcomes to wider populations, quantitative methods do not have to be inherently oppressive or unconcerned with emancipatory aims (Fawcett et al., 2010: 151–152). Quantitative methods can generate descriptive information that can be a way of informing and influencing decision makers by investigating the prevalence of patterns of privilege and inequality, such as how much a problem or issue is being experienced and by whom: for example, pay inequities between men and women (Australian Government, www.eowa.

gov.au/Pay_Equity/Pay_Equity_Information.asp); 'poverty ratios for private and disposable income' for selected countries, 'ranked by poverty
reduction' (Fawcett et al., 2010: 92, citing Mahler and Jesuit, 2006); 'global
violence against women' (Fraser and Craik, 2009: 237–239); patterns of
diversity and disadvantage among older Australian people (Black, 2009:
182–184); 'lesbian health inequalities' (McNair, 2003); 'learning about shifts
in household income by gender and race, unemployment figures, crime
patterns ... migration and immigration' (Agger, 2007: 454); and the political
and critical possibilities of 'quantitative history', using existing secondary
data to examine patterns of inheritance and wealth in families (Anderson,
2007: 248).

It is only when quantitative methods rely on experimental designs that aim
to show through laboratory conditions how human beings are engaged in
services and their outcomes, or that treat research participants as objects of
scrutiny, that it becomes problematic. An example of this concern is the contemporary trend to promote 'evidence-based practice', as research that focuses
on practical problems related to social regulation, productivity, and alloca-
tion and use of resources (Humphries, 2008: 5). Hence statistical data that
attend to cause–effect designs and claims of effectiveness and efficacy of interventions are preferred over qualitative approaches that investigate problems
experienced by people in socio-economic and cultural contexts. Humphries
(2008: 5–6) argues that it is difficult to ensure smooth application between
'evidence-based findings' and actual practice as contexts may differ in many
ways (time, place, particular populations).

Qualitative methods are those that produce data concerning quality (Bryman,
2008: 21–23, 366–399, 538–563). It is probably easier to describe qualitative
methods as what they are *not* – that is, not quantifiable – because there is no
exhaustive list of what they *are*. However, they include an exploration of values, processes, experiences, language and meaning, among other things. There
is a focus on the 'qualities of entities and on processes and meanings that are
not experimentally examined or measured (if measured at all) ... (Denzin and
Lincoln, 2005b: 7). The numbers of informants are usually limited, to be able
to cope with the volume of data, which is usually in text (words, language,
images).

Denzin and Lincoln (2005b: 3) describe qualitative research as:

> a situated activity that locates the observer in the world. It consists of a set of
> interpretive, material practices that make the world visible. These practices trans-
> form the world. They turn the world into a series of representations, including
> field notes, interviews, conversations, photographs, recordings, and memos to
> the self. At this level, qualitative research involves an interpretive, naturalistic
> approach to the world. This means that qualitative researchers study things in

their natural settings, attempting to make sense of, or interpret, phenomena in terms of the meanings people bring to them.

Denzin and Lincoln (2005b: 6–7) go on to say that qualitative research does not 'privilege' one methodology over any other, and is not influenced by a single paradigm or theory. As we saw in Chapter 3, there are many theories and perspectives informing qualitative methods, including those that aim to be emancipatory. Citing Flick (1998: 2–3), Denzin and Ryan (2007: 583) say that qualitative research is an inductive approach that is emerging as an alternative to quantitative (and deductive) approaches to keep pace with rapid social change and diversity. Blaikie (2000: 247–253) summarizes the 'preoccupations of qualitative researchers' as 'using the social actors' point of view', 'describing thickly', 'focusing on social processes', 'adopting a flexible approach' and 'developing concepts and theory'.

Qualitative methods are usually relatively unstructured or semi-structured, relying on open-ended questions or themes to elicit responses in questionnaires, surveys, interviews, observations and text analysis, and may draw on different approaches, including narrative, discourse and content analysis (Denzin and Lincoln, 2005b: 7). While statistics, tables, graphs and numbers are not usually the main form of data sought in a qualitative study, sometimes statistics may be the subject of a qualitative study to ascertain the diversity of meaning that may be masked by statistical categories. Qualitative studies may also explore the processes by which statistics are produced by people in various forms of social organization and through social processes: for example, see Cicourel (1974), Garfinkel (1974), Government Statisticians' Collective (1993), Ahmad and Sheldon (1993), Thorpe (1994), Harrison and Cameron-Traub (1994), Thomas (1996), and D'Cruz (2004a).

It is also important to realize that qualitative methods are not inherently emancipatory, unless researchers consciously construct their research with those aims and engage with participants with an awareness of the ethical and political context of research, and their own positioning within the research process.

In summary, methodology is the set of assumptions related to ethics and politics, epistemology and ontology that contextualizes the methods by which research is practised. Methods on their own are the practical ways in which information (or 'data') is (are) generated so that the questions of interest may be properly investigated and later analysed. You can do research by just focusing on methods related to research questions. But if you are doing emancipatory research, you do need to be explicit about the methodology informing your study and overall approach. We look at methods of data generation and analysis in Chapters 6 and 7, respectively.

Quantitative or qualitative? The debates about methods

Choosing whether to use *qualitative* or *quantitative* approaches to research is not a neutral exercise. Instead, each approach is associated with perceived or actual differences that are influenced by particular paradigms or ways of knowing. Basically, the arguments for or against qualitative and quantitative methods relate to judgements about trustworthy research that are informed by beliefs about reality and how one knows about and investigates that reality, with those making such judgements positioned within different paradigms (Bryman, 2008; Denzin and Lincoln, 1994, 2005a; Reason and Bradbury, 2008a). In the previous edition of this book, we summarized key aspects of the debates about the value and worth of quantitative and qualitative methods, drawing on Bryman (1988), who extends this discussion related to research as a practice in Bryman (2008: 588–601).

Quantitative studies, particularly those associated with experimental designs, aim to test or confirm hypotheses (Bryman, 2008: 141). The aim in the first instance is to disprove the theory by showing that there is *no* relationship between the variables of interest (Neuman and Kreuger, 2003: 143–144). For example, if you are running a family support programme and want to know if it is effective or not, in an experimental design you would want to show that there is no relationship between the programme and the outcomes for families. If your research shows that there *is* a relationship, this confirms the theory. Qualitative research, on the other hand, is said to rely on inductive theories – those that come from life or are grounded in human experience. Some critics would argue that it is impossible to produce entirely emergent or grounded theory untouched by the researcher's own intellectual positioning (Bryman, 2008: 548–549; Denzin, 1994: 508).

Statistical analyses are fundamental to quantitative methods to allow generalization of the results to the wider population (a nomothetic scope). They rely on probability sampling so that statistical rules for data quality and generalizability can be applied (Bryman, 2008: 167–182). Qualitative research does not seek to generalize to populations but, instead, looks at alternative ways of generating theory about human experiences and the contexts in which they occur. Hence, both probability and purposive sampling methods may be appropriate, depending on the aims of the research and the methods used (Bryman, 2008: 375–376).

However, while these apparent distinctions can be made in *methods*, associated with the types of data sought, quantitative and qualitative methods are not inherently positivist, oppressive or emancipatory. Denzin and Ryan (2007: 582–589) point out that historically, quantitative *and* qualitative research have been influenced by positivist and postpositivist approaches initially associated with the physical sciences and that later informed social science research. Early qualitative research was framed within the positivist paradigm, with the aim of 'doing good positivist research with less rigorous methods and procedures' (Denzin and Ryan, 2007: 583), citing, for example, Becker et al.'s (1961) report of participant observation as using 'quasi-statistics', and Strauss and Corbin's (1998, cited by Denzin and Ryan (2007) as 1999) attempt to make grounded theory fit more closely the standards for good positivist and scientific research.

It is also possible to use both approaches simultaneously even if the assumptions about reality and ways of knowing (as methods) differ so significantly, for example, see Bryman (2008: 602–626), Plano Clark et al. (2008), Teddlie et al. (2008), Fawcett et al. (2010: 151–152), as long as the differences are known and clearly justified.

The reflexive researcher: linking paradigm and method

To make informed choices in achieving methodologically and ethically sound research, you need to know what the criteria are for trustworthy research within different paradigms. Being aware of different criteria for trustworthy research can help in strategic designs that will convince powerful stakeholders, without losing your ethical stance. So it is possible to use quantitative methods, qualitative methods, or a combination, to achieve emancipatory aims, as long as you attend to the relational ethics with participants and that you have the appropriate skills yourself or on your research team to meet the criteria for trustworthy research.

Exercise: Quantitative and qualitative data – critiques

Below is an activity to raise awareness of the sorts of responses generated to quantitative and qualitative methods by people who may be opposed to one or the other. The activity may help you develop responses to these critiques. It aims to trigger your reactions and further reflections to explore your subjectivity and positioning as a researcher. The critical statements are derived from various scholarly texts that discuss such debates (for example, Bryman, 2008; Denzin and Lincoln, 1994; Humphries and Truman, 1994; Rubin and Babbie, 2007: 250–251; Silverman, 1998).

1 Read the statements below and repeat the following steps for each in turn.
2 What is your reaction to the statement (emotionally and/or intellectually)? (There is no right or wrong reaction. It is important to be aware of your

reactions because they indicate your personal positioning in relation to knowledge and ways of knowing.)

3   Identify the paradigm(s) represented by the statement.
4   Which stakeholders are more likely to make such a statement? Why might they make such a statement? (Consider what their knowledge and political and ethical positions might be. What's in it for them?)
5   To what extent is the statement valid or true?
6   To what extent could you challenge the statement?
7   How might you challenge the statement in terms of alternative assumptions about different ways of knowing? (To do this, you will need to set out what the assumptions are in the statement and what some alternative assumptions might be.)
8   How might you explain your reactions to the statement and the response that you made to it? (Think about what you have learnt, past experiences, and so on.)

Critical statements about quantitative approaches

Your data are meaningless because they are only numbers.

It is impossible to generalize about whole populations on the basis of responses provided by a sample population.

How can you control for what goes on in 'the real world'?

There is no truth in the claim that your design and data are unbiased.

There is no truth in the claim that you have succeeded in separating your values from the facts generated by the research.

How can you say that you have been able to measure people's experiences?

Critical statements about qualitative approaches

Your data are anecdotal and do not provide any real evidence of true experiences.

Your data are biased and subjective because your informants are talking about their own experiences.

Your informants are not being objective; they have a vested interest in what they are telling you.

You have used a small sample so your participants are not typical of the population of interest.

There is no consistency in your data because informants have told their stories in their own way.

You have not used a random way of finding your informants so your research is biased.

(Continued)

(Continued)

How can a few stories be useful to bring about change?

How can one story tell us anything of value? It is only one example.

How might you respond to the following comment?

'...if a researcher reports that the members of a club tend to be conservative, know that such a judgment is unavoidably linked to the researcher's own politics. However, researchers who use qualitative techniques can be conscious of this issue and take pains to address it. Not only are individual researchers able to sort out their own biases and points of view but also the communal nature of science means that their colleagues will help them in that regard.' (Rubin and Babbie, 2007: 250)

Traditional criteria for trustworthy research

Four criteria usually deemed necessary for trustworthy research are reliability, validity, generalizability and objectivity. They are often used for both quantitative and qualitative approaches. Critics of research that is controversial may also use these criteria to undermine the claims made, by claiming the methodology is deficient on one or more of these grounds.

Reliability

A test of good (reliable) research is the replicability of the research process and outcomes (Bryman, 2008: 149–150). The consistency of research instruments is the primary concern, because they aim to measure the phenomena of interest through surveys or observation. Any differences that may emerge in the study must be related to the actual phenomena and not to inconsistencies in the research instruments (Marlow, 2011: 184–185).

Moser and Kalton (1989: 353, in Kumar, 2011: 181) state:

> ... a scale or test is reliable to the extent that repeat measurements made by it under constant conditions will give the same result.

Marlow (2011: 185) uses the example of a ruler that remains consistent over time (and is therefore reliable) as a research instrument. Similarly, the research instruments that you as a researcher will develop to investigate your question – surveys or observation criteria, for example – need to be reliable over time and place as a way of ensuring the replicability of the results. The idea of replicability as it is related to reliability means that another researcher may want to repeat your study. Therefore, if they use exactly the same research instruments, they should get the same results, which is a way of confirming the trustworthiness of your research and its outcomes.

Sources of error

Researchers using these assumptions about the trustworthiness of their research process and methods seek to maximize reliability by minimizing sources of error (Marlow, 2011: 185–186), namely, (1) unclear definitions of variables, (2) use of retrospective information, (3) variations in conditions for collecting data, and (4) structure of the instrument.

Unclear definitions of variables It is essential to define the variables being investigated. If the variables remain loose or nebulous, then you will not develop appropriate questions that address the phenomena you are interested in and you may not be sure that you are measuring what you think you are measuring. Furthermore, respondents may interpret the questions in particular ways that, under these assumptions about reliability, are considered to be problematic.

Problems of reliable definitions may be more easily addressed if you are undertaking a scientific study where the variables perhaps lend themselves to clear definition – for example, blood pressure or income levels. However, for social work research, most of the issues of interest are abstract concepts, such as poverty or self-esteem or emotional abuse, that remain controversial as well as extremely difficult to operationalize (define in ways that make them seem concrete and physically real and, therefore, measurable) (see for example, Blunt-Williams, Meshelemiah and Venable, 2011: 780–783).

Use of retrospective information Reliability is seen as problematic if you rely on informants' recollections of events or experiences from the past or case records.

If you are using such material, it is essential to justify intellectually and ethically why you are using a retrospective approach – that is, you cannot conduct a prospective study for ethical, legal or methodological reasons. You must also discuss such limitations as they affect your conclusions.

Variations in conditions for collecting data One source of variation may be related to whether you have mailed out your questionnaires or are conducting face-to-face interviews. Face-to-face interviews introduce additional variations, such as the characteristics of the researcher (gender, age and ethnicity) or place of the interview, which may influence the responses given.

In research that seeks consistency throughout the process, these variations are problematic and should be minimized.

Structure of the instrument For a higher degree of reliability it is better to have structured methods of enquiry (using closed questions in questionnaires or interviews, for example) to control the degree to which informants may interpret what is meant by the questions. More open-ended questions that require categories to be developed by the researcher from the free-flowing responses given by informants pose problems for reliability.

Testing reliability

Researchers who wish to ensure reliability (consistency) of their research instruments may test for it using (1) test–retest, (2) alternate (or parallel) form, (3) split half, and (4) observer reliability (Kumar, 2011: 182–184; Marlow, 2011: 186–187).

The first three approaches are different versions of a pilot study. This is a technique that assumes that it is possible to develop questions that will generate similar responses if asked at different times and across a group of people who are not the research participants. The same set of questions may be asked on two occasions, or different but equivalent forms of the questions may be asked (Marlow, 2011: 186–187). The aim is to achieve consistent responses from the participants in the pilot study to questions that have been developed for a survey or questionnaire. If the sets of responses are very similar, this indicates that the questions have a high degree of reliability. Studies that have used such tests of reliability are Hudson (1990) and Teare et al. (1998) (both cited in Marlow and Boone, 2005: 190, 192).

Observer reliability refers to consistency of observations if more than one person is involved in observations of settings and interactions. Observers are usually trained in what is to be observed and how it is to be recorded. Additionally, predetermined criteria are used by at least two other people to code each of the observers' responses.

As can be seen, these approaches to testing reliability are influenced by assumptions that there is an absolute reality that can be ascertained by means of appropriately generated data. Furthermore, it is assumed that other researchers who wish to replicate the research will make use of the same research instruments with the aim of testing the replicability of the initial research outcomes. Questions and observations are therefore understood to be neutral techniques that can generate objective truths by minimizing inconsistencies in how questions are interpreted by informants. It does not consider how context may influence responses.

Validity

Validity refers to the actual structure and content of whatever method is used to elicit the information needed to answer the research questions. In positivist/quantitative studies, this is described as the 'measuring instrument', and may be defined as 'the extent to which you are measuring what you think you are measuring' (Marlow, 2011: 187) or 'whether a measure of a concept really measures that concept' (Bryman, 2008: 151). The method of data collection (a research instrument) must meet three kinds of internal validity: (1) criterion, (2) content, and (3) construct validity (Blunt-Williams et al., 2011: 780–783; Marlow, 2011: 187–189).

Criterion validity

Criterion validity, also known as 'concurrent and predictive validity' (Kumar, 2011: 180), involves comparing a research measure that you develop with another measure that also claims to represent the criteria being investigated, such as a scale or standardized measure. If the comparisons are similar, then the indicators that you have developed may be claimed to have high validity.

These types of comparison establish two types of validity: predictive and concurrent. *Predictive validity* is judged by the degree to which an instrument can forecast an outcome. *Concurrent validity* is judged by how well an instrument compares with a second assessment done concurrently (Kumar, 2011: 180).

Content validity

Content validity, also known as 'face validity' (Kumar, 2011: 179–180), 'is concerned with the representativeness of the content of the instrument' (Marlow, 2011: 188). It is 'based upon the logical link between the questions and the objectives of the study' (Kumar, 2011: 179). This means that the questions you ask informants or the themes that structure your observations must be directly associated with the research questions.

Construct validity

Construct validity:

> describes the extent to which an instrument measures a theoretical construct. … With construct validity, we are looking not only at the instrument but also at the theory underlying it. The instrument must reflect this theory. (Marlow, 2011: 189)

This definition shows the importance of the literature review in helping you to develop the conceptual and practical aspects of your research.

However, there are many concepts in social work that may have theoretical explanations, such as aggression, sociability and self-esteem, but may be difficult to define.

Generalizability

Generalizability, or external validity, is concerned with being able to draw conclusions and inferences about the wider population based on what is found by the research study via a sample of informants or sources. This is particularly important in quantitative studies that use statistical techniques to select samples so that the analysis and conclusions may then be applicable (generalizable), within statistical laws, to the wider population (Bryman, 2008: 156–157; Marlow, 2011: 10; Schofield, 1993). It is an important consideration in group designs, particularly in programme evaluations where you may want to explore or compare the outcomes (effectiveness) of services provided to different, but comparable, client groups (Marlow, 2011: 91–92). (See the section on sampling in Chapter 5, Designing Research). This is why representative samples are important, especially in quantitative research (Bryman, 2008: 33). Marlow argues that external validity or generalizability:

> depend on two conditions: first, ensuring the equivalency [comparability] of the groups [We ask, is this possible or desirable? Why or why not?] and second, ensuring that nothing happens during the evaluation to jeopardize the equivalence of the groups [We ask, is this possible or desirable? Why or why not?]. (Marlow, 2011: 91).

Objectivity

Objectivity is a principle that aims to minimize the influences of the researcher's values, beliefs and potentially vested interests in the topic being researched. Someone who is not seen as objective under this definition is described as biased (Marlow, 2011: 7, 163). One aim of objectivity is to foster an attitude of disinterest as a dispassionate enquirer whose primary task to search for knowledge is about curiosity and discovery, rather than trying to prove what you as researcher believe to be true. This is clearly an important ethical consideration. However, the principle also seeks to separate values from knowledge. As social workers, we need to consider how to be open-minded about knowledge while being aware of the need 'to take sides' to achieve social justice (Hurley, 2007: 167–169). We argue that the theoretical and ethical assumptions influencing all research should be made explicit.

Criteria for trustworthy research: critiques and alternatives

You may have noticed from the preceding section that the four criteria usually cited for ensuring trustworthy research focus on issues such as measurement, instruments, accuracy, predictability, value neutrality, and distance between 'researcher' and 'researched'. The assumptions about truth and reality and ways of knowing about reality that inform these criteria are primarily associated with positivism.

Many qualitative researchers and scholars who write about theoretical issues associated with research methodology have argued that the parameters for ensuring trustworthy research need to be reconsidered beyond positivism and its usual application in the form of quantitative methods. In a very influential article, Guba and Lincoln (1982) have set out an argument for an alternative way of ensuring trustworthy qualitative research that may be appropriate to emancipatory approaches. Their approach has informed their later work on evaluation (Guba and Lincoln, 1989), and other researchers who have developed the conceptual and practical ways of applying the 'naturalistic' criteria for trustworthiness in qualitative research (for example, Morrow, 2005; Morse, Barrett, Mayan, Olson and Spiers, 2002; Seale, 2002; Shenton, 2004). Guba and Lincoln (1982) have simplified the distinctions between positivism and competing paradigms that we explored in Chapter 3. They make a dichotomy between positivism, which they call 'rationalism', and alternatives, which they call 'naturalism' and we have called emancipatory approaches.

In developing alternative criteria for trustworthy 'naturalistic' research, Guba and Lincoln (1982: 246) identify four obligations that underpin *all* research, *regardless of paradigm*. These obligations are:

1 **Truth value**: establishing confidence in the outcomes for participants within their context.
2 **Applicability**: how applicable the research outcomes are for different contexts or with other participants.
3 **Consistency**: whether it is possible to replicate the findings if the study is repeated with the same or similar participants, and in the same or similar contexts.
4 **Neutrality**: how to establish that the findings are representative of participants' perspectives and the extent to which the researcher's positioning has been influential.

While all researchers must attend to these obligations, the criteria for claiming or judging 'trustworthiness' will depend upon the paradigm informing such judgements. Instead of the four criteria traditionally used and discussed above, Guba and Lincoln (1982) suggest alternatives relevant to the naturalistic paradigm.

Alternative criteria for trustworthy research

The naturalistic alternatives that Guba and Lincoln (1982: 246–249) propose are credibility (for validity), transferability (for generalizability or external validity), dependability (for reliability), and confirmability (for objectivity).

Credibility

The researcher must be able to show that the data of enquiry do represent appropriately 'the phenomena those data represent' (Guba and Lincoln, 1982: 246). However, because the naturalistic paradigm understands that social reality is only meaningful to the people who participate in that reality, the researcher can ask the informants whether or not 'their realities have been represented appropriately' (Guba and Lincoln, 1982: 246). Is the analysis believable within their understandings and experience of reality? This possibility is not open to researchers in a rationalistic, positivist paradigm because this would be seen as being biased or subjective.

Transferability

Knowledge generated from naturalistic research, for example, human behaviour or the meanings that people give to social events, is not generalizable beyond the context in which it is meaningful. However, some form of transferability is possible and even necessary under certain conditions. These conditions exist when the context in which the research is carried out shares sufficient features with another context that may allow some transfer of knowledge gained. Also, the conditions under which particular knowledge claims are made must be acknowledged. For example, if you have conducted research in a child welfare statutory organization, there may be some practice principles that are relevant broadly across the child welfare field, but they would also be limited by the differences between statutory and non-statutory organizations and their effects on social work practice. These contextual conditions must be integral to the claims made and conclusions drawn.

Schofield (1993: 208), an educational researcher, asks:

To what do we [qualitative researchers] want to generalize?

How can we design qualitative studies in a way that maximizes their generalizability?

She suggests 'three targets for generalization ... *what is*, to *what may be*, and to *what could be*' (Schofield, 1993: 208, 221, original emphasis) and continues:

Studying *what is* refers to studying the typical, the common, or the ordinary. ... Studying *what may be* refers to designing studies so that their fit with future trends and issues is maximized. ... Studying *what could be* refers to locating situations that we know or expect to be ideal or exceptional on some *a priori* basis and studying them to see what is actually going on there.

Dependability

Dependability is the alternative concept to reliability associated with replicability of rationalistic research: 'under the same circumstances in another place and time ..., and where discrepancies or deviations between two repetitions of the same study ... are charged to unreliability (error)' (Guba and Lincoln, 1982: 247). Within the naturalistic paradigm, an expectation of exact replicability is contextually impossible, if not intellectually unsound. Research designs ought not to be repeated automatically in a different context. Most designs emerge consciously to account for contextual differences.

Confirmability

Naturalistic researchers argue that it is impossible to separate values (the researcher's positioning) from how the research question is formulated and how the research is conducted. A related concept is 'strong objectivity' (Naples, 2007: 554–555, citing Harding, 1987) that proposes that all participants' points of view should be taken into account, a collective process that acknowledges 'epistemic communities' (Stanley and Wise, 1993: 200). 'Strong objectivity recognizes social situatedness of all knowledge ... and some social situations are capable of generating more objective accounts than others' (Hekman, 2007: 544).

Sometimes the rationalistic paradigm relies on findings that show 'quantitative agreement' (Guba and Lincoln, 1982: 247) – for example, the numbers of respondents who ticked this or that category as a response to a structured question. 'What is important is not that there be quantitative agreement but qualitative confirmability' (Guba and Lincoln, 1982: 247). Again, asking the informants by means of a process of consultation is a way of achieving confirmability.

Strategies for achieving trustworthy research: triangulation, transferability and reflexivity

Triangulation is not solely associated with naturalistic approaches and qualitative data, as it is also recommended in quantitative studies, as a 'validation strategy' (Clarke 2009: 297) that aims to 'minimize systematic measurement error' (Rubin and Babbie, 2011: 94, 298, 452, 584, 630). However, in naturalistic studies, triangulation involves combining 'multiple observers, theoretical perspectives, sources of data, and methodologies' (Denzin, 1970: 310, in Bryman, 2008: 379). Clarke (2009: 297) describes this approach as complementary designs ('connected contributions') between methods and approaches, or multiple case studies, that might alleviate the pressure for validation between quantitative and qualitative approaches, with one potentially dominating the other.

For example, triangulation improves the trustworthiness of the research if there is more than one observer of an interaction or context. It also helps to discuss observations, responses or conclusions with peers who are not directly involved in the research or with other informants. You may find approaching the research from different theoretical perspectives could increase the credibility, although such an approach might complicate the methodology considerably. You may use multiple methods, for example, by not relying solely on interviews, but adding observation, documentary analysis and other media to give alternative or complementary views (Hughes, 2011: 689–693). You may also combine quantitative and qualitative approaches. It is essential that you document all research processes and keep a diary of your reflections as you proceed as a way of auditing the trustworthiness of the research (Denzin, 1994: 513; Huberman and Miles, 1994: 439).

An alternative to triangulation is mixed-genre texts, described using a metaphor of 'the crystal' (Richardson and St Pierre, 2005: 959–978, in Denzin and Lincoln, 2005b: 5–6), which proposes that mixed-genre texts, like crystals, give multiple sides and facets (Richardson, 2000: 934, cited in Denzin and Lincoln, 2005b: 5–6). Examples of mixed-genre texts, whereby 'the same tale is told from different points of view', involve a combination of 'fiction, field notes and a scientific article', as in Wolf's *A Thrice-Told Tale* (1992), and a play by Smith *Fires in the Mirror* (1993), where the actors tell about the same incident from different points of view, representing people with a range of interests and perspectives (Denzin and Lincoln, 2005b: 6). Or as the narrator in *The Life of Pi* (Martel, 2003: 292–319) asks his disbelieving interrogators of his fantastic tale about a set of 'facts': 'which version of the facts would you like?'

Transferability relies on the following strategies, discussed by Schofield (1993: 208–220) in relation to the three domains of generalizability in qualitative research.

1 'Studying what is' involves studying what is typical and/or using multiple sites.
2 'Studying what may be' investigates changes that may be happening in a context, what may 'differentiate the present from the future', and considering the 'life cycle of phenomena' at a site.
3 'Studying what could be' involves studying a site that offers opportunities to investigate 'what could be' and/or using knowledge gained in a more unusual context for its application in another context.

Reflexivity is a process by which the researcher continually reflects on his or her participation in the process of knowledge production – that is, the research enquiry and the conclusions that are drawn (Fuchs, 1992; Smith, 1999: 137; Stanley and Wise, 1993). This includes an overt expression of values and assumptions (positioning) informing the choice of question, design, data collection and analysis and conclusions.

Reflexivity may be enhanced by the use of a research diary (mentioned above) as it is a way for the researcher to make explicit his or her thoughts, emerging hypotheses, and tentative theories as the research proceeds, making important links between process and outcome (conclusions).

Emancipatory methodologies and transformative research

In the first edition of this book, we included a discussion of 'decolonizing methodologies' (D'Cruz and Jones, 2004: 77–80), drawing on Smith (1999), who showed through many examples of research conducted in indigenous communities how research may be both a process of, and resistance to, colonization. Resistance includes challenging the role that research has played in maintaining dominance of colonizers' cultures over indigenous cultures and knowledge:

> Significant spaces have been opened up within the academy and within some disciplines to talk more creatively about research with particular groups and

communities – women, the economically oppressed, ethnic minorities and indigenous people. These discussions have been informed as much by the politics of groups outside the academy as by engagement with the problems which research with real, living, breathing, thinking people actually involves. Communities and indigenous activists have openly challenged the research community about such things as racist practices and attitudes, ethnocentric assumptions and exploitative research, sounding warning bells that research can no longer be conducted with indigenous communities as if their views did not count or their lives did not matter. (Smith, 1999: 9)

Processes involving 'decolonizing methodologies' to promote emancipatory and transformative research are relevant to all silenced groups (Smith, 2005: 87–88). However, decolonizing methodologies go beyond an intellectual process of linking knowledge and theoretical perspectives to research methods. Instead, the fundamental assumptions of knowledge itself are challenged – how you know and what you know related to your positioning within 'socially organized hierarchies' (Chapman, 2011: 725) that include gender, race, ethnicity, ability, age, class, sexualities, as well as institutionalized roles such as supervisor, boss, social worker or researcher.

Trustworthy research that relies on 'decolonizing methodologies' privileges marginalized and objectified people's concerns, practices and participation as both researchers and researched (Smith, 1999: 107). For research that aims to be empowering and emancipatory, we draw on different scholars who provide some useful principles and reflective questions to aid researchers (Humphries, 1994: 185–204; Mertens, 2010: 5–8; Smith, 1999: 9–10, 173).

Power: structural and situated

Naples (2007: 552, citing Wolf, 1996) summarizes three ways in which power and domination may be exercised in the research process: (1) power differences between the researcher and participants in relation to class, race, gender, ethnicity, sexualities, age, nations, among other dimensions; (2) the researcher's power to define the relationship and potential to exploit participants; and (3) the power to construct the meaning of participants' knowledge and shape their representations in the text. While the researcher is in a structurally-dominant position, there may be complexities related to other intersecting identities between researcher and participants, and participants can also resist and subvert the research relationship. It is also possible for researchers to subvert empowerment and emancipatory objectives while claiming the opposite, for example, through 'accommodation, accumulation and appropriation' (Humphries, 1994: 190–191, citing Said, 1978).

Accommodation refers to research practices that conform with, and do not challenge, ideas that represent dominant ways of knowing that may be experienced by marginal groups as oppressive. The researcher then engages in 'reconstruction' or 'repetition' (Said, 1978, in Humphries, 1994: 191) of structures that maintain the dominant perspective and that claim to understand and explain all experiences within that perspective (Humphries, 1994: 191).

Accumulation refers to a form of colonialism and imperialism in which materials from 'the Orient' or 'the East' (read as marginal or disadvantaged groups) are acquired, organized and disseminated as specialized knowledge by researchers external to those cultures or groups. The communication about the lives of oppressed groups in specialized language 'results in surveillance and regulation rather than "empowerment"' (Humphries, 1994: 198).

Appropriation of power is 'the purpose and effect of ... *accommodation* and *accumulation* ...' (Humphries, 1994: 200, original emphasis). Appropriation means that there is the potential for researchers to act oppressively. This is particularly the case if researchers from dominant groups conduct research on or about marginalized groups, and for marginalized groups' experiences to be conceptualized, analysed, and explained using the dominant groups' theoretical and value frameworks. Hence, marginal groups' experiences, knowledge and voices become codified as scholarship and knowledge, become the 'property' of dominant groups, and objectified as 'the Other', as objects of research, and part of a particular ideological position and relationship to dominant groups.

A synthesis of structural and postmodern and poststructural theories of power allows appreciation of structural power related to the positioning of dominant groups and their place in a social setting (society, community, workplace, family), and the situated relations of domination and resistance that are also possible in micro-contexts and interactions (Humphries, 1994: 186). Power can therefore be productive and also may be exercised as domination and oppression.

> This view of power can result in a clearer understanding of, for example, power relations inherent in the researcher–researched relationship, and reveals not a simple hierarchical loading based on socially ascribed characteristics, but complex multifaceted power relations that have both structural dominance and structural subordination play *on both sides*. (Humphries, 1994: 187, original emphasis)

It cannot be emphasized enough that social workers need to develop a theory of power because, without such an understanding, all social work approaches to social problems, including those made through research, become part of the problem rather than contributing to solutions.

Where discussions of empowerment are not grounded in a theory of power and in the wider nexus of political, economic and social power relationships, too easily concerns about social justice can be incorporated into existing beliefs and ideologies. The beneficiaries are more likely to be the research professionals than the research subjects. (Humphries, 1994: 203)

Asking critical questions in emancipatory and transformational research

We have developed a set of questions to guide reflective and reflexive research combining Smith's (1999: 9–10, 173) 'critical questions' and Mertens' (2010: 5–8) 'transformational paradigm'.

Researchers reflecting on *ethical issues* may consider:

- What are the ethical principles that guide my work? For example, whose research is it? Who 'owns' it? To whom is the researcher accountable? What processes have been established to support the research, participants and the researcher?
- What is the connection between those ethical principles and issues of social justice? Whose interests does the research serve? Who will benefit? Who refined the research problem?
- How do the ethical principles reflect issues of culture and power differences?
- How can this research contribute to social justice and human rights?
- If I accept that this is a desirable goal for the research, what would I do differently in terms of methodology?

Researchers reflecting on *ontological assumptions* may consider:

- To what extent did the researcher reveal different versions of reality?
- How did the researcher determine those versions of reality that have the potential either to support or impede progress towards social justice and human rights? What are some likely positive outcomes from this study? What are some possible negative outcomes? How can the negative outcomes be eliminated?
- What were the consequences of identifying these versions of reality?
- How did this research contribute to the change in understandings of what is real?

Researchers reflecting on *epistemological assumptions* may consider:

- What is the nature of the relationship between the researcher and the stakeholders?
- What evidence is there that the researcher addressed issues of power differentials explicitly and that the voices of the least powerful are accurately expressed and acted upon? Who decides the worth and value of the research and its outcomes?
- How did the evaluator establish a trusting relationship with the stakeholders?

Researchers reflecting on *methodological assumptions* may consider:

- How [did] a cyclical design ... use interim findings throughout the study?
- To what extent did researchers engage with the full range of stakeholders to gather qualitative data that enhance [*sic*] their understandings of the community? For example, who designed the scope and questions? Who will do the research?
- To what extent were the methods used responsive to the specific needs of the different stakeholder groups? What knowledge will the community gain from this study? What knowledge will the researcher gain from this study?
- How were the methodologies designed to enhance use of the research findings to support ... social justice and human rights? For example, who will write up the research and disseminate the results?

While the general principles for emancipatory research methodologies may be resonant for different activist communities, there may be specific considerations related to each groups' experiences historically and in contemporary contexts, for example, indigenous people (Smith, 1999: 10); or children (Colls and Hörschelmann, 2010: 6–10).

Putting it all together

In this chapter we have extended the theoretical discussion of paradigms we set out in Chapter 3 to include their relevance for research design, data collection and analysis, discussing the differences between methodology and method and why this matters. We have considered that methods by which data may be collected are directly, if not always explicitly, linked to beliefs about the problem being explored and what is valid knowledge about that problem. We have looked at ways of ensuring credible research, exploring the more traditional criteria and also some alternatives within different sets of assumptions. Finally, we have proposed an approach to doing emancipatory research that connects these theoretical and practical aspects in good social work practice.

Further reading

Agger, B. (2007) 'Does postmodernism make you mad? Or, did you flunk statistics?' in W. Outhwaite and S. P. Turner (eds), *The Sage Handbook of Social Science Methodology*, Los Angeles and New York: Sage (pp. 443–456, especially section on 'Meaning, not method', pp. 453–455).

Bryman, A. (2008) *Social Research Methods* (3rd edition), Oxford: Oxford University Press (Chapter 24, 'Breaking down the quantitative/qualitative divide', pp. 587–601).

Fawcett, B., Goodwin, S., Meagher, G. and Phillips, R. (2010) *Social Policy for Social Change*, South Yarra, Victoria: Palgrave Macmillan (Chapter 8, 'Evidence: the role of research in policy and practice').

Smith, A. and Pitts, M. (2007) 'Researching the margins: An introduction', in M. Pitts and A. Smith (eds), *Researching the Margins: Strategies for Ethical and Rigorous Research with Marginalised Communities*, Basingstoke, Hampshire: Palgrave Macmillan (pp. 3–41).

5

Designing Research

Introduction

The previous chapter considered how procedures and techniques (methods) of research are embedded in assumptions regarding how one may legitimately investigate the social world (methodology). In the next chapter, you will be introduced to commonly used methods for collecting and generating data. We need to consider our purpose for using such procedures so that they are appropriate for achieving research goals – and also the ethical and political implications of doing so. Research design makes connections between the research question, the approach to different ways of enquiring into social issues, and use of research methods.

In this chapter, we distil complex literature on research design, and offer signposts on:

1   Showing the relationship of research design to paradigms and methodology.
2   Setting out the main elements of design, including key decision points, sampling approaches and recruiting participants.
3   Discussing approaches to ethical research, including governance and relational ethics.

Designing as part of the research process

You have a research question(s), you have reflected on different ways of enquiring into social issues and how your own social position locates you as a researcher, and now some kind of plan is needed as to how you will go about your research. Let us first consider if there are general principles that can guide you in generating an appropriate and workable plan.

Exercise: Thinking about general directions for your research design

If you still have some interest in the research questions you developed in Chapter 2, return to these and make a few quick notes on how you would proceed to enquire into them. (If you have lost a bit of interest in them now, come up with a couple of new ones!)

Quite often, beginning (and not so beginning) researchers jump ahead to think of commonly used methods at this point. 'I'll do some interviews' or 'I'll send around a questionnaire'. The discipline of research design asks us to pause and clarify: 'What for?'; 'What will I be able to do with this information?'; 'How will it assist me in answering my question?' Designing research involves clarifying our rationale for adopting certain procedures and techniques, leaving us better placed to meet the tests for trustworthy research discussed in Chapter 4.

While there may be some differences in how the term 'research design' is defined, according to Punch (1998: 66) it generally means considering 'all the issues involved in planning and executing a research project' and, more specifically, 'the way a researcher ... tries to rule out alternative interpretation of results'. However, the main idea is that through design the researcher is situated 'in the empirical world and connecting research questions to data' (Punch, 1998: 66).

The idea of 'situating the researcher in the empirical world' depicts research design as a bridge between conceptualizing and operationalizing research. A research design is highly theorized and yet extremely practical. It becomes a means of defining what will be done to address the research question, making explicit what is to be studied, why it is to be studied and how it is to be studied (Blaikie, 2009). Expressing it in these terms emphasizes the significance of considering who is involved in creating the design and the social context(s) in which the research is to take place.

The time and effort involved in creating a research design contrasts starkly with a common perception that doing research is about conducting a survey or carrying out some interviews or focus groups. For many people, research methods are the concrete expression of research and perhaps the point at which they have experienced research being done. However, methods are an outcome of a complex design process that requires engagement with those challenging questions as to how we can know and study the social world. Crotty (1998) depicts research methods as the tip of a pyramid that has its foundation in epistemology and is built upwards through theoretical perspectives and methodology.

We have drawn on Sim and Wright (2000: 18) to depict in Figure 5.1, the 'complex relationship between theory, a research question, research methodology, research design and research methods'.

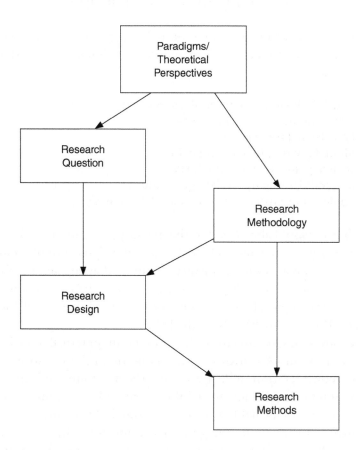

FIGURE 5.1 Locating research design

Source: Adapted from Sim and Wright (2000:18)

Wadsworth (2011: 44) explains that:

A good research design ensures you will get the best evidence – the most relevant, credible, valid, trustworthy, reliable and authentic possible – and also that you haven't overlooked possible sources of criticism or possible counter-evidence. It matches up the sources available, and the questions needing answers, with the kinds and amounts of observations, evidence and conversations needed to generate new understandings and insights, and show how and why you came to them. It allows time for reflection to creatively develop plausible explanations and proposals and for testing new ideas in practice to ensure the purposes of the research are properly met.

Elements of research design

Research design, as a basic plan for a research project, includes a 'logical structure' and a plan to be followed (Sim and Wright, 2000: 27, 38, adapted) that should consider:

- What entities, phenomena or variables to study
- Under what conditions to generate data
- What types(s) of data to generate
- From whom (or what) to generate data
- At what time points to generate the data
- What methods to employ for data generation
- What implications ensue for subsequent data analysis

A research plan would also attend to the practical and administrative arrangements necessary for the research to be completed successfully. This might include, for example, ensuring adequate staffing, drawing up a viable timetable, processes for accessing participants or data sources, attending to any necessary ethical approvals, and overall costing and budgeting of the project (Alston and Bowles, 2012; Wadsworth, 2011).

The research design grounds the project in practical considerations that may require modifications to the scope or to the question itself. An important consideration will always be the feasibility of the research, which includes time, money, availability of suitable equipment, and number and expertise of available researchers (Sim and Wright, 2000: 28). The process involves the researcher going back and forth between designing for trustworthy research and planning for its implementation, refining the research question and focus on the way. Again, we are led to ask who is contributing to this process and how decisions are made in these formative stages.

The design process provides an important window on to the ways in which research knowledge is constructed. Decisions present themselves in particular ways as a consequence of the methodological principles that stake a claim on their capacities to render 'truths' of some kind. Decision making about designs occurs within these discourses but also attends to the social contexts (economic, political, cultural) of their application: the principles have to be made to 'work' in particular circumstances, and require continuing re-interpretation to cast a study as 'good research'. At the same time, the design also has to 'work' in terms of furthering the overall purposes of the research. As discussed previously, this may well mean a process through which consideration is given as to which design options connect best with the (often diverse) interests and preferences of key stakeholders, including the users and recipients of social work services.

From a conceptual perspective, a good design in social work research requires purposeful thinking through of the core ontological and epistemological assumptions being brought to the study of the topic – the 'ways of knowing' discussed in Chapter 3. A strong grounding here will help guide the myriad of decisions that will need to be made in constructing a congruent and fitting research design that is ethically and politically informed and also feasible in the time, resources and relationships that can be dedicated to it. Further, a good research design must consider the ethics and politics of how participants are treated, beyond legalistic ethical criteria.

Types of research design

There is no one accepted classification of research designs. It can become a bewildering exercise to find one's way through the maze of possibilities. Learning to research therefore involves learning to identify key decisions that are made in the process of determining a design appropriate to the research question and focus. Humphries (2008: 190–192, drawing on Yin, 1994) tabulates different strategies related to the research question and some of their features. This approach assists in building a design that is fit for purpose (see Table 5.1).

TABLE 5.1   Relevant situations for different research strategies

Strategy	Form of research question	Requires control over behavioural events?	Focuses on contemporary events?
Experiment	How? Why?	Yes	Yes
Survey	Who? What? Where? How many? How much?	No	Yes
Archival analysis	Who? What? Where? How many? How much?	No	Yes / No
History	How? Why?	No	No
Case study	How? Why	No	Yes

Source: Yin (1994)

Research designs may be most simply described as 'experimental' and 'non-experimental'. *Experimental designs* follow the tenets of (positivist) scientific method. They seek to either establish causality (cause–effect) or correlation between variables, testing hypotheses about these relationships (hypothetico-deductive designs). *Non-experimental designs* are informed by methodologies more concerned with description or exploration. (You can see how the naming of these designs and their purpose suggests the dominance of natural science as the norm.)

Therefore, an 'appropriate' design is one that is best to answer the question of interest to us. That is, if we want to explore a newly identified social issue, then we might employ a non-experimental design. If we wanted to determine whether an intervention causes certain outcomes, then we would most likely use an experimental design. What we will be able to contribute to knowledge about the question is dependent on what the design (with its strengths and limitations) can deliver, and the extent to which we have been able to implement it in ways consistent with the criteria that pertain to the methodologies underpinning it.

Understanding research design in this way is a good starting point. However, any straightforward classification of design according to purpose is likely to break down on closer examination (Blaikie, 2009). As we hope has become evident by now, quantitative methodologies are not bound to hypothesis testing and experimental design. We might employ a quantitative approach descriptively, for example, to research trends and patterns in rates of homelessness or disparities in household income. Alternatively, we might employ a qualitative approach in search of an explanation, which, while not seeking to find causes or correlations, may well produce compelling narratives that carry their own explanatory power.

Key decision points in research design

Drawing on Sim and Wright (2000) and Blaikie (2009: 10), here are some questions for reflection as key decision points in research design:

- Is the *research strategy* to explore, describe or explain?
- Is the research question asking, 'what', 'how', or 'why'?
- How does the research strategy establish the *conditions under which data need to be generated*?
- What *type of data* to generate? Qualitative, quantitative, or both?
- From *whom or what* to generate data?
- What are the *time points* for generating data? Is it from a single point in time (cross-sectional) or over time (longitudinal)?
- What is the *choice of methods* for generating data?

Considering whether our research question is primarily about 'what', 'how' or 'why' will help in establishing the research strategy and the conditions under which data need to be generated. If the strategy concerns establishing cause–effect relationships, then the conditions will involve a high degree of control by the researcher over the entities being studied, and may require an experimental approach. Under these 'experimental' conditions, the researcher will actively manipulate the situation to accord with required procedures. On the other hand, if the strategy is exploratory, then the research will be attempting to create conditions more akin to encounter and dialogue, rather than control.

One has to consider whether the data should be in the form of numbers that can be used statistically to demonstrate certain patterns or correlations, or whether the data need to be in a form that it can be analysed for meaning, lived experiences, cultural practices, and so on. In many instances, particularly in more descriptive research and some evaluations, the research question may well point both ways.

The decisions about the type of research questions and form of data also influence where or from whom you will generate data (sources of data). Data sources include people, files, newspapers, and so on. Finding and accessing sources of data, the criteria to be used for inclusion and exclusion, and size of the data source, all relate to the matter of 'sampling', which will be discussed below.

Consideration may also be given as to whether the data source is to be a 'primary' or 'secondary' one. Commonly, a source that is accessed for the first time for a particular project is a primary data source. Primary sources include people who are participants or informants (for example, service users, service providers, policy makers, funding bodies). However, we should avoid where possible overburdening oft-researched populations, or being invasive, or expending resources unnecessarily on creating new data sources when existing ones may be more than adequate. The judicious use of secondary data sources, where the data has been generated previously and is ready to hand, can be extremely productive. Secondary sources include existing case files, case statistics held by organizations, library archives of organizational policy documents, video and audio records, or increasingly social media repositories such as Twitter or Facebook (with the journal *Mass Communication and Society*, for instance, being dedicated to social media analysis). For example, working with existing databases of social statistics (such as found in the Australian Bureau of Statistics or the Australian Institute of Health and Welfare) can add breadth to a project that may not be realizable otherwise.

Sources, then, have to do with *where* you will get your data. This is not to be confused with 'methods', which have to do with *how* you will get your data and then conduct the analysis. You need to be able to connect the source of your data to appropriate methods for collecting such data. For example, if you are recruiting people as your informants, you can use interview, surveys, focus groups, or journals. If you are using secondary sources where you will already have the data available, it is then how you organize it for your research that becomes important. We will be discussing methods of data generation and analysis between primary and secondary sources in Chapters 6 and 7 respectively.

Cross-sectional approaches generate data pertaining to one specific time and participants are consequently all involved once over the same period. Where trends, patterns or changes over time are sought, longitudinal approaches generate data at one or more predetermined or emergent points over a period of time. Generally, a longitudinal study will be 'prospective', tracing changes into the future. Participants are invited to take part over a length of time, usually with a beginning and end date given. Projects can have a longitudinal character but be 'retrospective', studying back into the past, where participants might be asked to reflect on past events for their views and experiences. Life history research would be one example.

The choice of methods for generating data will be considered in detail in the next chapter. The choices we make about how to generate data are central to any research design. Ultimately, what we can legitimately say from our research will depend on the nature and quality of the data we have generated. It can be perplexing if we go straight to one of the many handbooks on research methods for inspiration – there are so many options from which to choose. But if we have thought through the theoretical perspectives that are informing our research, the kind of research question we are posing, and the resources at our disposal, then we will have a way of arriving at sensible and appropriate methods for generating the data required.

Surveys and interviews are among the most commonly used methods, and there is good reason for this. Surveys can generate data that will assist us to get a fix on a particular issue and illuminate in descriptive fashion what is occurring, how prevalent it is and what people's expressed attitude is towards it. That fits very well with many research questions and the paradigms in which they rest. Loosely structured interviews, by contrast, can take us into the meanings through which people construct their personal and interpersonal worlds, and so generate data for a rather different kind of research question. The range of methods is expanding as researchers engage new technologies or cross boundaries. For example, use of digital cameras or video recorders by participants can provide another kind of cultural insight altogether. Or again, auto-ethnography has emerged, controversially, as a blend of autobiography and ethnography. Here, stories are told about personal experiences but analysed as part of a broader cultural and political understanding. We might be attracted to such novel approaches, but the question remains: Will the data so generated serve us well in addressing the questions we are posing and the core assumptions we bring to our research?

As social work researchers, we are interested in topics and issues that are likely to be complex and multifaceted. We may also wish to gain the attention of diverse audiences. This opens up possibilities for employing a mixture of methods to generate data. Mixed-method approaches are becoming increasingly popular, and increasingly accepted. As we hope will be evident from preceding chapters, what once may have been seen as an irreconcilable split between quantitative and qualitative research can now look like a somewhat false dichotomy. We have shown how different paradigms may rest on competing assumptions about how to know and study personal and social realms. If we are sure of our footing in this respect, we can construct a coherent research design that employs a considerable mix of methods. Our rationale may be to 'triangulate' across those methods to strengthen our analysis. Or, it may be to draw on methods that complement one another in their investigation of various dimensions of our topic to better capture the whole. Clarke (2009), for instance, argues that a mixed-method approach is the way to gain a comprehensive picture of a chronic disabling condition (stroke) – and is explicit in the ontological and epistemological position from which she designs this integration.

The sets of decisions discussed so far represent designs that might be structured to address research questions of a what, how or why nature. If you wish to look in more detail at research designs for conducting 'Needs assessments and evaluations', you can follow Weblink 5.1.

 Weblink 5.1 Designing for needs assessment and for evaluations

Where the research purpose is to move beyond generating knowledge and into the immediate use of that knowledge for achieving beneficial change with and among the research 'participants', then other sets of decisions also come into play.

Designing for action

It is possible to construe the research process as one of not only generating knowledge but also as a process for achieving social change. Here, research is not supplementary to practice and policy development, or simply a source of informed recommendations. Rather, research becomes a vehicle by which development, improvement and change occurs. In such approaches, there is a deliberate designing of the research process in order to maximize the possibilities for incorporating research into agendas for change and improving situations by involving those most affected, 'action research' having become perhaps the foremost of these (Alston and Bowles, 2012: 198; Reason and Bradbury, 2008a).

Action research stems out of a number of traditions. In some respects, it is an attempt to challenge dichotomies such as 'theory–practice', 'ideas–actions', 'researcher–researched', and so on. These are substituted with concepts of 'praxis', 'ideas-in-action', 'collaborative enquiry' and 'co-researchers', language that constitutes alternative paradigms for the researcher as change agent. Of course, this raises the question as to how change itself is conceived. As Hart and Bond (1995: 14) discuss, there is a continuing debate regarding the work of the commonly accepted founder of action research, Kurt Lewin, and to what extent his approach to the integration of social research and social action was 'democratic or manipulative'. Hence, the term 'participatory action research' is often used by those who wish to associate themselves explicitly with the more democratic and emancipatory versions.

Hart and Bond (1995: 39–43) construct a typology of action research, and argue that these types emanate from contrasting 'models of society', varying along a spectrum from a consensus model, which is aligned with rational social management, to a conflict model, aligned with structural change. Accordingly, the four types of action research – 'experimental', 'organizational', 'professionalizing' and 'empowering' – differ as to who defines the problems, how change interventions are pursued, degrees of collaboration, and so on. These all represent variations on designing research for action. The variations can be seen to reflect differing power relations between stakeholders, and between 'researchers' and 'participants'.

Participatory, collaborative action research has specific design elements that involve a thematic concern (rather than a research question), and four 'moments' (Kemmis and McTaggart, 1988: 9, 10). This approach takes account of the responsive and evolving character of action research and design is set within a cyclical process of planning, acting, observing, reflecting.

In action research, a group and its members undertake:

- to develop a plan of critically informed action to improve what is already happening
- to act to implement the plan
- to observe the effects of the critically informed action in the context in which it occurs, and

- to reflect on these effects as a basis for further planning, subsequently informed critically informed action and so on, through a succession of cycles (Kemmis and McTaggart, 1988: 10)

Kemmis and McTaggart (2005) posit eight key features of participatory action research:

1 A spiral and cyclic self-reflective process
2 Social process
3 Participation
4 Practicality and collaboration
5 Emancipation
6 A critical approach
7 Reflexivity
8 Transformation of theory and practice

For many, such features align readily with social work values and practice approaches, and action research has proved to be an attractive option. But realizing those values in research is as challenging as it is in everyday practice, especially given the diverse organizational and cultural contexts in which social welfare occurs (Healy, 2001).

While the cyclical process provides a conceptual framework for carrying out research, the participatory dimension inevitably means this itself will be subject to interpretation and negotiation. Describing their experience of engaging in this kind of research with families of children with disabilities, Bray and Mirfin-Veitch (2003: 80) comment:

> We also had to be wary, as researchers, of being captured by our methodology. While we were concerned with issues of research design and methodology, the parents were focused on the action – what we could do to bring about positive changes for families. Thus conforming to particular requirements of action research models, such as formal action-reflection cycles, was not the concern of the parents, even though it inevitably happened within the range of data-gathering, discussion and resultant actions.

The possibility of being 'captured' by one's methodology is highlighted by the tenets of participatory action research. Here, the methodology is not only being appraised for its potential to generate certain ways of knowing, but also for its potential to engage with others in a participatory movement towards certain social changes. There is a complex interplay in the processes of designing for action between constructing trustworthy research and facilitating change. Negotiating this path is a distinctive matter of political and ethical practice, and one that requires requisite epistemological grounding (Hammersley, 1995).

Sampling and research design

One of the key decisions in research design is: 'from whom (or what) to collect data?' Sampling is relevant to all varieties of research design, though arguably the more participatory they are the less appropriate the term itself becomes. 'Sampling is necessary because you usually cannot include everyone in the study' (Marlow, 2011: 138). Approaches to sampling differ markedly and depend upon the research aims.

Within experimental designs that rely on quantitative methods, the numbers of participants (sample size) and their recruitment and selection are influenced by the need to make statistically derived generalizations from the group studied to the wider population. Probability sampling is the approach best suited as it aims for representativeness in the sample and is crucial to the 'external validity' of the study. This contrasts with the requirements of qualitative methodologies, where the attempt is to obtain what Marlow (2011: 146) refers to as an 'information rich' sample that is sought deliberately with some theoretical purpose. The resultant approach is termed non-probability or purposive sampling. The features of probability and non-probability sampling (Alston and Bowles, 2012) are shown in Box 5.1.

Box 5.1   Features of probability and non-probability sampling

Probability sampling

- Each population unit has an equal, or known, chance of selection
- There is a high degree of representativeness
- It allows the researcher to generalize results
- It is favoured by quantitative researchers
- There are four main types:

  - Simple random sampling
  - Systematic random sampling
  - Stratified random sampling
  - Cluster random sampling

Non-probability sampling

- Each population unit does not have an equal chance of selection
- There is no claim to be representative
- It does not necessarily allow the researcher to generalize results

- It is favoured by qualitative researchers
- There are four examples:
  - Accidental (or convenience or availability) sampling
  - Quota sampling
  - Purposive sampling
  - Snowball sampling

Source: Alston and Bowles (2012: 90, 95, amended)

Probability sampling to achieve a representative sample and the requisite sample size uses random sampling procedures. This is very much a technical process. Varieties of random sampling have been developed to cater for such factors as: the need to build certain 'strata' into the sample (age bands, for example); the absence of an accessible or suitable 'database' from which to draw the sample; and the difficulty in identifying the population under study. Requisite size depends upon the forms of statistical analysis that are to be employed and the diversity of the population. The greater the diversity, the larger the sample size needed (Alston and Bowles, 2012: 99). Generalizability of results will be affected by the adequacy of the numbers of participants involved in the research. Numbers from 30 upwards are intimated, though, in general terms, the larger the representative sample relative to the population the smaller the margin of error (Alston and Bowles, 2012: 98).

Non-probability sampling does not aim to produce findings that can be generalized through statistical analysis. However, the researcher must connect the size, recruitment and selection of the sample to the aims of the research focus, purpose and methodology. We may want to ensure, for example, that within our sample there are 'quotas' of certain characteristics. We may deliberately seek a kind of 'typicality' in a 'case study', or we may purposely engage people who meet some 'eligibility criteria' in having experienced particular events or through living in a given community or specific set of circumstances. We may be constructing our research in respect of those whom we readily come across in our work. Our research interests might concern people to whom we have limited access, or people who have an identified area of expertise. Broadly, in exploratory and qualitative descriptive studies, we would be concerned with generating new ideas and understandings. The basis of sampling therefore becomes 'theoretical' rather than 'statistical'. Within participatory action research, the basis of 'sampling' would be rather more action-oriented and those engaged in the research identified perhaps as much by virtue of their shared interests in developing new actions as new theory.

The timing of sample selection similarly varies according to the research design. Experimental designs of differing kinds determine the sample structure at the outset. This may be the case too for some studies in the ethnographic-inductive traditions (Kellehear, 1993) — for example, in certain descriptive strategies. Designs that aim to develop theory, on the other hand, adopt what Flick (1998: 65) calls a 'gradual definition of sample structure', also known as *theoretical sampling*:

> [I]ndividuals, groups, etc. are selected according to their (expected) level of new insights for the developing theory, in relation to the state of theory elaboration so far. Sampling decisions aim at that material which promises the greatest insights, viewed in the light of the material already used and the knowledge drawn from it.

Developed for grounded theory by Glaser (1992: 101), with colleague Strauss, theoretical sampling is:

> the process of data collection for generating theory, whereby the analyst jointly collects, codes and analyses his [*sic*] data and decides what data to collect next and where to find them, in order to develop his theory as it emerges. The process of data collection is controlled by theoretical sampling according to the emerging theory.

Whether one is pursuing a statistically based sampling approach or a theoretically purposive one, the pragmatics of research will be encountered. Flick (1998: 71), in discussing how one balances breadth and depth in sampling decisions, describes how such decisions can be affected by limited resources (money and time).

Ethical considerations in research design

This section discusses three main areas: (1) ethical protocols for conducting research that pertain especially to design issues; (2) relational ethics, including brief discussions of ethical research practice with children and with indigenous communities, and on sensitive topics with vulnerable populations; and (3) negotiating, maintaining and terminating access as an overview of the ethics and politics of research throughout the process.

Ethical protocols

While we use examples of ethical codes from Australia, we believe that their principles are recognizable elsewhere. Ethical protocols demonstrate how research occurs within a set of institutional arrangements that, in this instance, prescribe or encourage certain research practices deemed 'ethical'. As with all such institutional arrangements, there is a history and context to their existence, and controversy concerning their content and impact (Ife, 2001).

Research governance that monitors standards of ethical behaviour through Committees and Boards tends to operate in a legalistic way to protect the rights of participants. This is described as a principalist approach, which assumes an ethical universalism and individualized focus and tries to find a balance between often conflicting moral principles (King, Henderson and Stein, 1999). Committees determining whether or not to approve a project scrutinize the design submitted to them, accompanied by an assessment of the associated ethical risks and mitigation strategies being proposed. This procedure tends to suit research designs of the 'predetermined' rather than 'emergent' type, since the policy is largely one of approving (or not) specific steps that the researcher explains they will be taking in managing the risks.

The two formal statements that perhaps impact most on social work researchers seeking ethics approval in Australia are:

- National Statement on Ethical Conduct in Human Research (NHMRC, 2007)
- Australian Association of Social Workers' Code of Ethics (AASW, 2010)

The 'National Statement on Ethical Conduct in Human Research' ('National Statement') replaces the statement issued by the National Health and Medical Research Council (NHMRC) in Australia in 1999. The National Statement sets out principles of ethical conduct and the composition and procedures for Human Research Ethics Committees (HRECs). It includes particular sections on, for example, research involving children and young people; people with cognitive impairment, an intellectual disability, or a mental illness; Aboriginal and Torres Strait Islander Peoples; and people in dependent or unequal relationships. The revised statement includes new topics such as qualitative methods; researching with people in other countries; and research with people who may be involved in illegal activities.

The National Statement, similar to many such others, reaffirms three values fundamental to the design and review of human research:

- Respect for human beings is a recognition of their intrinsic value. ... Respect requires having due regard for the welfare, rights, beliefs, perceptions, customs and cultural heritage, both individual and collective, of those involved in research.
- Beneficence. The likely benefit of the research must justify any risks of harm or discomfort to participants.
- Justice. There is no unfair burden of participation in research on particular groups; there is fair distribution of the benefits of participation in research. (NHMRC, 2007: 12–13)

The National Statement also includes a fourth value: research merit and integrity. It asserts that 'unless proposed research has merit, and the researchers who are to carry out the research have integrity, the involvement of human participants in the research cannot be ethically justifiable' (NHMRC, 2007: 11). This is assessed by ensuring the methods of the research are appropriate for its aims, basing the research on a study of current and past literature, and having researchers with the necessary experience, qualifications and competence to carry it out.

Since the Nuremberg trials at the end of the Second World War, which examined the horrific experimentation that had occurred in prisoner of war camps, informed consent has been a core component in codes for ethical research. The National Statement adopts the following:

> The requirement for consent … has the following conditions: consent should be a voluntary choice, and should be based on sufficient information and adequate understanding of both the proposed research and the implications of participation in it. … The process of communicating information to participants and seeking their consent should not be merely a matter of satisfying a formal requirement. The aim is mutual understanding between researchers and participants. (NHMRC, 2007: 19)

On this issue, in relation to children and young people, the Statement advises:

> Being responsive to developmental levels is important not only for judging when children or young people are able to give their consent for research: even young children with very limited cognitive capacity should be engaged at their level in discussion about the research and its likely outcomes. (NHMRC, 2007: 55)

The professional association for social work in Australia (Australian Association of Social Workers, or AASW) accepted a revised Code of Ethics in 2010, which is binding on all members. Unsurprisingly, the underlying values of the code replicate those of the National Statement. The Code states that 'in the determination and pursuit of its aims, social work is committed to three core values, which give rise to general and specific ethical responsibilities. These values are: respect for persons, social justice, professional integrity' (AASW, 2010: 12).

The AASW Code of Ethics covers all aspects of social work practice. Special ethical responsibilities of social workers engaged in research comprise over 20 items, which include the following:

- Protecting the privacy and dignity of research participants
- Obtaining informed consent to participation
- Assessing, minimizing and actively managing risk for harm, discomfort and inconvenience

- Ensuring anonymity and/or confidentiality of research participants and data
- Accurately and fully disseminating research findings
- Bringing research results that indicate or demonstrate social inequalities for injustices to the attention of relevant bodies (AASW, 2010: 36–38; see website, www.aasw.asn.au)

From this list and the requirements of the National Statement, you can see how compliance impacts upon all aspects of research design. You are invited to investigate other relevant comparable Statements and Codes and related resources (see Weblink 5.2).

 ## Weblink 5.2 Examples of ethical codes and statements

The complexity of the social worlds where research is conducted, however, ensures that ethical practice in research is not guaranteed by the enunciation of ethical codes (Humphries and Martin, 2000; Ife, 2002). Even as research-ers are exhorted to use these codes, it is evident that the relational dimension between researcher and participant is paramount – and, we would contend, this relational dimension is intimately about power and ethics.

Relational ethics

Critics of approaches that rely on administrative compliance with institutional or professional requirements emphasize relational ethics. Iphofen (2009: 4) says: 'a responsible researcher is one who understands and examines the ways in which the moral and methodological principles of their work are interwoven.' Within this frame, Iphofen believes 'all too often institutional caution has taken precedence over ethical concerns, and ethical review has been confused with risk aversion, damage limitation and managerial accountability' (Iphofen, 2009: 5). Kellehear (1993: 13–14) argues that a bureaucratized committee procedure 'may abrogate the researcher from the responsibility of seeing ethics as part of the ongoing process of research'.

By contrast, a relationship-based approach to ethics emphasizes consultation, mutual understanding, recognition, involvement and agreement – a rather more promising basis for engaging with cultural and social diversity (Smith, 2005).

Recognizing the limitations of bureaucratic committee procedures, and the principalist approach that tends to dominate the moral reasoning of such committees, Iphofen (2009: 10) suggests that we adopt a 'rapid review of raised ethical awareness' by asking 'what are the "threats" to the principles we are attempting to balance?' To guide this review, he proposes a set of questions:

- What threatens our autonomy – as researchers and as subjects of research?
- What might threaten our interests?
- What are the threats to the interests of all 'stakeholders'?
- Are there any threats to participants' capacity to consent to participate in research?
- What threatens the possibility that research can be of benefit to 'us' (as individuals, groups or members of a particular society)?
- What are the threats to making sure that research does not do us any harm? (Iphofen, 2009: 10)

We have discussed at some length in Chapters 3 and 4 the principles of transformational and emancipatory research, which are consistent with Humphries and Martin's (2000: 78–83) 'feminist and anti-imperialist ethics'. These are:

- The principle of partiality
- Locating the researcher
- Research subjects are active, reflexive beings
- Representing others
- Encompassing difference
- Contextualizing research
- Accountability to communities

Research with children

The idea of establishing a mutual understanding between researchers and participants in the communication process around consent, and extending this to the way in which children and young people are to be engaged, is suggestive of an approach that is very much based on the quality of the relationship established by the researcher. This is resonant with an 'ethic of care' (Tronto, 1993) that in real-world contexts requires 'reflection on the best course of action in specific circumstances and the best way to express and interpret moral problems' (Moss, 2006: 190, citing Sevenhuijsen, 1998: 59).

Combined with an 'ethics of encounter', as associated with the philosophical works of Emmanuel Levinas, Moss emphasizes how this is about relationships, 'in particular how to relate to the Other without making the Other into the same' (2006: 190); and this leads to creating 'connections between provisions for children and ethical concepts and practices … a relational self … spaces where children can speak and be heard …' (2006: 191). Prout and Tisdall (2006: 43) put it this way:

The relational dimension of [children's] participation ... requires information sharing and dialogue ... based on mutual respect and power sharing. ...
Professional adults should inform their relationships with children through
practising 'ethics of care' or 'ethics of encounter'.

Indigenous research ethics

Smith (2005: 97), writing from Aotearoa/New Zealand, reminds us:

> For indigenous and other marginalized communities, research ethics is at a
> very basic level about establishing, maintaining, and nurturing reciprocal and
> respectful relationships, not just among people as individuals but also with
> people as individual, as collectives, and as members of communities, and with
> humans who live in and with other entities in the environment.

Smith questions the processes whereby ethical codes are produced and generated. She suggests that this remains primarily a 'top-down' process whereby
'the discussions, dialogues, and conversations about what ethical research conduct looks like are conducted in the meeting rooms of the powerful' (Smith,
2005: 97). She offers a critique of the way terms such as *respect* and *beneficence*
and *informed consent* are pursued without allowing for a 'bottom-up' defining
of ethical behaviours. Out of such a critique emerges an 'alternative way of
knowing and thinking about research ethics, research relationships, personal
conduct and researcher integrity' (Smith, 2005: 101).

An example of indigenous research ethics is contained in a memorandum of
good practice that was developed by the Institute of Koorie Education (IKE)
at Deakin University, Australia, in the mid-1990s. The paper asks all researchers to be mindful of 'the history of past research practices into Aboriginal and
Torres Strait Islander affairs which have been exploitative and, in so many
cases, of little value to the families, clans and communities associated with
the research' (IKE, 1994: 2) The Institute is 'committed to research activities
which advance the processes of empowerment and self-determination for
Indigenous people' (IKE, 1994: 1). Guidelines for ethical research practice
are provided, differentiating between the responsibilities of Koorie and non-
Koorie researchers.

Koorie researchers have to negotiate a path that has tended primarily to
'serve the cultural interests of colonial Australia' (IKE, 1994: 2) while engaging in otherwise legitimate research activity. The following understandings,
attitudes and practices are among those encouraged:

> Community consultation takes time; sit down and listen rather than take on a
> controlling role whereby the project is run purely to outsiders' timetables and
> agenda.

The success or failure of the project will ultimately be decided within the authority structure of the Koorie community; respect the authority of the elders in the community and be prepared to take direction from their advice.

Koorie community members expect to be involved in open and equal (symmetrical) communication about projects that affect their lives; accept and facilitate the need for open and equal interactions with community members, interactions which secure community input into defining the actual work of the research project. (IKE, 1994: 3)

Koorie cultural practices to be respected include, among others:

- Personal, as distinct from professional, relationships in establishing conditions for further interactions.
- The need for extended timeframes in which decisions are made and the collective nature of those decisions.
- The status of individual autonomy within a cultural system of collective responsibility for social action.
- The publication of only appropriate pictorial material and texts. (IKE, 1994: 5)

When addressing ethical matters for non-Koorie researchers, the paper emphasizes how Koorie research:

must now be inclusive of Koorie community interests … must be non-invasive of Koorie people's lived experiences and cultural practices … must be non-exploitative of Koorie knowledge … must move from the positivistic positioning of Koories as objects of others' enquiries. (IKE, 1994: 4)

Ethical practice by non-Koorie researchers entails 'cross-cultural sensitivity; that is, researcher preparedness to honour culturally different values, needs, practices and perspectives' (IKE, 1994: 4). More recently, the Australian Institute of Aboriginal and Torres Strait Islander Studies (AIATSIS, 2011) has produced 'guidelines for ethical research in Australian Indigenous Studies'. Fourteen principles are presented to guide research, grouped under broad categories that include:

- Rights, respect and recognition
- Negotiation, consultation, agreement and mutual understanding
- Participation, collaboration and partnership
- Benefits, outcomes and giving back

A fundamental challenge for ethical practice by non-Koorie researchers arises from an acknowledgement that in the past 'research has not served the interests of Koorie communities through critical understandings of their socio-political circumstances. It has, however, served to build academic reputations within the research community and universities' (IKE, 1994: 4). Two decades later, it is salutary to consider whether significant progress has been achieved in this respect. While awareness of such issues for ethical research with indigenous communities has grown, as is reflected, for example, in the National Statement and its ethical considerations specific to Aboriginal and Torres Strait Islander peoples (NHMRC, 2007: Chapter 4.7), the overall benefit that has been rendered to those communities remains at best equivocal.

Sensitive topics and vulnerable populations

Increased ethical regulation has become a broader concern for those whose research involves what are deemed to be 'sensitive' topics and 'vulnerable' populations – as will be the case with much social work research. Melrose (2011) reflects on her many years as a critical social researcher and argues that 'the consequences of increased ethical regulation may contradict its intention and place 'vulnerable' participants at greater risk than 'sensitive' research undertaken with such groups in earlier historical periods' (2011: abstract). She concludes that a 'formulaic and proceduralist' approach 'ignores the fact that ethical dilemmas arise within social contexts and that their resolution is inherently political' (2011: paragraph 9.1).

Formal and institutionalized ethical codes and statements extol values of respect, beneficence and justice as fundamental to ethical research practice. As we consider critically the enactment of these values with regard to people who are marginalized and potentially vulnerable, we are encouraged to think about these easily espoused values anew – and, we would argue, to consider the possibility that a relational approach fused with an appreciation of the ethics of power sharing is more likely to generate research that will be respectful, beneficial and just for those populations to whom social work claims to be committed.

Negotiating, maintaining and terminating access: relationships of power

Negotiating, maintaining and terminating access is a special example of the ethics and politics of research, within relational ethics.

It is important that no harm is done to people who are key informants, or archival, historical or private materials that have public or private significance.

Researchers are usually required to submit proposals to ethics committees out-
lining their plans for accessing data and how they will protect their sources,
people in particular. These legalistic forms of ethical protections are contrasted
with 'relational ethics' that are respectful of cultural values and social relations
(Smith, 1999, 2005; Stanley and Wise, 1993).

The processes for negotiating, maintaining and terminating access
are courteous and proper ways of establishing research credibility and
integral to the design, for example, see Donnelly (2010) on 'maximising
participation in international community-level project evaluation' and
Mertens (2010) on 'social transformation and evaluation' with the Deaf
community.

Milgram's (1963) 'study of obedience' and Humphreys' (1970) 'study of
men's sexual behaviour' are used by many researchers to discuss the ethical and political complexities associated with informed consent, privacy
and deception that are part of negotiating access (Humphries and Martin,
2000: 75–76; Neuman and Kreuger, 2003: 100–105; Punch, 1986; Rubin
and Babbie, 2007: 80–86). Although Milgram (1963) and Humphreys
(1970) argued that it was necessary to deceive their informants to discover
important knowledge that would otherwise be unknown, other researchers
show that there is a complicated argument that can disguise and entrench
the researcher's power in relation to informants. For example, Everitt et al.
(1992: 86) ask:

> Do all participants have equal rights to be informed about the research-minded
> process? … Participation has to be understood in the context of power rela-
> tions. … There may well be situations in which research-minded practitioners
> wish to reflect critically on the practices of those more powerful than them-
> selves. … Research-minded practitioners, critically reflecting on the practice
> of social welfare, may well be less powerful, both in themselves and in their
> emancipatory ideas, in organizations and contexts which are fundamentally
> sexist, heterosexist and racist.

There are specialized procedures for negotiating access with children, much
of it regulated by institutional ethics committees administering legal protections of children. We just want to comment here that sometimes legal protections of children institutionalized through ethics committees may work to
prevent children's participation under the guise of their protection (Graham
and Fitzgerald, 2010a: 140–143).

Bell (1993: 58–59) explains to novice researchers why it is important to
negotiate access, providing practical tips and mentioning possible pitfalls (see
Table 5.2). While Bell focuses on research done by someone who works for

TABLE 5.2 Negotiating access: practical tips and possible pitfalls (Bell, 1993: 58–59)

Practical tips	Possible pitfalls
Clear official channels by formally requesting permission to carry out your investigation as soon as you have an agreed project outline. Speak to the people who will be asked to cooperate. ... Remember that people who agree to help are doing you a favour. ...	Getting the management's permission is one thing, but you need to have the support of the people who will be asked to give interviews or complete questionnaires. ... Even if you explain the purpose of the study and the conditions/guarantees verbally, participants may forget. If you say an interview will last ten minutes, you will break faith if it lasts an hour. If you are conducting the investigations as part of a degree or diploma course, say so. ...

an organization (insider researcher), her guidelines are also useful for researchers whose research focus is outside their employing organization, or who may work in one section of an organization, for example, policy, but want to involve participants from another section, for example, practitioners. This is an important consideration because of knowledge and positioning related to insider and outsider status.

Through an 'insider–outsider continuum' (Boulton, 2000: 89–91), knowledge may shift between participants, and the outsider has to learn and negotiate with insiders. Sometimes the researcher may be insider or outsider, and sometimes both insider and outsider at different times in the research process (Morgenshtern and Novotna, 2012).

The mutual recognition of the researcher's outsider status by both researcher and respondent can be seen to mark a boundary between their worlds. The extent to which such boundaries become barriers to understanding must be considered.

Researchers who argue for awareness of inequalities between researchers and participants also recognize that informants and gatekeepers exercise their own versions of power (Barn, 1994; Byrne-Armstrong, 2001; D'Cruz, 2000; Delaney, 1988; Scanlon, 1993; Skeggs, 1994; van Maanen, 1988), for example, by denying access to the site or participants, limiting access to key people, documents or places, and withholding information that is sought by the researcher. Kellehear (1989: 66) describes the experience of the university-based researcher this way:

> From the moment you enter the research setting, be it a village, a hospital or someone's doorstep, you quickly realise you are on someone else's 'territory'. You are no longer in the familiar setting of the university but rather on someone else's 'turf'.

In some cases, it may not be possible to negotiate, maintain and terminate access in a formal way that implies there are clearly identifiable informants who can consent to the research and the researcher's presence in their setting: see, for example, the politics and ethics of fieldwork in criminal justice systems as a participant observer of public protests and police practices (Punch, 1986). The normal expectations that individuals involved in research should give informed consent are not particularly meaningful in such research.

As we have shown, in designing research and situating ourselves in the empirical world, many ethical matters confront us. Codes of practice can seem tiresome, bureaucratic and socially uncritical, in place to guard against litigation or otherwise protect institutions as much as researchers and participants. Yet, formal ethical procedures can prompt us to consider important ethical issues that we may have overlooked in planning our research. They can also act to curb some oppressive practices that might otherwise go unchecked (Ife, 2001). Engagement with the positions of those for whom research practice has proven insensitive or exploitative might also help combat the dangers of ethical complacency.

You might like to try the reflective exercise below to think through some of the issues that arise when seeking 'informed consent'.

Exercise: Reflecting on the issues involved in providing informed consent

Imagine you have been invited to participate in a research study:

- What would you want to know about the research and the way it is to be conducted before deciding whether or not to participate?
- How would you want this information to be conveyed to you?
- How might the information you require, and the way it needs to be communicated, vary according to your social position and community membership?
- Can you think of any circumstances under which you might find it hard to decline the researcher's invitation to participate?
- What might the researcher do to reduce any sense of coercion or inducement that you might be feeling?

Contingencies and contexts in research design

The term 'design' may conjure up the image of a relatively safe and comfortable process. There is a question to be investigated and the researcher draws upon his or her expertise to design a way of doing so, mindful of practical limitations but more or less in charge and uncluttered by extraneous interference. There might be the occasional 'site visit' or consultation meeting, but the information gained is smoothly incorporated into the design process.

If the term does conjure up such an image, then it is arguably somewhat misleading. Reflecting on his experience of researching advocacy within psychiatric services, Healy (1996: 70, citing Taylor, 1993: 123) suggests the metaphor of a journey to complement that of design: 'the researcher who searches for and discovers a research method is similar to a traveller who sets out on a journey with an anticipated itinerary; sometimes things go to plan and sometimes things change according to contingencies along the way.'

Commenting on the difference between idealized approaches to research design and the reality, Healy (1996: 72–73):

> ... tells the story of a research project which at first sight is a sad and sorry tale of frustration, many failures and some successes. The process has been the very antithesis of the idealized model – convoluted, intensely complicated, enmeshed in politics and driven by passion. As well it reveals that these experiences directly mirror the world of its investigations and that in consequence the findings of the project are based as much in the process of attempting to study the world as in the formal, explicit process of research.

Putting it all together

In this chapter, we have begun to explore what is meant by research design, the connection with differing ways of knowing and methodologies, and some of the varying types of research design and accompanying ways of selecting a sample. We have shown how ethical and political considerations permeate these matters and have introduced you to some of the more formalized ethical procedures for research and a range of debates that surround them. Some of the concepts may not have been easy to grasp, but if you are able to read a piece of research and think through the methodological preferences and ethical issues at play, whether the research design appears to make sense in relation to the research question and whether the sampling looks appropriate, then you are beginning to appreciate the range of considerations that inform research activity. We hope you are also beginning to understand how our approach to research as a political and ethical practice provides an important insight into the decision making involved in research design. The path followed by the researcher is not one that can be dictated solely by technical considerations. Rather, it is imbued with moral choices, the positioning of the researcher as a knowledge maker and agent of change, and the requirement to be adept in meeting unexpected contingencies within changing contexts.

Further reading

AIATSIS (2011) *Guidelines for Ethical Research in Australian Indigenous Studies* (2nd edition), Canberra: Australian Institute of Aboriginal and Torres Strait Islander Studies.

Blaikie, N. (2009) *Designing Social Research: The Logic of Anticipation* (2nd edition), Cambridge, UK: Polity Press (Chapters 1 and 2).

Ethics and Social Welfare – a journal first published in 2007 of contemporary critical and reflective articles covering a range of ethical issues.

Iphofen, R. (2009) *Ethical Decision-making in Social Research*, Basingstoke, Hampshire: Palgrave Macmillan (Chapter 1).

6

Generating Data

Introduction

In Chapters 4 and 5, we looked at how different ways of knowing are important in designing a research study.

In this chapter, we shall be:

1 Looking at how to generate data (methods), through different sources, including people, organizations and places where people live and work, archives, and statistical collections.
2 Taking a perspective that sees data generation as a process by which the researcher is as much a 'participant' through his or her positioning – through choice of topic, framing of questions, conceptual approach. It is not a neutral activity.
3 Placing data generation in a context in which both ethical and political issues are important considerations.

This chapter aims to show that 'methods' can generate both qualitative and quantitative data, depending on the degree of structure that you, as the researcher, design into your methods. We show that structured methods generate quantitative data, while lesser structure generates qualitative data. We have included a chart that links method, degree of structure and the type of data generated.

Data generation: some considerations

In choosing your methods of data generation, you should consider the following:

- Is the design and methodology going to convince all stakeholders, especially those who control funding and policy decisions about services? Mixed-methods may be an option to attend to a range of interests

- What is your own position in relation to types of data and what is trustworthy? (Refer to Chapters 3 and 4)
- What is your relationship with the research participants/informants?

A greater degree of structure in the methods gives the researcher greater control over the participants' responses than more open-ended methods do. However, sometimes relatively structured approaches associated with large-scale quantitative studies are necessary to achieve anti-oppressive aims, for example, understanding gender inequality (Fraser and Craik, 2009: 237–239) or social indicators related to patterns of health and employment among social groups (Agger, 2007: 454).

The researcher must consider carefully the connections between research aims, data generation and analysis. The methodology gives direction, helping the researcher to think critically and reflexively about why particular methods are selected to meet pragmatic, theoretical, political and ethical aims. We take the position that data are generated as a result of social processes between the researcher, informants and other data sources, such as policy documents or client files. What we generate as data is related to how we have conceptualized the research, the research focus, and the content, type and structure of questions by which we explore the topic with informants and engage with documentary sources.

Ways of generating data

Data may be generated in many ways that can be used on their own or combined. Familiar methods include interviews, questionnaires and surveys, scales, observation, logs and journals, visual technologies, and secondary data (Harper, 2005; Marlow, 2011: 180–182; Neuman and Kreuger, 2003). It is important not to select methods that set out 'to prove a particular perspective or manipulate data to arrive at a predisposed truth' (Patton, 1990: 55), while appreciating the nuances of 'objectivity' (see Chapters 3 and 4).

Also, researchers may be insiders, outsiders, and a shifting combination of both identities, depending on their organizational and other affiliations (Hellawell, 2006; Kanuha, 2000; Labaree, 2002; Taylor, 2011). The nuanced and complex relationship between being both insider and outsider is described as a 'continuum' (Boulton, 2000: 89–91) or 'the space between' (Corbin Dwyer and Buckle, 2009). Sometimes, researchers are outsiders who have to negotiate with insiders (Labaree, 2002), and sometimes the researcher may be both outsider and insider, for example, as a member of an indigenous community (Kanuha, 2000) or a friend 'researching queer culture' (Taylor, 2011: abstract). However, insider researchers need to recognize that what they take for granted as 'ordinary, routine, everyday things' (Boulton, 2000: 90–1) are data to be critically questioned. Thus, an insider researcher may become an outsider by asking critical questions about what is known and why and how these things are known.

While awareness of insider–outsider complexities is often associated with qualitative/emancipatory approaches, Brannick and Coghlan (2007) examine the acceptability of insider research in organizations, from positivist, hermeneutics and action research approaches. They conclude that 'there is no inherent reason why being native is an issue [in any of these approaches] and that the value of insider research is worth reaffirming' (2007: abstract).

Linking methods of enquiry with types of data

How you generate data (the method) may be the same for both quantitative and qualitative approaches. However, the *degree of structure* in the enquiry process is usually linked to the type of data that are necessary to answer the research question: quantitative, qualitative, or both? (The differences between quantitative and qualitative methods were discussed in Chapter 4). Table 6.1 summarizes the connections between the degree of structure, the methods of enquiry, and the types of data that will be generated (qualitative or quantitative). It provides a guide for thinking about what sort of data you need to best answer your research question and enable you to design your methods of enquiry to generate data that are 'fit for purpose' (Humphries, 2008: 190–192).

In Table 6.1, six methods of enquiry are listed in the left-hand column. Three columns are labelled according to the degree of structure in the different methods of enquiry. It shows that while the same methods of enquiry

TABLE 6.1 Methods of enquiry, degree of structure and types of data generated

	DEGREE OF STRUCTURE		
	Structured	Semi-structured	Unstructured
Methods of enquiry			
Interviews (face to face or through electronic means)	quantitative	quantitative and/or qualitative	qualitative
Questionnaires, surveys and scales (face to face, mailed or online)	quantitative	qualitative (if questionnaires or surveys include open-ended questions)	n/a
Observation	quantitative	quantitative and/or qualitative	qualitative
Logs and journals	quantitative	quantitative and/or qualitative	qualitative
Visual technologies, including photography	quantitative (e.g. content analysis)	n/a	qualitative
Secondary sources	quantitative	n/a	qualitative

may be used in different research studies, the types of data generated will depend on how structured the methods are. For example, a structured interview where the researcher controls the range and content of responses using closed questions and fixed-response categories will generate data in a different format from unstructured or semi-structured interviews using open-ended questions, where the participant controls the range and content of responses. Some methods of enquiry can generate *only* quantitative *or* qualitative data. For example, scales can only generate quantitative data, while unstructured or semi-structured interviews can only generate qualitative data, such as stories or oral histories. Most of the other methods of enquiry have some scope for generating a mixture of qualitative and/or quantitative data, depending on the purpose of the research. For example, some researchers derive the categories they use in large-scale surveys from qualitative studies or exploratory research. Kumar (1996: 109) discusses this approach as a way of ensuring that the categories used in the survey are reasonably representative of the range of possible responses. Feminist researchers Martin (1994) and Truman (2000) have demonstrated how they involved 'the researched' in community-based, mixed-methods studies and large-scale quantitative studies, respectively.

Interviews

Social workers are very familiar with interviewing because it is one of the main ways in which we work with people as clients. This familiarity with interviewing as a 'social work skill' shows how social workers already have some connection with a key ability required for social work research, although D'Cruz (2009: 87–88) reflects on possible similarities and differences between a social work research interview and an interview with a client seeking help.

The most familiar understanding of interviews is that they are processes in which one person asks questions and the other person answers them. The questions are seen as eliciting truth from the informant and it is assumed that there is a neutral relationship between the interviewer and informant. For example, child protection forensic interviews (Parton et al., 1997: 15, 19) seek to uncover facts about what happened to a child and meet legal tests of truth (Parton et al., 1997: 31, 36). Some research writers (such as Holstein and Gubrium, 1995; Humphries and Martin, 2000: 80) would argue that interviews are interactive processes between researcher and informant(s) where the researcher and participant are positioned within particular ways of knowing (Chandler, 1990; D'Cruz, 2000, 2009: 73–88; Humphries and Martin, 2000; Skeggs, 1994).

Interviews may be categorized according to structure (Patton, 1987: 110–117; Payne and Payne, 2004: 131–132):

- Informal conversational, that is relatively unstructured and non-directive
- General interview guide that is in-depth and semi-structured
- Standardized open-ended
- Closed quantitative

The *informal conversational interview* occurs in a spontaneous way and is often part of participant observation, where the researcher may notice a particular interaction. She or he then informally approaches people in the setting and clarifies the meaning of the interaction using a spontaneous conversational style of questioning (Pithouse, 1987). This approach is essential to avoid the researcher imposing his or her meaning on events that may be understood differently in the context. There are no predetermined questions because they are generated from what is going on immediately in the context. For example, Ostrander and Chapin-Hogue (2011) used unstructured interviews as conversations to reflect on 'an unsuccessful university–community collaboration' so that they could 'learn from [their] mistakes'.

Some writers may argue that this form of interviewing poses ethical dilemmas because informants may not realize that they are being 'interviewed' – unlike in more formal interviews where consent is sought and there is a clear start and finish (Patton, 1987: 110). However, if the participants in the setting have agreed to your presence as a researcher and know what the purpose of the research is, this may alleviate concerns about informed consent.

An *interview guide* is more structured than an informal conversational interview because it relies on general themes to be explored with all informants (Kumar, 1996: 109). These 'semi-structured' interviews are more formal, have a clear start and finish time, and participants are usually asked to sign consent forms, agreeing to participate. However, while there is some structure, the interaction relies on a non-directive, conversational style because the topics covered are a guide and not a set of questions asked in exactly the same way for every participant (Patton, 1987: 111; Payne and Payne, 2004: 131). The researcher can also ask probing questions to understand responses more deeply: for example, in oral/life histories and narratives/stories of people's experiences (Payne and Payne, 2004: 25).

 Weblink 6.1 Examples of studies that used in-depth, semi-structured interviews

The *standardized open-ended interview* is more structured than the interview guide, using a set of carefully worded questions (Patton, 1987: 112–113). Each informant is asked the questions in the same order and using the same wording for each question. There is less opportunity for probing and flexibility. This form of interview is used when there are many interviewers to ensure that all interviewers ask the questions in the same way, to limit variations in responses (Patton, 1987: 112–113).

Finally, *closed quantitative interviews* (Patton, 1987: 117) characterize quantitative studies. These interviews are very structured, with 'questions and categories … determined in advance'. The informants must choose from a set of fixed responses in the interview schedule (Patton, 1987: 117).

Computers can be used to conduct structured interviews (Babbie, 2007: 270–275), which may involve an interviewer, for example, through Computer-Assisted Telephone Interviewing (CATI) or Computer-Assisted Personal Interviewing (CAPI). Sometimes an interviewer is not needed, and an informant can enter or voice-record his or her responses directly into a computer, for example, through Computer-Assisted Self-Interviewing (CASI) and Voice Recognition (VR).

Interviewing children involves special considerations related to ethics and methods. We have discussed the ethical issues when involving children as research participants in Chapters 3 and 5, particularly informed consent. Interviews would need to take into account the variations of cognitive and linguistic abilities related to both chronological and developmental age of children (Colls and Hörschelmann, 2010: 6–8).

 Weblink 6.2 Examples of research where children as participants were interviewed

Questionnaires, surveys and scales

Questionnaires, surveys and scales are usually structured methods that generate quantitative data.

Questionnaires and surveys

Questionnaires are questions on paper that may be used in face-to-face interviews, mailed, or distributed through electronic means, such as email or the internet (Payne and Payne, 2004: 186). The Question Bank (http://qb.soc.surrey.ac.uk) (Payne and Payne, 2004: 186) is recommended as a good place to start to avoid the usual pitfalls, such as asking leading or ambiguous questions

(Babbie, 2007: 244–264; Kumar, 2011: 154–155; Marlow, 2011: 169; Payne and Payne, 2004: 186–190).

Exercise: Designing questions

Table 6.2 has sets of sample questions. Assess the appropriateness of the questions, some of which have actually been used in social research surveys and interviews. Table 6.3 provides guidelines for constructing good questions, and uses the examples in Table 6.2 to show why they are not appropriate.

Questionnaires and surveys are normally completed by participants without intervention by the researcher (Bryman, 2008: 216–229). Usually, a letter is attached explaining the research and covering ethical issues such as informed consent and anonymity. Mailed questionnaires should include a stamped, addressed envelope for the return of the questionnaire (Babbie, 2007: 260–261).

Mailed questionnaires do not usually have a high return rate (Bryman, 2008: 219). An acceptable response rate for mailed questionnaires ranges from 'barely acceptable' if 50–59 per cent are returned; 'acceptable' if 60–69 per cent are returned; and 'very good' if 70–85 per cent are returned (Bryman, 2008: 219). To have enough data for analysis and reporting, the researcher should follow up with informants. Individuals should not be identified on their returned questionnaires, so an appropriate follow-up procedure would be to send reminder letters to all members of the sample, thank those who have already returned questionnaires, and encourage others to do so (Babbie, 2007: 262; Bryman, 2008: 221).

Surveys may also be conducted by 'internet polling'. Participants may be sent a survey by email or message boards, or through a website that previously recruited participants can access (Payne and Payne, 2004: 125–128). Internet polling may be used with people who are intended to represent the general population's views, for example, voting intentions or opinion surveys, or with people who may be otherwise difficult to contact due to sensitive issues being investigated (Payne and Payne, 2004: 126), for example, 'self-harming' people and drug-dealers (Coomber, 1997; Payne and Payne, 2004: 128, citing Fox et al., 2003). New technologies also allow for Computerized Self-Administered questionnaire (CSAQ) and Touchstone Data Entry (TDE) (Babbie, 2007: 272–275). CSAQ uses a CD-ROM or similar electronic device to mail a set of questions to a participant, who loads the device onto their own computer, records and saves their answers to the questions and returns the device to the

TABLE 6.2 Examples of badly designed questions

Graham (1993: 137–138)	Royse (1999: 183–190)	Payne and Payne (2004: 186–190)	Kumar (2011: 154–155)
How healthy are you?	Have you donated blood or gone to the dentist this month?	What do you think about this area?	Is anyone in your family a *dipsomaniac*?
Are the health practices in your household run on matriarchal or patriarchal lines?	Yes ☐ No ☐ Dont know ☐	Youth crime is a problem in this area, isn't it?	Is your work made more difficult because you are expecting a baby?
Has it happened to you that, over a long period of time when you neither practised abstinence nor used birth control, you did not conceive?	Don't you agree with the president that the federal government should not overspend?	Do you think there should be more recreational facilities and daycare centres for children and older people?	Yes ☐ No ☐
	Agree ☐ Disagree ☐ Dont know ☐		Are you satisfied with your canteen?
How often do your parents visit the doctor?	How many hours of television did you watch last year?	What is the average age of people in your household?	How often and how much time do you spend on each visit to the child care centre?
Do you oppose or favour cutting health spending, even if cuts threaten the health of children and pensioners?	Do you feel that Freud's structural hypothesis is an improvement over his topographic hypothesis?		Does your department have a special recruitment policy for racial minorities and women?
	How do you black people feel about Jesse Jackson?		Unemployment is increasing, isn't it?
Do you agree or disagree with the following statement? 'Abortions after 28 weeks should not be decriminalized.'	Are you a religious fanatic?		Smoking is bad, isn't it?
	How many times in the past year have you seen a social worker?		How many cigarettes do you smoke in a day?
Do you agree or disagree with the government's policy on the funding of medical training?	Are you always in bed by 11.oo p.m.?		What contraceptives do you use?
Have you ever murdered your grandmother?	Marijuana should not be decriminalized.		

TABLE 6.3 Guidelines for constructing questions

Guidelines for constructing questionnaires	Guidelines of what not to do, with examples
Keep the questions short.	Do not use ambiguous questions.
Keep the questions clear and focused.	'How healthy are you?' (Graham, 1993: 318)
'Questions must be easily understandable to all respondents ... each question should mean the same to everyone involved so that comparable answers are obtained' (Payne and Payne, 2004: 186).	'Has it happened to you that, over a long period of time when you neither practised abstinence nor used birth control, you did not conceive?' (Graham, 1993: 138)
	'How many times in the past year have you seen a social worker?' (Royse, 1999: 189)
	'Is your work made difficult because you are expecting a baby?' (Moser and Kalton, 1989: 323, in Kumar, 2011)
'As a general rule, whenever the word *and* appears in a question or ... statement, check whether you're asking a double-barrelled question' (Babbie, 2007: 247, original emphasis).	'Are you satisfied with your canteen?' (Moser and Kalton, 1989: 319)
	'What do you think about the proposed peace plan?' (Babbie, 2007: 247)
	Babbie (2007: 247) gives examples of common terms that may be misinterpreted by respondents, for example, 'Native American', that some people interpreted as 'born in the USA' and others as 'American Indian'.
	'Families should insist that women wear the veil' covers two topics: that 'women should wear the veil' and that 'families should insist on it' (Payne and Payne, 2004: 20).
	Avoid double-barrelled questions.
	'How often and how much time do you spend on each visit?' (Kumar, 2011: 155)
	'Does your department have a special recruitment policy for racial minorities and women?' (Bailey, 1978: 97)
	'How often do your parents visit the doctor?' (Graham, 1993: 138)
	'Have you donated blood or gone to the dentist this month?' (Royse, 1999: 183)
	'Do you oppose or favour cutting health spending, even if cuts threaten the health of children and pensioners?' (Graham, 1993: 138)
First ascertain whether or not a respondent is a member of a group in which you are interested.	Do not ask questions that are based on presumptions about informants.
	'How many cigarettes do you smoke in a day?'
	'What contraceptives do you use?' (Moser and Kalton, 1989: 325)

(Continued)

TABLE 6.3 (Continued)

Guidelines for constructing questionnaires	Guidelines of what not to do, with examples
Use questions that are sensitively phrased and appreciate and validate difference and diversity of experiences.	Avoid asking direct questions on sensitive issues. 'Have you ever murdered your grandmother?' (Graham, 1993: 138) Avoid insensitive, discriminatory or inflammatory language or 'loaded' terms. 'How do you black people feel about Jesse Jackson?' (Jesse Jackson is an African-American politician in the USA) (Royse, 1999: 187) 'Are you a religious fanatic?' (Royse, 1999: 187)
Ask questions in a way that does not suggest to respondents the way in which they are being expected to respond. This includes the social desirability of some responses, regardless of what the respondents actually think (Babbie, 2007: 251).	Avoid leading questions. 'Do you oppose or favour cutting health spending, even if cuts threaten the health of children and pensioners?' (Graham, 1993: 138) 'Don't you agree with the president that the federal government should not overspend?' (Royse, 1999: 184) 'Unemployment is increasing, isn't it?' (Kumar, 2011: 155) 'Smoking is bad, isn't it?' (Kumar, 2011: 155)
Be aware that the wording and terminology of questions may influence the responses you get (Babbie, 2007: 250–251).	Citing analysis by Rasinski (1989) of terminology in a US General Social Survey of attitudes towards government spending, Babbie (2007: 250–251) shows how 'assistance to the poor' and 'halting the rising crime rate' generated more support, while the opposite, such as 'welfare' and 'law enforcement' attracted less support. Another example is the use of names in hypothetical scenarios, for example, male names can produce different responses to female names (Kasof, 1993, cited in Babbie, 2007: 251).
Questions should be relevant to the respondents in order to avoid people making up answers because they feel they ought to have an opinion.	

Guidelines for constructing questionnaires	Guidelines of what not to do, with examples
The respondents are willing and able ('competent') to answer the questions.	Avoid questions that assume the informants have the necessary background knowledge. 'Do you agree or disagree with the government's policy on the funding of medical training?' (Graham, 1993:137) 'How many hours of television did you watch last year?' (Royse, 1999:184) Babbie (2007: 249, citing Bian, 1994) gives the example of Chinese respondents being fearful of answering questions candidly as they believed their responses would be traced to them and there would be repercussions.
The questions are focused on the present.	Avoid questions where information may be unavailable. 'How many hours of television did you watch last year?' (Royse, 1999:184)
Construct questions without the word 'not' in their structure.	Avoid questions with double negatives. 'Do you agree or disagree with the following statement? "Abortions after 28 weeks should not be decriminalized"' (Graham, 1993:138) 'Marijuana should not be decriminalized' (Royse, 1999:190). 'Does it seem possible or does it seem impossible to you that the Nazi extermination of the Jews never happened?' (National Survey commissioned in 1993 by the American Jewish Community, 1 in 5 polled [sic] doubt on Holocaust, cited by Babbie, 2007: 250)
Use simple language with familiar words from everyday speech.	Avoid jargon or complicated language. 'Are the health practices in your household run on matriarchal or patriarchal lines?' (Graham, 1993:138) 'Is anyone in your family a *dipsomaniac*?' (Kumar, 2011:154) 'Do you feel that Freud's structural hypothesis is an improvement over his topographic hypothesis?' (Royse, 1999:186)

Sources: Derived from Babbie (2007); Graham (1993); Kumar (2011); Marlow (2011); Payne and Payne (2004); and Royse (1999)

researcher. TDE requires a participant to phone a given number and then use the keypad on their phone to respond to questions asked by a computer.

Beyond appropriate question design (see Table 6.3), using the internet requires consideration of technical issues that may affect access a successful completion. For example, different hardware platforms (MACs and PCs), internet software that may or may not be compatible with participants' systems, and server crashes that may affect timeliness (Payne and Payne, 2004: 126–127). Babbie (2007: 274–275) provides a list of dos and don'ts when using the internet for surveys (see www.worldopinion.com/the-frame/frame4.html).

In addition to the ethical procedures for all approaches to questionnaires and surveys, researchers need to be mindful that:

> promises of anonymity are less credible [in emailed surveys] when [respondents] e-mail replies will contain names and electronic addresses. Confidentiality is easier to deliver: although the emerging data-set will … be at risk to [sic] hackers, it is not significantly more vulnerable than other data-sets held on computers. (Payne and Payne, 2004: 127)

Here are some sources about designing questionnaires and surveys with children:

- Bell (2007) 'Designing and testing questionnaires for children'
- Early Years Foundation Stage Forum, http://eyfs.info/forums/index.php?showtopic=9750 (accessed 2 February 2012) – a discussion group on the pros and cons of using questionnaires with children
- London School of Economics (2011) *EUKids Online: Questionnaires for Children and Parents*, www2.lse.ac.uk/media@lse/research/EUKidsOnline/EUKidsII%20(2009-11)/Survey/Master%20questionnaires.aspx (accessed 2 February 2012)

Scales

Scales measure informants' attitudes. They provide a quantitative summary of scores applied by researchers to people's responses to sets of statements about particular topics (Payne and Payne, 2004: 17). Common features of scales are:

- The presentation of a series of stimuli (usually *statements*).
- A requirement that the response to each must be one selected from a fixed and *limited* choice (e.g. 'strongly agree'; 'agree'; 'undecided'; 'disagree'; or 'strongly disagree').
- The *scoring* of responses into a numerical value (e.g. 1 to 5 on each statement).

- Some *combination* of these numerical scores into a *single number* on a 'scale'. (Payne and Payne, 2004: 19, citing Kumar, 1999: 127–135, original emphasis)

Scales are often embedded in questionnaires along with other structured questions (Babbie, 2007: 246): for example, Renzetti's (1992) study on partner abuse in lesbian relationships. The design of scales relies on the same rules as for questionnaires, such as not using jargon and keeping language simple (Babbie, 2007: 245–251; Payne and Payne, 2004: 20) (see Table 6.3). Refer to Kumar (2011: 167–176) for in-depth advice on designing scales.

Attitude scales (also known as 'indexes' or 'ratings': Hoinville et al., 1982: 33–37; Schutt, 1999: 75–81, both cited in Payne and Payne, 2004: 18): participants respond to particular statements or questions 'set externally' by the researcher, choosing from a fixed set of responses from positive to negative.

Likert scales are the most commonly used scale (Kumar, 2011: 170–174; Marlow, 2011: 178). A Likert scale is:

a series of statements [given to a respondent who] is then asked to respond using one of five response alternatives, for example, 'strongly agree', 'agree', 'no opinion', 'disagree', 'strongly disagree', or some variant of these. (Marlow, 2011: 178)

Usually, Likert scales are meant to include up to 100 statements, derived from a more extensive list of possible statements that have already been tested through a pilot study with a representative sample (Payne and Payne, 2004: 19–21). If Likert scales are part of a bigger questionnaire, fewer scale items may be required. You may have come across examples of a Likert scale in your everyday experience – questionnaires regarding your satisfaction with a service, for example.

Exercise: Developing your own Likert scale

You may like to develop Likert scales to find out:

- social work students' level of satisfaction with a research programme
- service users' level of agreement that a family support programme is meeting their needs
- a topic of your choice

What sorts of issues would you need to look at to be able to develop a thorough approach to the questions you ask? You may like to list these issues before you begin designing your questions.

Scales useful for practice evaluation

- Target problem scales (Marlow, 2011: 179):

   are a means to track changes in a client's target behaviour. This type of scale is particularly useful when actual outcomes are difficult to identify. The scale involves identifying a problem, applying an intervention, and then repeatedly rating the extent to which the target problem has changed.

- Rapid assessment instrument (Marlow, 2011: 180):

   is a standardized series of structured questions or statements administered to the client to collect [data in practice evaluations]. Rapid assessment instruments are short, easy to administer, and easy to complete. ... The Multi-Problem Screening Inventory (MPSI) (Hudson and McMurtry, 1997) is an example.

Other scales used in social work research

- Thurstone scales
- Semantic Differential Scale
- Guttman Scale
- Bogardus Social Distance Scale

The Bogardus Social Distance Scale (Payne and Payne, 2004: 21) works on a 'hierarchy of attitudes', whereby if a participant agrees with a statement at one level of the scale, it is assumed that he or she will agree with all statements that appear at levels below that. This scale has been used in race relations research, and where:

   hypothetical acceptance of someone from a minority ethnic group as a marriage partner presupposes acceptance as a friend, a neighbor and a work colleague, whereas acceptance as a neighbor presupposes only acceptance as a work colleague. (Payne and Payne, 2004: 21)

Scales that have been used in social work research and practice evaluation (Royse, 1999: 109–130):

- Community living skills scale
- Children's motivation scale
- Quality of life questionnaire
- Job satisfaction scale
- Rating scale for aggressive behaviour in the elderly
- Adult children of alcoholics tool

Chambers and Johnston (2002) discuss 'developmental differences in children's use of rating scales'. They conclude that younger children are unable to easily differentiate between levels on a Likert scale and instead tend to choose extremes. Other scales tend to be developed for use by adults (parents, teachers, child care providers) in assessing children: for example, ADHD (National Resource Center on ADHD); children's physical environments (Moore et al., 2003); and screening for mental illness (Massachusetts General Hospital, 2010), although the latter does provide rating scales for children to use for self-assessment.

Observation

Observation may differ according to the degree of structure. In very structured forms of observation, the researcher sits detached from those being observed and uses a grid or scale to record particular items of interest as they occur, such as behaviour within a period of time. Examples are child development where children's behaviour and development may be observed according to particular actions on a checklist to ascertain whether or not they are consistent with 'normal development' (Colls and Hörschelmann, 2010: 4–5; Rose, 1999b: 135–154). Bryman (2008: 254–257) discusses examples of structured observation, including 'observing jobs' (Jenkins et al., 1975), 'incidents' (LaPiere, 1934), and 'contrived observations' where researchers set up a scenario and observe what people do in response to it (Webb et al., 1966). However, Robson (2010) has shown in her study of sub-Saharan children's daily work and caring activities that observation can be conducted without using a predetermined checklist to generate descriptions of items of interest as they occur.

Participant observation is a less structured form of observation, where the 'participant' and the 'observer' roles of the researcher may shift depending on the context and the particular situations and people within that context. The researcher may be a 'participant-as-observer', which may shift to 'observer-as-participant' and back again (Atkinson, 1990; Gold, 1958). The identities of the researcher as 'insider' or 'outsider' (Smith, 1999: 5, 10, 137–141) become quite explicit and, in indigenous research, are crucial with regard to relationships of power and how this links with knowledge in research (Smith, 1999). For example, if the researcher also happens to be a member of the indigenous community, there may be complicated expectations about the researcher's role, especially if there are personal relationships involved. It cannot be assumed that community members will automatically accept someone from their own community as a researcher. In fact, they may sometimes prefer someone who is not an indigenous person to be the researcher.

Our position is that while a (participant) observer has a particular research interest and conceptual approach, observation is an active process where knowledge is negotiated and generated in the interaction between the researcher and the informant(s) (Holstein and Gubrium, 1995; Humphries and Martin, 2000; Wood and Kroger, 2000: 72–73). The researcher must be open to what may emerge from the context which then may be analysed using the conceptual approach informing the research (for example, Pithouse, 1987; Robson, 2010). Participant observation (usually combined with interviewing and local artefacts) is a basic method used in auto/ ethnographic research (Holt, 2010: 204; Morgenshtern and Novotna, 2012; Payne and Payne, 2004: 71–75; Robson, 2010: 150, 154–156; van Blerk, 2010: 234–235).

 Weblink 6.3 Examples of studies that included (participant) observation with children

Logs and journals

Logs and journals (and diaries) can be used with varying degrees of structure (Marlow, 2011: 175–177). For example, informants (including clients) may be asked to keep diaries of patterns of behaviour, such as 'health experience' (Elliott, 1997), or a social worker's record describing a client's use of alcohol (Marlow, 2011: 176), combined with structured entries of time-linked use of alcohol, or daily diaries using open and closed format to record 'everyday prejudice' (Hyers et al., 2006).

Elliott (1997: abstract) explained that the diary:

> offered a means to 'observe' behaviour which is inaccessible to participant observation. … Five key advantages [include] the potential of the 'diary-interview' method to accommodate different response modes; the extent to which the method captured diarists' own priorities; the importance of the research process in illuminating the contexts within which helpseeking took place; the role of the diaries as both a record of and reflection on the experience of illness and the value of the diary interview method as a means of understanding what is 'taken for granted' in accounts of health and illness.

Reflective journals may be used for experiential learning, for example, by social work academics examining their teaching (Norton et al., 2011) and social work students on field placements (Baum, 2012).

Weblink 6.4 Examples of journals and diaries

Journals and diaries may be the basis for oral/life histories, biographies and ethnographies (for example, Armstrong, 2001; Edwards, with Howard and Miller, 2001; Holman Jones, 2005: 763–91), recording 'individuals' personal experiences and the connections between them and past social events' (Payne and Payne, 2004: 23). A special form of research that can be seen as 'journalling' is when researchers write reflectively/reflexively about their own experiences, which may then become critical essays, auto/biographies and autoethnographies.

Autoethnography is 'an autobiographical genre of writing and research that displays multiple layers of consciousness, connecting the personal to the cultural' (Ellis and Bochner, 2000: 739; see also Ellis et al., 2011), and 'making the personal, political' (Holman Jones, 2005: 763–791). In doing an autoethnography, as with auto/biography, the 'data generation' process cannot be easily separated from the 'data analysis' process. This is because the researcher is also a participant in his or her own research process, in investigating particular aspects of lived experience and how that is located within context (time and place of its unfolding). 'Data generation' methods for autoethnography and auto/biography may involve a range of personal and public documents (diaries, reports), images (photographs, videotapes, audiotapes, and so on) that the researcher/participant draws on to construct meaning. Reflexivity and critical reflection are integral to the process as the researcher becomes an instrument of the research process (Crawford, 1997; Delamont, 2009; Gair, 2008).

Weblink 6.5 Examples of journalling, stories, autoethnographies and essays by social workers and others

Children have been asked to use forms of journals, for example, 'young commercial sex workers in Ethiopia' who were asked to document their everyday lives using 'mobility maps' (van Blerk, 2010: 235); 'compositions' written in English supplemented by drawings about their daily work and caring duties by children in sub-Saharan Africa (Robson, 2010: 150–154); young people who combined a diary with photographs and interviews about their lives (Bagnoli, 2004).

Innovative approaches to data generation: visual methods, the Pocket Chart, Ten Seeds Technique

Payne and Payne (2004: 238) describe visual methods as:

> ... all uses of images, with or without accompanying words, such as photographs, video, film, television, or hand-drawn artwork, whether pre-existing or generated as part of the research process.

Harper (2005) discusses 'what's new visually?' as an emergent approach to generating information from and by research participants, which is important in empowerment research. For example, Fudge Schormans (2010) used visual imagery with 'people with intellectual disabilities' to enable them to challenge negative portrayals in the media.

Images generated for research may be those:

- that already exist, for example, family photographs, works in art galleries, photographs in newspapers, pamphlets and posters that advertise services at social work offices. These images are secondary data, and interpreted for their meaning (known as 'semiotics', Payne and Payne, 2004: 239, citing Rose, 2001)
- that are generated collaboratively with participants as a way of eliciting information (Payne and Payne, 2004: 239, citing Harrison, 1996)
- that are generated by the researcher as part of fieldwork, for example, photographs, maps or videos in ethnographic studies or community development profiles
- that are complementary to words, in communicating research findings

Visual methods have been particularly useful when working with children of various age groups. Citing Schratz and Steiner-Löffler (1998) and Wetton and McWhirter (1998), Payne and Payne (2004: 241) discuss the uses of photography with primary-school aged children and their feelings about places in the school 'where they felt good or bad', and the 'Draw and Write technique', where children used 'annotated drawings of what they did to make and keep themselves healthy'. Children as Photographers is a large-scale research project looking at how and why children take photographs. Undertaken jointly by the National Museum of Photography, Film & Television, the University of Birmingham, and Kodak, the project features the photographs of 180 children from five European countries and their comments about their work (www.cap.ac.uk/cap.asp, accessed 7 September 2011). There are also examples of community photography with 'marginalized communities throughout the world' (Community Photography Outreach) and Kids with Cameras (www. kids-with-cameras.org/community/culturalagents-toolkit.pdf).

Weblink 6.6 Examples of research using photography and other methods with children

Visual images should not be regarded as objective facts but as subjectively constructed. For example, in photography or video recordings, the selection and framing of the subject, and editing that is subsequently done, which may distort or change the images shown, may be intentional in a wish to mislead or simply because of positioning as a field of perception (Haraway, 1991; Payne and Payne, 2004: 239–240).

In contrast with the generally accepted idea of 'visual methods' discussed above, we have interpreted two 'strengths-based approaches' developed for 'international community-level project evaluation' (Donnelly, 2010) as 'visual methods', as the descriptions below will show. These approaches are Pocket Chart and Ten Seed Technique (TST), which Donnelly used with focus groups.

Pocket Chart:

> involves a person placing a voting token into a pocket on which an issue or subject they wish to vote for or support is depicted ... *in a way that could be understood by all and was most often pictorial.* Women and men used different voting tokens to allow for disaggregation of data. [This can also be done for different age or minority groups]. The Pocket Chart also provide[s] a degree of quantification to issues that [lend] themselves more to qualitative data collection methods ... without intrusive questioning ... [and] can be used more than once. ... The tokens [are] counted publicly and results displayed openly at a final meeting. (Donnelly, 2010: 46–47, emphasis added)

Ten Seed Technique (TST) is:

> a participatory tool ... used for rapid assessments related to the current status of the community in relation to an issue (Jayakaran, 2002). [Use 10 seeds or similar tools to represent an entire relevant population in a community.] The seeds are placed on a contrasting background of a depiction of the issue ... *The group (focus group size or larger mixed groups) ... move the seeds to represent the proportion of the population depicted (or otherwise) by the picture/question.* (Donnelly, 2010: 47, emphasis added)

Examples of TST in practice include ascertaining the proportion of children of school age:

- not attending school
- who do not attend due to cost
- who are girls who do not attend due to cost

Individuals are not identified. Discussion allows for some degree of consensus by community participants. TST can be conducted as part of a focus group, and results can be communicated at a final public meeting when other results are displayed (Donnelly, 2010: 47).

Secondary sources

Sometimes researchers who have generated data for their own studies may not analyse all of it for various reasons (Payne and Payne, 2004: 214–218). These unanalysed data can be used by other researchers to conduct their own analyses, including using existing data for a different purpose. Payne and Payne (2004: 214), citing Bloor (2002), give the examples of oral histories of Welsh miners being re-analysed to look at theories of social capital and, citing Iganski et al. (2001), of employment data being re-analysed to look at racism from a socio-economic perspective.

Secondary sources valuable for social work research include documents such as case files and agency statistics (Burgen, 2010; Pockett et al., 2010); policies (McLaughlin, 2010; Takahashi, 2011; Xu, 2011); or statistics such as social indicators (Saunders, 2002); census data; comparative international data from the World Health Organization or the Organization for Economic Co-operation and Development, and even parliamentary debates found in *Hansard* (Cockburn, 2000; Marlow, 2011: 180–182; Payne and Payne, 2004: 215–216).

 Weblink 6.7 Examples of research where secondary sources were used

Mixed-methods

It is recommended that mixed-methods are used, whether in quantitative *or* qualitative studies, to maximize the trustworthiness of the data generated, as 'measurement' (Rubin and Babbie, 2011: 94), or emergent theories through 'naturalistic' approaches (Bryman, 2008: 21–24; 603–626). Qualitative and quantitative strategies may be combined:

1 if only one approach or the other will not allow you to answer the research questions adequately (Bryman, 2008; Clarke, 2009; Marlow, 2011: 183)
2 to be 'democratically engaged' (Greene, 2002)
3 to convince key stakeholders (Cockburn, 2000; Kaufman Hall, 2001; Silverman, 1998).

> The combination of multiple methodological practices, empirical materials, perspectives and observers in a single study is best understood, then, as a strategy that adds rigor, breadth, complexity, richness and depth to any inquiry (see Flick, 2002, p. 229). (Denzin and Lincoln, 2005b: 5)

Bryman (2008: 606–607) discusses Hammersley's (1996) classification of approaches to multi-strategy research.

1 *Triangulation*: when quantitative research is used to corroborate qualitative research findings and vice versa, using different methods (see Chapter 4).
2 *Facilitation*: when one approach is used to aid another. For example, qualitative research may precede a quantitative study by providing hypotheses to be explored further or enhance the design of interview questions. Quantitative research may also facilitate qualitative research – by identifying a selection of people to be interviewed in-depth following a more structured survey and analysis.
3 *Complementarity*: mixed-methods to address different aspects of a study or research question. Examples: population-based survey combined with focused interviews with stroke patients (Clarke, 2009: 298); participant observation of 100 elementary school-age children in the UK, some of whom were diagnosed with 'Special Educational Needs' combined with 'semi-structured interviews and a semi-projective exercise' with 44 of the children (Holt, 2010: 204); participant observation combined with focus groups, semi-structured interviews, 'mobility maps', and informal discussions with 'young commercial sex workers in Ethiopia' (van Blerk, 2010: 234–235).

Regardless of the reasons for using mixed-methods, it is important to be aware of the assumptions informing qualitative and quantitative approaches: see, for example, Clarke (2009), which we discuss in Chapter 7 on data analysis.

Categorizing people: identity, diversity and positioning

It is usual in most research for informants to be asked at the start or end of the interview or questionnaire to indicate details about themselves by means of tick boxes, scales or one-word answers: for example, sex (female or male), gender (man or woman), age (group or specified), ethnicity, religion, disability, marital status, and so on. The responses made by each informant may appear later as summarized or aggregated descriptions of the participants, separated from what are set out as responses to the main questions about the research topic. In other words, informants are not asked how 'being particular identities' (men or women, for example) relates to their experiences of whatever is being researched.

Truman and Humphries (1994: 3) use the example of racism and cite Graham (1993: 32) who says:

> most typologies do not invite people to record their experiences of racism, but to define themselves in terms of physical and cultural attributes ... 'race' typologies typically combine a complex of dimensions [political boundaries, geographical definitions and colour] into a single scale.

Research approaches that use the 'categorizing people' method tend to silence those who are marginalized or disadvantaged. The categories are fixed and usually derived for bureaucratic purposes rather than necessarily representing the *meaning* of identity for individuals and groups and their lived experiences. The categories treat all individuals categorized in particular ways as exactly the same, stereotyping them: for example, assuming that all 'Indian' people in hospital would like particular food rather than asking them how their religious and regional backgrounds may influence food habits (Ahmad and Sheldon, 1993). The categories do not necessarily allow people to belong to multiple identity categories, as argued in the example above regarding 'race'. Furthermore, the categories that claim to represent particular groups may be used to treat those groups as problems or deviant, and the research may reinforce these perceptions (Hurley, 2007) – for example, using ethnicity or race profiling to identify 'criminals'. There is also the potential for categories that are used thoughtlessly in social research to be taken over by people with more repressive agendas, such as racist or anti-women groups. Awareness of the politics and ethics of categorizing people is essential when framing research questions to ensure that they are participatory and can achieve emancipatory objectives. Notice the differences between the questions in the two columns in Table 6.4.

TABLE 6.4 Categorizing people and research perspectives

Categorizing people	Critique-based alternatives – using categories in a non-discriminatory way
As deviant	
'Why do battered women stay with partners who abuse them?' (Renzetti and Lee, 1993: 28)	'What factors make battering possible or even permissible?' (Renzetti and Lee, 1993: 28)

Categorizing people	Critique-based alternatives – using categories in a non-discriminatory way
By excluding or misrepresenting groups	
The General Household Survey in the UK that asks informants to classify their personal relationships in the context of the household in which they live using categories that refer to legal definitions of marriage: 'married', 'cohabiting', 'single', 'widowed', 'divorced' or 'separated' (Truman and Humphries, 1994: 5–6)	'How useful is the legal definition of marriage in understanding personal relationships?' (Truman and Humphries, 1994)
By keeping invisible what is considered to be the normal identity category, such as looking at lesbianism	Explicitly conceptualize and explore heterosexuality (Truman and Humphries, 1994: 10)
'What is lesbianism and why is it so common? How does lesbianism affect the whole of a woman's life?' (Truman and Humphries, 1994: 10, based on Kitzinger and Wilkinson, 1993)	'What is heterosexuality and why is it so common? How does heterosexuality affect the whole of a woman's life?' (Kitzinger and Wilkinson, 1993)
As a problem group	
'Why are there so many black children [in Britain] in foster care?' (Barn, 1994)	'What are the processes that involved the entry of black children into care?' (Barn, 1994)
Stereotyping	
'Why are black people more vulnerable to schizophrenia than white people?' (Truman and Humphries, 1994: 16)	'What are the social processes which lead to a disproportionate number of black people being diagnosed as schizophrenic?' (Truman and Humphries, 1994: 16)

Putting it all together

In this chapter we have looked at how to generate data ('methods'). We have looked at how researchers can use the same methods, but the level of structure designed into the enquiry process influences whether the data produced will be quantitative, qualitative, or both. We have also looked at both primary and secondary data sources.

However, we have also extended the understanding of data generation beyond methods to a focus on politics and ethics. Regardless of how a researcher may seek to conduct ethical research, the process of enquiry and its outcome as knowledge is always embedded in power relationships between the researcher and the researched.

Further reading

Bogdewic, S. (1999) 'Participant observation', in B. F. Crabtree and W. L. Miller (eds), *Doing Qualitative Research* (2nd edition), Thousand Oaks, CA: Sage (pp. 47–69).

Bryman, A. (2008) *Social Research Methods* (3rd edition), Oxford: Oxford University Press (Chapter 25, 'Mixed methods research: combining quantitative and qualitative research', pp. 603–626).

Clarke, P. (2009) 'Understanding the experience of stroke: A mixed-method research agenda', *The Gerontologist*, 49 (3): 293–302.

Hellawell, D. (2006) 'Inside–out: analysis of the insider–outsider concept as a heuristic device to develop reflexivity in students doing qualitative research', *Teaching in Higher Education*, 11 (4): 483–494, doi: 10.1080/13562510600874292.

Kayrooz, C. and Trevitt, C. (2005) *Research in Organizations and Communities: Tales from the Real World*, Crow's Nest, NSW: Allen & Unwin (pp. 93–97) (compares six case studies according to aims, design, methods, contexts, and political and ethical issues).

Payne, G. and Payne, J. (2004) *Key Concepts in Social Research*, London: Sage (documentary sources: pp. 61–65; interviewing: pp. 129–134; questionnaires: pp. 186–190).

7

Making Sense of Data: Analysis

Introduction

In this chapter, we shall be:

1 Discussing the differences between quantitative and qualitative data analysis.
2 Discussing approaches to managing and organizing quantitative and qualitative data and the relationship to analysis.
3 Looking at approaches to quantitative and qualitative analysis consistent with research aims and methods of data generation.
4 Discussing the implicit ethical and political issues in data analysis.

What is data analysis? Why is it necessary?

Data analysis is a process of making sense of the responses you have received as a result of using various methods of data generation. In quantitative studies, and in some qualitative studies that use positivist and/or quantitative methods as the model for research, analysis is represented as a separate and subsequent stage to data generation. In qualitative studies informed by naturalistic and/or emancipatory paradigms, data generation and analysis are regarded as interrelated processes.

After you have completed the data generation process, the data will be a collection of information – whether about multiple individuals or sites, or multiple data sets from individual informants or sites. The data will be either numbers (quantitative) or text (words or images) as video and audiotapes and transcripts, case files, field notes or diaries, or a combination. To be able to answer your research question, you first must identify the *patterns* – similarities, differences, contradictions, negative cases – connecting cases or within a single case. You should then draw appropriate conclusions related to 'epistemic communities'

(Stanley and Wise, 1993: 200), and how your research has contributed to knowledge about the topic. What contribution to existing knowledge has your research made? Does it replicate and support existing knowledge, or extend it? Does it identify gaps and/or challenge claims in existing knowledge? Depending on the paradigm, the analysis may be seen as generating absolute 'truth' and objective facts, or a partial version.

Mixed-methods and complementary data sets

In Chapter 4, we discussed triangulation, along with transferability and reflexivity as strategies for achieving trustworthy research. Among other things, triangulation involves using more than one method of data collection, sometimes combining quantitative and qualitative methods ('mixed-methods'). If using mixed-methods, researchers must consider sampling and recruitment, methods of data generation and their complementarity, that for the purposes of this chapter, are directly relevant to methods of interpretation and analysis (Evans et al., 2011; Irwin, 2008). Basically, if you have combined quantitative and qualitative approaches, and different methods, you will have different data sets, with each set corresponding with its particular method of enquiry. These data sets are complementary or 'connected contributions' (Clarke, 2009: 297), for example, to 'understand the experience of stroke', mixed-methods may be integrated to give appropriate weight to data from different methods so that a well-integrated analysis is developed.

> Quantitative investigators have typically had to speculate about the unseen processes that account for the observed relationships between variables. The use of qualitative data in a separate sample of community-dwelling seniors helped to shed light on the underlying reasons *why* and *how* these factors operate to affect well-being following a stroke. (Clarke, 2009: 298)

In Chapter 4, we introduced the idea of 'mixed-genre texts' (Richardson and St Pierre, 2005: 959–978, in Denzin and Lincoln, 2005b: 5–6) that may be useful in analysing and re-presenting the research outcomes.

Exercise: Linking paradigms, methods, data sets and criteria for trustworthiness

In the first edition of this book (D'Cruz and Jones, 2004: 133–134), we provided a simple example of relating data sets to methods. You may like to refer to that if you are a beginner, before you attempt this exercise.

> Why should you not use each data set as a check of the validity of other sets? If you were to use statistical collections, case files and interviews with clients or social workers, what are the different assumptions that apply to these methods in terms of how 'reality' is understood and explained?
>
> Have you concluded that you cannot use the different data sets as checks on each other because:
>
> - a statistical collection relies on an understanding of a reality that is measurable and 'objective'?
> - case files only record what is 'relevant' for an organization and it is usually someone's recorded version of events within organizational requirements?
> - interviews about files and practices are another version/reinterpretation of what is on file?
>
> How might these three data sets complement each other in answering the research question?

Three questions for researchers to guide analysis involving different data sources are:

1 Data on what? *What* do these data tell me and, crucially, what can they *not* tell me about?
2 Strength of claim. *How well* do these data tell me this? How convincing are claims I want to make on the basis of the data? How can I make the strongest claims possible without pushing the data 'too far' by making claims which are beyond their capacity?
3 Integration of data. How best can I integrate and make sense of different forms of qualitative data? How can I integrate quantitative and qualitative material? The answer to this must take full account of, and be consistent with, the researcher's answers to (1) and (2). (Mason, 1994: 99–107, original emphasis)

 ## Weblink 7.1 Examples of research using mixed-methods

Working with people: negotiating knowledge and meaning

Ideally, participants should be involved in the data analysis (Reason and Bradbury, 2008b: 1–13; Ward et al., 2010: 67–69). Apart from practical considerations related to the institutional contexts in which many researchers work

(Ward et al., 2010: 71–78), researchers also need to consider the relations of power in resolving differences between participants' perspectives.

While acknowledging multiple perspectives, as social workers it is often difficult to avoid taking sides. Ethically, the researcher should declare his or her positioning and use a journal to aid critically reflective and reflexive practice throughout the process. The researcher should be aware of the politics of knowledge and that through a 'hierarchy of credibility' (Becker, 1970), individuals and groups positioned in structurally powerful positions may be seen as 'having the full truth', while those with less powerful positions may be disregarded.

However, it is simplistic to take the view that 'truth' lies solely with subordinated groups. Nor should researchers marginalize participants in dominant positions as they are entitled to their views. It is appropriate for researchers to point out the consequences of privileged perspectives for those who are less powerful. The test for social work research is how to design, analyse and present conclusions from research that can address ethical commitments to disadvantaged groups while also addressing the political dimension (the ability to convince powerful stakeholders). A political approach may include judicious selection of data generation strategies and ways of getting the message across in the conclusions and reporting. There is no guarantee that these strategies will influence powerful interests and, therefore, additional strategies may include community work, advocacy and lobbying for change based on the research (Naples, 2007: 557–559). For example, see 'Exemplars' in Reason and Bradbury (2008c: Part III), Kaufman Hall (2001), and Fawcett et al., (2010: 143–158).

Organizing and analysing quantitative data

Usually quantitative studies involve responses from a large number of informants, which is necessary if valid statistical analyses are to be conducted. Researchers must do three things to arrive at their conclusions: (1) organize raw data into a format suitable for computer analysis; (2) present data in tables and graphs to summarize the patterns; and (3) interpret the data for theoretical implications (Neuman and Kreuger, 2003: 326).

Data organization involves:

1 *Coding*: systematic organization of data through *coding procedures* and *codebooks* into a format that is computer-readable.
2 *Data entry* into a computer file in a spreadsheet or grid format with data linked to variables described in the codebook.
3 *Data cleaning* that is done to check there are no inaccurate entries, to maximize the trustworthiness of the analysis and conclusions (Neuman and Kreuger, 2003: 326–329; Rubin and Babbie, 2011: 504–508).

While data from structured methods are already in computer-ready form, researchers who have asked semi-structured questions to complement structured questions must translate the open-ended responses into categories or themes that can then be coded into an appropriate form to conduct statistical analysis (Kumar, 2011: 266–268). See for example, Bryman (2008: 233–234) on coding open questions.

In looking at quantitative data analysis, we will not be doing any more than identifying key concepts and processes. See Kumar (2011: 253–277), Sarantakos (2005), Bryman (2008: 314–362), Rubin and Babbie (2011: 501–569), and Neuman and Kreuger (2003: 325–355) for introductions to quantitative data organization and analysis and the use of computers: for example, SPSS for Windows, for Mac and PC.

As there is quite specialized knowledge required to undertake sound quantitative analyses, if you are uncertain about basic statistical concepts, you may like to read the following books, which we have found helpful:

- A. Graham (2008) *Teach Yourself Statistics*, New York: McGraw-Hill.
- D. Rowntree (2004) *Statistics without Tears: An Introduction for Non-mathematicians*, Boston, MA: Pearson.

We strongly recommend that you consult a statistician or someone with proven experience in undertaking quantitative research, unless you have a thorough understanding of the complexities of statistical logic that inform data collection and analysis. For example, statisticians were part of the research team in Mason (1994: 107–108) and D'Cruz et al. (2002). It is essential to get the design technically correct from the start to ensure methodologically trustworthy research and conclusions. However, if you involve a statistician, as a social work researcher must know what kinds of questions you want answered and how to interpret the statistical patterns related to literature and theory (Neuman and Kreuger, 2003: 354).

Do not trawl through the raw data just to see what emerges ('trawling' means running every possible form of analysis with selected tests of significance). This is costly as well as bad research. It is costly because of the time it takes to produce and print every possible statistical test on large quantities of data. It is bad research because it suggests that you are unclear about your research question and how the data you have generated answers it. It also suggests that you are trying to find significance in your data to prove the relationships in the data rather than knowing what relationships you require and doing appropriate tests to explore the significance of these relationships.

Quantitative data analysis uses statistics (1) *to describe* informants and their responses, and (2) *to draw inferences* about the significance of relationships between variables and the extent to which the hypothesis is confirmed or not. The analysis may examine whether or not the patterns relate to only one variable (*univariate analysis*), two variables (*bivariate analysis*), or more than two variables (*multivariate analysis*) (Bryman, 2008: 322–332). Table 7.1 shows the links between the purpose of the analysis, methods and complexity related to the number of variables.

TABLE 7.1   Quantitative data analysis: linking the purpose of the analysis, methods and complexity in relation to the number of variables

Purpose of the analysis	Type of analysis	Number of variables involved
How many? What is the proportional distribution?	Frequency (absolute and relative)	Univariate
How many? Where do the main clusters appear?	Measures of central tendency – mean, mode, median, normal distribution	Univariate
How many? What is the distribution and its variation?	Measures of dispersion or variability – normal distribution, range, standard deviation	Univariate
How many? How does one variable relate to other variables? Relationships, not causality (cause and effect)	Contingency tables; Pearson's coefficient and Spearman's rho (correlation tests, for strength and direction of the relationship between variables)	Bivariate
Is the relationship between two variables spurious? Is there an intervening variable in the apparent relationship between two variables? Is a third variable moderating the relationship between two variables?	Refer to texts on advanced statistical techniques (see, for example, Bryman and Cramer, 2001) or a statistician	Multivariate

Sources: Bryman (2008: 322–332); DeRoos (2011), in Marlow (2011: 236–256)

Descriptive statistics

Descriptive statistical analyses ask the question 'How many?' in relation to the actual and proportional distribution in the sample of participants; the clustering, distribution and variation in the emerging patterns; and relationships between variables. While descriptive statistics are normally associated with quantitative analyses, it is also possible to use descriptive statistics in qualitative analyses to complement written descriptions of people's experiences and to offer greater precision to the word-descriptions (Rubin and Babbie, 2011: 520–523). In quantitative studies, these descriptive patterns may be in different formats, known as *levels of measurement*, indicating how often something occurs and/or the strength and direction of change and/or the relative differences between events or people. These different levels of measurement generate different kinds of data: (1) nominal or categorical (for example, sex: M or F); (2) ordinal (for example, Likert scales); (3) interval (for example, IQ, or Thurstone Scales); and (4) ratio (for example, age in years or months, or income). These different levels of measurement are associated with mathematical relationships and the degree of sophistication of the statistical analysis increases with each level of measurement as listed. Refer to definitions and examples of these different data types in Bryman (2008: 321–322), DeRoos (2011: 237–238), and Kumar (2011: 62–79).

How many? What is the proportional distribution?

Frequency counts of *categorical/nominal variables* describe participants' characteristics, such as age, gender or ethnicity, and the distribution of responses across participants. These descriptions of participants' characteristics can be used in both quantitative and qualitative analyses (Rubin and Babbie, 2011: 520–523). The researcher can present the *absolute frequency* (head count) and *relative frequency* (percentage or proportion of participants) in each category. The absolute frequency alone is helpful, while including the percentages gives a greater understanding of the patterns of representation. It is not appropriate to present only the percentages as it gives a misleading impression of the actual numbers they represent.

For example, you have interviewed 50 people about their experiences with a family support service and represent their responses as absolute (N) and relative (%) frequencies (see Table 7.2).

While a frequency table is a helpful description of patterns of participants' responses, we discussed in Chapter 6 critiques of approaches that present participants' characteristics unrelated to their experiences of phenomena being investigated (Truman and Humphries, 1994), instead recommending that analysis should show how these characteristics may be associated with topics of interest to the research, for example, how participants' gender may be related to their experiences of family support services.

TABLE 7.2 Example of a simple frequency table describing patterns of responses

Experiences of family support services	N (%)
Improved circumstances	30 (60)
No difference	10 (20)
Made things worse	10 (20)
TOTAL	50 (100)

How many? Where do the main clusters appear?

In addition to simple statistical counts, researchers also need to know where the data clusters, known as *measures of central tendency*: (1) mean, (2) mode, and (3) median (Rubin and Babbie, 2011: 509–512; www.mathsteacher.com.au/year8/ch17_stat/02_mean/mean.htm, accessed 28 February 2012).

The *mean* is the arithmetical average. The mean (average) can only be used with interval or ratio data, such as age or income. For example, you may need to know average age or income of participants related to a research question about homeless youth or seniors seeking in-home care.

The *mode* is the most frequently occurring response. The mode can be used with any form of data and is easiest to use. It shows you the most popular response. For example, if you look at Table 7.2, the modal category is 'improved circumstances'. It can also show you the most commonly occurring characteristics, for example, most simply, whether there are more men than women with mobility disabilities. It is possible to have more than one mode in a distribution – it means that there is more than one popular response pattern.

The *median* is the middle response, if you think of it as (hypothetically) setting out every single response you have received in a row, from lowest to highest. (You can do this yourself with very small samples but, normally, a computer can work it out for you.) You then take the middle response or score. The median can be used with ordinal, interval and ratio data. For example, you may be interested in where the middle point is in housing prices to better understand the consequences for low-income earners wanting to buy a property.

While it is useful to know the patterns of clustering in the data, it is also helpful to understand their distribution and the spread between lowest and highest scores (or responses).

How many? What is the distribution and its variation?

The patterns of distribution and variation within the data complement knowledge about the clustering or central tendencies. *Measures of dispersion* or *variability* refer to the *range* and *standard deviation*. The *normal distribution* is used to understand the patterns of distribution and variations between individuals or events within a group.

The *normal distribution* assumes that there is a standard way in which responses ought to be arranged that produce a symmetrical pattern. This pattern, when associated with the sample of respondents, is assumed to replicate the patterns in the main population and allows conclusions drawn from the study to be generalized to the whole population (Bryman, 2001: 94). In the normal distribution, the mean (the average), the mode (most frequently occurring) and the median (central point) all occur in the same place in the pattern, this being the mid-point. Then, all other responses are distributed within the range of the available responses (the lowest to highest points) with a pattern of variation between the responses known as the standard deviation.

It is proposed that approximately 68 per cent of all scores/responses lie within one standard error on either side of the mean (or average) with a further (approximately) 28 per cent within two standard errors on either side of the mean. (Three standard errors on both sides of the mean account for around 95 per cent of the sample (Rubin and Babbie, 2011: 528–535)). Another way of explaining it is that about 50 per cent of responses ought to be below the mean and the other 50 per cent above it. Of the 50 per cent on each side of the mean, 34 per cent would be one standard error below and 34 per cent one standard error above (that is, the majority of responses).

When the measures for a study are combined in relation to different variables, a pattern that is specific to that study/variable is generated that has its own 'height' (mode, median and mean) and 'width' (range), although the overall shape may conform to the bell-shaped curve of the normal distribution. However, if the clustering does not conform, the distribution will be described as 'skewed'. Refer to www.google.com.au/search?q=normal+distribution&hl=en&prmd=imvns&tbm=isch&tbo=u&source=univ&sa=X&ei=Sv9KT_CoFZGhiQfufzZDw&sqi=2&ved=0CE4QsAQ&biw=1366&bih=628 (the normal and skewed distributions) (accessed 27 February 2012).

Hacking (1990) and Rose (1998: 109–10, 120, and 1999b) critique the political and ethical implications associated with the normal distribution and its applications in the social control of populations and individuals, especially with the increasing reliance on risk assessment in many aspects of social life. Additionally, policymaking that looks at where the greatest demand seems to exist, based on the clusters around the mean or average as being the 'real' extent of a problem (the mainstream or the norm), disregards people who sit on the 'outliers' (at the margins) (Bryman, 2008: 325), and, because of small numbers, are seen as unrepresentative of the norm or general experience of a problem or issue. The danger of relying solely on numerical majorities as representative of the extent of a problem (as 'demand') is that people who are 'on the margins' may be denied services, although numerical representation alone does not determine whether a group is 'marginal' (Hurley, 2007; Smith and Pitts, 2007). For example, men may be forgotten in service provision among the elderly because more women than men survive into old age (Arber and Ginn, 1991; Thompson, 1994), but heterosexual men may be marginal in research about HIV/AIDS because the problem is associated solely with gay men (Smith and Pitts, 2007: 6).

How many? How does one variable relate to other variables?

It is important in social work research to understand relationships between variables. Most commonly there is interest in the extent of effectiveness of interventions and/or what the associations are between multiple problems. Descriptive statistics show relationships between variables as *measures of association*. The main relationships of interest are *causality* (for example, has this intervention caused an outcome?) and *correlation* (for example, the strength and direction of any association between mental illness, substance misuse and homelessness) (Neuman and Kreuger, 2003: 342–344).

Usually, relationships between two variables (bivariate analyses) are explored and described using *cross-tabulations* or *contingency tables*. Table 7.3 is an example of a bivariate contingency table (gender by income), in which Payne and Payne (2004: 56) use text instead of numbers to show how to represent data and read such tables. Normally, you would use numbers in the cells, but they would show the patterns expressed in words in the table.

TABLE 7.3   An example of a table without numbers: gender by income: people in paid employment

Income level	Men	Women	Totals
High	Lots	Few	All high earners
Middle	Some	Some	All middle earners
Low	Few	Lots	All low earners
Totals	All men	All women	All of our sample

Source: Payne and Payne (2004: 56, Table 1)

It is also possible to describe multivariate relationships using tables, but these are more complicated (see Kumar, 2011: 292–297, for examples of tables and advice on effective presentation).

In addition to tables or graphs to describe associations between variables, researchers doing quantitative analyses often wish to show whether the observed relationships are due to chance or an actual relationship, and the confidence in such relationships. You would use inferential statistics for this.

Inferential statistics

In experimental studies in particular, researchers aim to *test hypotheses* that causal and/or correlational relationships have not occurred by chance, but instead represent actual relationships between variables. Researchers support their conclusions by claims of *statistical significance*, or the probability of obtaining the results by chance (Neuman and Kreuger, 2003: 350–351; Royse, 1999: 36). However, even if tests are statistically significant, their theoretical relevance needs to be established (Bryman, 2008: 332–333). It is the researcher's role to draw meaningful conclusions about the contribution made by the apparent relationship between variables. It may be necessary to conduct multivariate analyses, which are rather more complicated and beyond the scope of this book.

A researcher can test a hypothesis *directly*, stated either as:

Two-tailed or non-directional, as a relationship between variables, without specifying the direction of the relationship: for example, 'gender has *an impact on the likelihood* of hospitalization for depression'. (Marlow and Boone, 2005: 252, emphasis added)

or:

One-tailed or *directional*, as a relationship between variables that has a particular 'direction': For example, 'women are *more likely than men* to be hospitalized for depression'. (Marlow and Boone, 2005: 252, emphasis added)

Hypotheses can also be tested *indirectly*, by seeking to confirm the *null hypothesis*, stated as 'there is no relationship between variables'. Researchers who use this approach make it 'more demanding' to make claims about the strength of the association between variables of interest (Neuman and Kreuger, 2003: 144). This approach emphasizes that an ethical researcher is a 'disinterested observer'. His or her interest in seeking confirmation of a relationship between variables should be sufficiently distanced to be prepared to find that there is no relationship, however desirable it may be to show the opposite. So, drawing on the examples given above, a null hypothesis would be 'there is *no relationship* between gender and hospitalization [for depression]' (Marlow and Boone, 2005: 253, emphasis added).

Hypotheses are developed and justified through connecting both professional and personal experiences and 'academic' and 'grey' literature (Hurley, 2007: 166–167; Jesson et al., 2011: 54–56), rather than relying uncritically on personal impressions or whims. Hypothesis testing relies on *tests of statistical significance*, which estimate the degree of confidence (probability) that the relationship between variables is due to an actual relationship, rather than by chance, and can be generalized to the wider population. It is possible for a researcher to falsely conclude that there is a relationship between variables by rejecting the null hypothesis – known as a Type I error. It is also possible to falsely conclude that there is no relationship between variables, instead accepting the null hypothesis – known as a Type II error. Ways of avoiding such errors include larger samples and levels of measurement – for example, ratio variables that allow for stronger statistical tests to be used (DeRoos, 2011: 263–265).

For a more detailed introduction to the types of statistical tests used for bivariate analysis refer to Marlow and Boone (2005: 255, Table 12.1) and Neuman and Kreuger (2003: 343–344, Box 12.5 and Table 12.4).

Quantitative research can meet pragmatic and strategic objectives, and researchers can work in emancipatory ways, making explicit the value base and relevance of method for the question. However, it is also possible for researchers to 'misuse and misinterpret inferential statistics' (Rubin and Babbie, 2011: 562–566), and inferential statistics can also be controversial (Rubin and Babbie, 2011: 566–569). Hacking (1999) gives the examples of statistical studies (Herrnstein and Murray, 1994; MacKenzie, 1981) that have been used to generate theories of causality that are applied uncritically and their abuse in meeting particular ideological agendas, such as race stereotypes (Hacking, 1999: 57).

Presenting your analysis

We have alluded to tables and graphs as important ways of presenting quantitative analyses (see Kumar, 2011: 291–309; Sarantakos, 2005: 367–373). See Tables 7.2 and 7.3 as examples of frequency and contingency tables, respectively. Figures 7.1–7.4 are some examples of commonly used graphs.

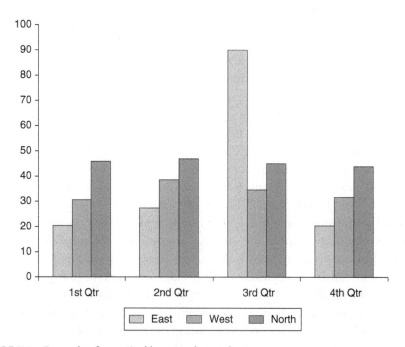

FIGURE 7.1   Example of a vertical bar or column chart

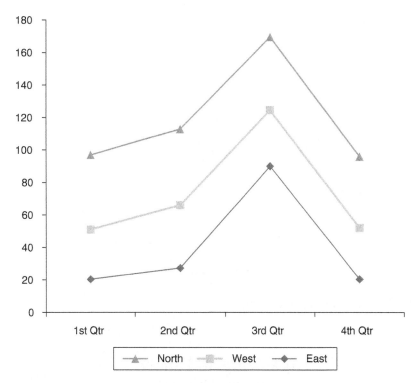

FIGURE 7.2   Example of line chart

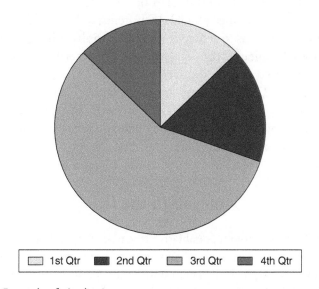

FIGURE 7.3   Example of pie chart

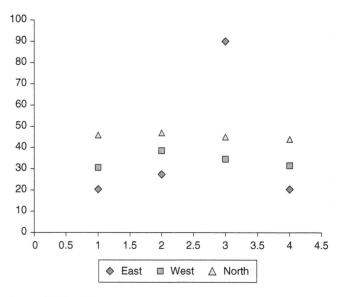

FIGURE 7.4   Example of scattergram

Organizing and analysing qualitative data

Qualitative data are usually in the form of text, such as notes taken of observations, interview transcripts, official documents, or 'conversion or linkage to words' of images such as videotapes or photographs (Huberman and Miles, 1994: 429–430). Qualitative data analysis has been described as 'messy' because, unlike in quantitative studies, the stages are dynamic and closely interrelated (Grbich, 2007: 20–25), with some arguing that the researcher is an 'instrument' in the process (Punch, 1993: 185–186). Bogdan and Biklen (1982, 1992) distinguish these interrelated aspects of qualitative data analysis as 'analysis in the field' and 'analysis after the field'.

'Analysis in the field'

From a practical point of view, qualitative researchers, whether working alone or in a team, should use a data management approach for good storage and retrieval of large volumes of data (Huberman and Miles, 1994) to ensure that they are not 'miscoded, mislabeled, mislinked and mislaid' (Wolfe, 1992: 293). A reliable system of data management will allow documentation of the analysis over the life of the research – a form of auditing the analysis as it proceeds (Grbich, 2007: 25–31; Guba and Lincoln, 1982).

Huberman and Miles (1994: 431, Table 27.1) recommend 'What to store, retrieve from and retain':

1 **Raw material**: field notes, tapes, site documents.
2 **Partially processed data**: write-ups, transcriptions. Ideally, these should appear in their initial version, and in subsequent corrected, 'cleaned', 'commented-on' versions. Write-ups may profitably include marginal or reflective remarks made by the researcher during or after data collection.
3 **Coded data**: write-ups with specific codes attached.
4 **The coding scheme or thesaurus**: in its successive iterations.
5 **Memos or other analytic material**: the researcher's reflections on the conceptual meaning of the data.
6 **Search and retrieval records**: information showing which coded chunks or data segments the researcher looked for during analysis, and the retrieved material, records of links made among segments.
7 **Data displays**: matrices, charts or networks used to display retrieved information in a more compressed, organized form, along with the associated analytic text. Typically, there are several revised versions of these.
8 **Analysis episodes**: documentation of what you did, step by step, to assemble the displays and write the analytic text.
9 **Report text**: successive drafts of what is written on the design, methods and findings of the study.
10 **General chronological log or documentation:** of data collection and analysis work.
11 **Index:** of all the above material.

Levine's (1985) approach to storage and retrieval supports interaction between data generation and data analysis.

> … **[1] formatting** (how materials are laid out, physically embodied, and structured into types of file(s)), **[2] cross-referral** (linkage across different files), **[3] indexing** (defining codes, organizing them into a structure, and pairing codes with specific parts of the database), **[4] abstracting** (condensed summaries of longer material, such as documents or extended field notes), and **[5] pagination** (numbers and letters locating specific material in field notes – for example, B J K 1 22 locates for Brookside Hospital the first interview with Dr Jameson by researcher Kennedy, page 22).

> These functions, historically accomplished with notebooks, index cards, file folders, and edge-punch cards, can be carried out far more easily and quickly with computer software. … Even so, a physical filing system is also needed for raw field notes, hard copies of transcriptions, audio tapes, memos, and the like. (Levine, 1985: 169–186, numbering and bold added)

This 'analysis in the field' (Bogdan and Biklen, 1982, 1992) means that the researcher ought to be 'constantly engaged in preliminary analytic strategies' (Bryman and Burgess, 1994: 7; Grbich, 2007: 25–31), being critically aware of the research in process and willing to modify aspects in response to contextual issues. For example, the research focus may need revision or the data might suggest new lines of enquiry. The researcher's journal that documents reflections about the research process and analytical insights that require further exploration integrates analysis with data generation and therefore broadens the meaning of both processes (Richardson, 1994: 525–526). See Grbich (2007: 25–31) for examples of preliminary analytic strategies.

'Analysis after the field'

The second aspect of qualitative analysis is 'analysis after the field' (Bogdan and Biklen, 1982, 1992). This process involves coding, categorizing, and other ways of pattern-making from data. The researcher must be aware of different perspectives on the data and conclusions that can be drawn, with awareness of the political implications of disagreements with the conclusions. Ethically, a researcher should use a journal to document his or her reflections on the process and positioning as a researcher, including seeking opportunities for reflexive commentary on the data, outcomes and conclusions. The peer-reviewed, electronic journal, *Sociological Research Online*, encourages this approach to research and its publication (see www.socresonline.org.uk/). It also means that, in practice, it is more difficult for qualitative data to be presented as 'findings' separate from the 'discussion', which is usually the format for quantitative studies. See Grbich (2007: 31–36), Bryman (2008: 550–557) and Maxwell and Miller (2008) for guidance on generating codes and themes.

Inductive approaches

Analytic induction is:

> an approach ... in which the researcher seeks universal explanations of phenomena by pursuing the collection of data until no cases that are inconsistent with a hypothetical explanation (deviant or negative cases) ... are found. (Bryman, 2008: 539)

It is 'a way of building explanations by constructing and testing a set of causal links between events, actions, etc., in one case and the iterative extension of this to further cases' (Gibbs, 2011). *Concepts and their definitions* are considered hypotheses to be tested, with concepts modified through the research process, and the aim of representing the meanings most relevant to the context (Gibbs, 2011, citing Ratcliff, n.d.). The researcher may wish to use flowcharts and other diagrammatic ways of representing relationships between concepts in building theory (Grbich, 2007: 32–34; van Rooyen, 2011: 275–276).

Hypotheses may be 'an approximation' rather than an exact fit with the data. In keeping with the strategies of 'rival and alternative hypotheses' and 'negative cases':

> when you encounter a case that does not fit your theory, ask yourself whether it is the result of (1) normal social variation, (2) your lack of knowledge about the range of appropriate behaviour, or (3) a genuinely unusual case. (van Rooyen, 2011: 227)

Grounded theory, attributed to Glaser and Strauss (1967), was developed as a set of 'procedures and techniques' (Strauss and Corbin, 1990). The main feature is 'the meshing of theorizing and data collection' (Bryman and Burgess, 1994: 4). The grounded theory approach comprises a series of steps, including 'open', or 'initial', and 'axial' coding (Bryman, 2008: 541–548; Charmaz, 2005, 2011; Strauss and Corbin, 1990). However, there are many criticisms of grounded theory (Bryman, 2008: 48–50), including the potential for the analysis to disregard context and treat data as neutral. Clarke (2007) proposes a situational analysis to extend the basic grounded theory approach.

Computers can assist with inductive approaches through a code-and-retrieve function, and coding and memo-writing in NVivo (Bryman, 2008: 565–584; Fielding, 2008; Hesse-Biber and Crofts, 2008). However, there are strengths and weaknesses in using computers for qualitative analysis (Bryman, 2008: 566–567; Sarantakos, 2005: 357–359), and many qualitative researchers who have used computers for organizing and coding their data return to the transcripts to conduct the interpretive aspects of analysis and get a contextual sense of their data (Bryman, 2008: 583).

Ethnography

Ethnography emerged from anthropology and literally means 'writing culture' (Mitchell, 2007: 55). An ethnographic study involves a range of methods, including extended participant observation, conversation-style interviews and documentary review. Data are collected primarily as field notes and diaries (Bogdewic, 1999), although in-depth interviews may be audio-taped with participants' permission and later transcribed (typed up) as text. The researcher gains an understanding of the symbolic world, including how people in the setting give meaning to their experiences, and seeks to understand the language and the patterns and rules of behaviour within that setting (Payne and Payne, 2004: 71–75); for example, in communities (Payne and Payne, 2004: 46–50) or professional practice (D'Cruz, 2004a: 27–30, 33–34, 106–130; Pithouse, 1987).

While the earliest ethnographies investigated 'exotic' cultures, more recently the approach has been to treat aspects of our own cultures as 'strange', to investigate the rules and conventions that are taken for granted as 'normal', and to critically question them (Mitchell, 2007). A very influential article by Miner (1956) [search 'Body ritual among the Nacirema'] is a classic in this regard. To explain why it is so would undermine the lessons it teaches from a first reading. However, once you have read the article, refer to www.oppapers.com/essays/Horace-Miner-Response/84848, which offers a succinct commentary on its aims.

Ethnography goes beyond the 'concrete [field] notes' recording events in sufficient detail 'as they happen'. A researcher engaged in participant observation normally records events and material artefacts in detail (for example, Robson, 2010), later engaging with the records to frame the written ethnography. Field notes act as *aides-memoires*, supplementing the 'headnotes' contained in the researcher's memory (Ottenberg, 1990, in Mitchell, 2007: 61–62). Ethnography relies on 'thick description' (Geertz, 1973a, 1973b, in Mitchell, 2007: 56–62), that is 'description-plus-interpretation' (Mitchell, 2007: 61). Hence, in analysing data/writing an ethnography, the researcher must include a reflection of his or her status as insider/outsider at different times in the process (Gill and Maclean, 2002; Ladino, 2002; McKenzie, 2009; Savvakis and Tzanakis, 2004).

Sometimes it can be overwhelming for a novice researcher to deal with a substantial volume of data.

 Weblink 7.2 A practical guide in organizing field notes, derived from Lofland (1971) and Bogdan and Biklen (1992)

Critical discourse analysis

Critical discourse analysis is an approach that looks at how language is used to produce versions of knowledge that then gain legitimacy politically, socially, culturally and professionally, while marginalizing others: '… words which are used and their meanings depend on where they were used, by whom and to whom' (McDonnell, 1986, in Jupp and Norris, 1993: 47). We would add that *when* particular words have particular meanings is also important because meanings can change within and between places over time (D'Cruz, 2004a:

75–105). Thus, there are no universal or fundamental truths that are meaningful to everyone, everywhere, every time. Critical discourse analysis uses direct methods of data generation, such as semi-structured interviews and participant observation, and secondary sources, such as policy documents or photographs.

Social work researchers can contribute to social change by investigating these sorts of questions through critical discourse analysis:

- What is considered to be legitimate knowledge at a particular time and place?
- How does it come to be legitimate?
- How is legitimate knowledge expressed? (words and syntax)
- What are other versions and what happens if there is disagreement about what may be accepted as the legitimate version?
- Whose voices and knowledge is silenced, by whom and why?

 Weblink 7.3 Examples of critical discourse analysis

Semiotic analysis, related to critical discourse analysis, looks at how words and material culture are representations of social and cultural reality: for example, Russell and Tyler's (2002) study of 'the construction of femininity [of 3–13 year old girls, by a retail chain] "... focusing on representations of femininity in marketing and sales literature, on the company website and in the stores themselves" (2002: 623–624)', cited in Payne and Payne (2004: 62–63).

Policy analysis

Secondary data in all formats – formal documents, such as archival materials, existing laws, policies, statistics, even *Hansard* (the verbatim printed and public record of debates by politicians in Parliament) – lends itself to policy analysis. These documents offer a particular perspective on social and political agendas and their consequences at a particular time and in a particular place. For example, Xu (2011) analysed the *Antiterrorism and Effective Death Penalty Act* (1996), and the *Illegal Immigration Reform and Immigrant Responsibility Act* (1996) in the USA, showing by graphs (2011: 187–191, 195) and case studies (2011: 196–203) 'the impact of deportation on Chinese Americans':

> The 1996 immigration law reforms and associated aggressive deportation practices have demoralized and prevented millions of immigrants from remaining

in U.S. society. Because of the expanded criminal grounds for deportation, criminal arrests are widely used ... and immigrants are ... detained for various amounts of time without the right to see their family members. Deporting a permanent resident is usually based on the ... most serious and demoralizing 'aggravated felony' criminal charges ... [which] could be two shoplifting convictions ... or tax evasion charges that result in the loss of more than $10,000. ... In these two examples, mandatory detention and deportation clearly outweigh the crimes that trigger it. (Xu, 2011: 187–188)

 Weblink 7.4 Examples of policy analysis using secondary data

Narratives, auto/biographies, autoethnographies and life/oral histories

Life stories, oral histories, biographies, and autoethnographies are different forms of narrative (Anderson, 2009; Crawford, 2012; Davidson, 2011; Morgenshtern and Novotna, 2012; Riessman, 1994b), when people tell their stories from their own points of view. Therefore, notions of absolute truth and objective fact are quite meaningless. Personal narratives give power to individuals to tell their lives in their own words, and offer insights into everyday experiences of inequality and oppression. They should articulate within 'a community of stories', expressing culture and history, to minimize a tendency to introspection, self-indulgence and reductionism associated with individual narratives (Atkinson, 2009; Delamont, 2009).

 Weblink 7.5 Examples of journalling, stories, autoethnographies, oral histories and essays by social workers and others

On the following page are three extracts showing how data generation and data analysis are almost inseparable processes in this form of research. 'Writing [becomes] a method of inquiry' (Richardson and St Pierre, 2005). Extract 1 is from a chapter written by three indigenous Australian women (Huggins et al., 2000). The extract is part of Huggins' story about her mother's experiences during the 1930s and 1940s with regard to 'the work of class and race' and what it means for her identity as an indigenous Australian woman (Huggins et al., 2000: 52):

> ... Aboriginal women were sent to work as domestic servants and nursemaids on station [large pastoral and grazing properties] homesteads and, in some cases, as stock-workers. ... This began when they were 13 and 14 years of age, and in some cases younger. Domestic service was a cruel time for my mother, as it was for so many women of her generation. The working relationship was of the master–slave order: the men were addressed as 'boss', the women as 'mistress'. Many women endured appalling treatment, including beatings, being locked up in cells, subjection to sexual abuse. It was an experience that stood in gruesome contrast to the loving companionship they had known among their own people.

Extract 2 is Chinell's (2011) re-presentation of the experiences of one participant in a Canadian study of 'reflections on homophobia and heterosexism in social work education':

> Sara talked about an article ... which referred to gay and lesbian lives as a 'chosen lifestyle' and 'new family form' which she found 'offensive', and stated:

> The language being everywhere, everything from social work research, all of the classes, and the fact that it wasn't done in an anti-discriminatory/anti-oppressive practice course [makes me ask] how then is it ever going to carry through as a theme for inclusivity, not tolerance. These are some of the words that I heard. Tolerance is homophobic, I don't want to be tolerated. (Chinell, 2011: 765)

Extract 3 is taken from life/oral histories of Australian women health workers 'enduring drought then coping with climate change', in rural areas (Anderson, 2009):

> **A**: It's certainly something that now with the farm that we've got now – my husband and I – I detach myself emotionally from it ... and I see my husband, he's emotionally attached to it and I talk to him at times and say, you know, 'look, it doesn't matter. If we lose the farm, we lose the farm. You know, as long as we've got our family, our health. We can move on ... we can start again. Don't worry about it!' ...

> **B**: And other farmers can't see that. They can't see that they could move on, even at, in their mid-40s, they can't see that there could be another life [out] there. This is the only life that they know. (Anderson, 2004, cited in Anderson, 2009: 347).

The truth of narratives, especially when used in public policy evaluations and commentaries, can be controversial: for example, the Human Rights and Equal Opportunity Commission's (1997) report, *Bringing Them Home* (D'Cruz and Jones, 2004: 34–37). As researchers, we can only acknowledge that 'our analytic interpretations are partial, alternative truths that aim for "believability, not certitude, for enlargement of understanding rather than control" (Stivers, 1993, p. 424)' (Riessman, 1993: 22–23).

Exercise: Narratives – truth or lies?

Are people's stories of lived experiences of oppression 'biased' or 'lies'? How might you respond to such claims as a researcher positioned within the values and ethics of social work? Would we describe stories of privilege in the same way? Why or why not? Think of other examples from your experience or of media reporting of current affairs or social issues – how are stories of people's lived experiences dealt with by people who occupy different positions, such as policymakers or service providers?

Content analysis

Content analysis aims to show the meaning in data generated by documentary and/or visual methods, including secondary sources, using detailed researcher-generated categories to quantify the instances of the categories and interpret the outcomes (Neuman and Kreuger, 2003: 304–305; Payne and Payne, 2004: 51). It is useful if wishing to examine the messages being conveyed in the text, for example, in newspaper coverage of politicians or policies. Some social work-related studies that have used content analysis are Petr and Barney (1993), Allen-Meares (1984), Ryan and Martyn (1996, 1997), and Ryan and Sheehan (2009). Refer to Neuman and Kreuger (2003: 304–313) for the steps in conducting content analysis.

Although van Rooyen (2011: 220) justifies content analysis as a *qualitative* method, as long as the data are 'considered in context' rather than as 'rigidly imposed categories', Bryman (2008: 274–293) includes content analysis as a *quantitative* method. Jupp and Norris (1993: 41) comment that content analysis is a positivist approach in which text is seen as an objective and unambiguous representation of 'attributes, attitudes and values relating to individuals', rather than accounting for different ways in which texts can be read, and the relationship to wider social and cultural relationships.

Exercise: Content analysis – which paradigm(s)?

Reflecting on what you have read above and in Chapters 3 and 4, how would you respond to the following questions: Is content analysis qualitative and interpretive, quantitative and positivist, or can it be both? How do you justify your conclusions?

Representation and re-presentation

Writing qualitative research is both a representation and a re-presentation (retelling in a reconstituted way) of participants' truths using the researcher's voice. It may be apparent that qualitative studies usually present 'findings' as integral to the 'discussion', unlike quantitative studies. However, the degree of researcher 'intervention' in the text may vary considerably, with narrative approaches being most likely to represent participants' stories as fully as possible and with the researcher offering minimal commentary. The researcher's positioning must be explicitly stated, and acknowledgement of the partial nature of the claims must be made.

Putting it all together

In this chapter we have discussed the differences between quantitative and qualitative data analysis, briefly introducing some approaches that may be applied to the data you have generated using various methods. We have tried to show the complexity of data analysis, because there are so many ways in which data can be 'made sense of' in relation to the research question. However, it is also important to understand that the analytical approach isn't just a case of producing some patterns in data. The researcher should also be clear about the messages to be conveyed and how best to describe, understand, explain and theorize about social problems and issues that are of interest to social workers and the people who experience them. You also need to consider how to work in a participatory and emancipatory way, using research as another social work strategy. This chapter has sought to do all of these things, as well as introduce you to the rich world of analytical resources for social work researchers.

Further reading

Bryman, A. (2008) *Social Research Methods* (3rd edition), Oxford: Oxford University Press (Chapter 14, 'Quantitative data analysis', pp. 314–338; Chapter 15, 'Using SPSS for Windows', pp. 340–362; Chapter 22, 'Qualitative data analysis', pp. 538–563; Chapter 23, 'Computer-assisted qualitative data analysis: using NVivo', pp. 565–584).

Emerson, R. M. (1995) *Writing Ethnographic Fieldnotes*, Chicago, IL: University of Chicago Press.

Grbich, C. (2007) *Qualitative Data Analysis: An Introduction*, London: Sage (Chapter 2).

Neuman, W. L. and Kreuger, L. W. (2003) *Social Work Research Methods: Qualitative and Quantitative Applications*, Boston, MA: Allyn & Bacon (Chapter 11, 'Nonreactive research and secondary analysis'; Chapter 12, 'Analysis of quantitative data').

Payne, G. and Payne, J. (2004) *Key Concepts in Social Research*, London: Sage (association and causation: pp. 13–17; attitude scales: pp. 17–22; auto/biography and life histories: pp. 23–27; coding qualitative data: pp. 36–41; community profiles: pp. 42–46; community studies: pp. 46–50; content analysis: pp. 51–55; contingency tables: pp. 55–60; documentary methods: pp. 60–66; ethnography: pp. 71–75; fieldwork: pp. 94–98; grounded theory: pp. 98–102; hypothesis: pp. 112–116; levels of measurement: pp. 138–143; secondary analysis: pp. 214–218).

Ethnography Journal, http://eth.sagepub.com/ (accessed 27 September 2012).

Journal of Contemporary Ethnography (from a variety of academic disciplines including, but not limited to, Anthropology, Communications, Criminal Justice, Education, Health Studies, Management, Marketing, and Sociology), http://jce.sagepub.com/ (accessed 27 September 2012).

Journal of Ethnographic and Qualitative Research, www.cedarville.edu/event/eqrc/journal/journal.htm (accessed 27 September 2012).

Journal of Mixed Methods Research (Sage).

8

Reporting and
Disseminating Research

Introduction

We shall be using this chapter to 'put it all together', as in some senses all components of research do come together in the reporting and disseminating phase. We shall be:

1 Exploring ambivalences about devoting important time and effort to the final phase of research.
2 Considering dissemination as part of a broader communication and change process.
3 Examining the way research is reported and how writing seeks to persuade and legitimize.
4 Looking at how to achieve impact from critical social work research while recognizing the challenges in doing so.
5 Inviting you to revisit your understandings of social work research.

Ambivalences

After all the struggles, satisfactions, exasperations and expended energy, you have made it to the final chapter. You might be thinking that it is almost time to gather up your things and look ahead to the next venture – that you can probably move through this last part pretty quickly, and it may not have that much more to add anyway. If any of these sentiments hold true for you, and that would be entirely understandable, you may well be mirroring a process that so frequently occurs in research. Little time and attention is left for the final and crucial phases, ensuring that the outcomes of research reach a wider audience.

Cheetham and her colleagues (1992: 120) argued:

> Research in the social work field will almost always be in some sense 'applied';
> which is to say that, if sensibly conceived and successfully carried out, it will
> contain some truths which have a purchase at some level on policy, manage-
> ment or practice. There is therefore a need to feed conclusions of studies into
> debates, in the various locations at which they take place, about policy and
> practice. More than this, there may be lessons to be learnt, and an opportu-
> nity afforded by research findings specifically to educate, persuade or otherwise
> influence policy makers, managers and practitioners towards more effective
> organization and practice.

Because of the potential for improving policy, management or practice,
those who facilitate your research, either by providing funds (for example,
external funding body), time (for example, the agency which employs you)
or access to participants or other sources of data ('gatekeepers'), may make
such resources possible on the condition that you report your findings to
them. In fact, writers such as Kellehear (1993) would argue that there is
an ethical imperative to disseminate one's research findings. There is also
a responsibility to 'give something back' to those who have participated
in the research and committed their time and attention to it; and a common condition of formal ethics approval for research is that participants
will receive some form of 'feedback'. Yet, as Fuller and Petch (1995: 87)
observe:

> Researchers have not always given [dissemination] the priority it deserves.
> There are several reasons for this, ranging from lack of time or energy once the
> study is completed, through diffidence about the importance of the findings,
> to (even) a misguidedly high-minded reluctance to communicate the rich
> subtleties of one's conclusions to audiences sometimes impatient for simple
> messages.

Reluctance may derive also from a concern felt by many social researchers
that, no matter how interesting they may believe their results, their audience
may not. This may well be a consideration if there have been long delays
between collecting the data and reporting the findings. The poignancy of
divergent time frames is captured by Cheetham et al. (1992: 121):

> ... given the tendency of research questions to be formulated in terms of today's
> issues and the equal tendency of research to reach fruition tomorrow; researchers
> will sometimes find they have an interesting story to tell to an audience which
> has long since departed.

However, should we allow ourselves these 'excuses'? Rabbitts and Fook (1996: 169) think not:

> How much work remains in draft form in the heads and filing cabinets of countless social workers? There are the standard excuses: 'not enough time'; 'it's easier said than done'; 'most of what is published is not useful to practitioners anyway'. These may all be true, but are not really excuses. We don't have much time, but why have we prioritized other activities over writing? Writing for publication can be excruciatingly difficult, but which social worker has not had to engage in painful activity? And if most of what is published is not useful to practitioners, isn't it up to us to begin to change that?

In the intervening decades, there has been a growing acceptance of the imperative to confront such challenges and to engage in purposeful research dissemination activities. In some respects, the momentum has been fuelled by an evidence-based movement that mandates greater accessibility to the outcomes of research studies in its quest to modernize the profession. The Social Care Institute for Excellence in the UK, branded with 'sharing knowledge, improving lives', has been a prime example of a concerted drive to cultivate research-minded practice and to generate a repository of user-friendly materials to support this. That it does its work primarily through online technologies is of course further comment on significant developments that have occurred in this area. While the media through which dissemination takes place is evolving rapidly, many of the fundamental issues to be addressed in its use remain strikingly familiar.

Dissemination: communication and change

You might like to pause at this point and consider your own thoughts about dissemination.

Exercise: Thinking about dissemination – some preliminary questions

Think back to some of the ideas you have had for research studies.

- Why, if at all, would you want to disseminate the messages from your research?
- Who would you want to reach? How might you go about this?
- Would different approaches to disseminating be required for different audiences? How might they differ?

Four straightforward reasons for dissemination are given by Fuller and Petch (1995: 88): (1) to inform others; (2) to ensure research is used; (3) to meet obligations to participants; and (4) to clarify interpretations and recommendations. Of course, these are not necessarily so straightforward in practice. It is possible that our research findings are controversial and sensitive. The perception of 'speaking truth to power' may evoke a range of responses in us: withdrawal, heroism or martyrdom, for example. Assessing the likely impact upon a range of involved parties may be highly complex. Similarly, the process of feeding back to participants holds both benefits and risks that can be time-consuming and demanding to manage.

For such reasons, thinking about dissemination is a 'front end' activity and not something we hope to fulfil by 'writing up'. Anticipating the 'readership' of our research, we would want to conduct the research in such a way that we create interested audiences as we go. Moreover, we will have been making judgements as to the kinds of research that our audience(s) will find persuasive and credible. This will have played its part in determining our methodologies and designs for the study. Then, we would want to draw upon our understandings of communication so that we can be as effective as possible in ensuring our messages are not only 'sent' but also 'received'.

Theoretical developments in this field offer us more sophisticated ways of conceptualizing both the form (or 'media') of communication and also the process, appreciating, for instance, the diversity in people's identities and positions as 'readers' and the significance of this for our dissemination strategies. The limitations of regarding dissemination as an instrumental and somewhat technical process are exposed by such understandings (Fox, Martin and Green, 2007), which again situate the activity as a *social practice to be accomplished* rather than a task to be performed.

The aim of 'informing others' relates to one particular view about the role of the researcher. As intimated, our aim might not only be to inform but to increase the possibilities that this information will be acted upon for the improvement of practice and policy; and, in some sense, move in emancipatory directions for service users and communities. Reporting and dissemination, therefore, are part of a broader consideration regarding the connections we draw between research and social and/or personal transformation. This brings into relief the ways we conceptualize processes of change and transformation, and the purposes we construe for research in this regard. The position of this book has been that social work research is a political and ethical practice and that it has a special place within wider transformative practices.

As regards different channels and media for dissemination, Fuller and Petch (1995: 96) offer the following list:

- Research reports
- Summary reports
- Pamphlets
- Items in newsletters
- Articles in social work press or professional journals
- Local/national press
- Academic journals
- Oral presentations (meetings in own agency, conferences, seminars, workshops)
- Poster displays

As we add in the use of newer communication technologies (for example, digital video or audio products, eye-catching presentational software) and online capabilities (websites, social networking, and so on), even this simple list becomes quite formidable. The conclusion reached by Fuller and Petch (1995: 96) is that:

> Researchers ... need to plan a dissemination strategy, take account of resources and time that can be made available, and decide on priorities. This really involves thinking clearly, once any advance undertakings have been met, about where the main interest of the research lies.

In this respect, Patton, a researcher with a long-standing interest in evaluation and the utilization of research findings, offers an observation from his own studies into this topic that underlines the importance of understanding processes of communication and change. He notes:

> Two factors emerged as consistently important in explaining utilization: (a) political considerations ... and (b) a factor we called the *personal factor*. ... The personal factor is the presence of an identifiable individual or group of people who personally care about the evaluation and the findings it generates. Where such a person or group was present, evaluations were used; where the personal factor was absent, there was a corresponding marked absence of evaluation impact. (Patton, 1997: 44, original emphasis)

From our point of view, this 'personal factor' will not be attributable to the personalities of individuals but rather to their social positioning towards the research and what it represents for them; and, to the craft with which the researchers have engaged others in the transformative potential of their research.

This discussion has focused upon dissemination from the vantage point of the researchers themselves. Dissemination is, of course, a matter of concern at other levels and in other forums. There are a number of agendas involved. Professional associations may be active in promoting research

activity and research findings among their members to increase the repu-
tation and status of the profession. Grant making organizations may be
committed to ensuring that their funded projects do promote effectively
the outcomes of their research. Government policies, particularly those
concerned with 'modernizing' welfare and enhancing performance, may
well establish infrastructure to support the wider dissemination of research
findings among human services practitioners and managers. As noted previously, Information Gateways on the internet have been established, providing new forms of access to current research. Thus, the environment
has been changing towards a scenario of too much rather than too little
information being readily available. As anticipated in the first edition of
this book, it has not been surprising to see salient areas of debate turn
increasingly to policies and processes for managing rather than making
knowledge.

Reporting: representation, persuasion and analytical work

The research report is customarily the foundation written document. Yet here,
as Punch (1998: 266) comments: 'the rethinking of research which has accompanied both the paradigm debates and the emergence of new perspectives has
included research writing: how the research is to be put into written form,
and communicated'.

There remains a relatively conventional format for reporting studies that
derives largely from quantitative methodologies. The format reflects underlying assumptions about ways of knowledge making; the bulk of the writing is
done once the research is completed; it represents that work through a series
of more or less pre-structured headings. Marlow (2011: 287) offers a typical
list of such headings for a research report:

- Statement of the research topic
- Literature review
- Research questions and hypotheses
- Research design
- Sampling strategy
- Data collection method(s)
- Results
- Discussion
- Limitations
- Recommendations for future research
- Implications for practice

Marlow suggests that this basic format can be applied to a range of different kinds of research study and believes that it holds good whether or not the methodological approach has been primarily quantitative or qualitative, allowing for some latitude under the 'results' or 'findings' section when it comes to qualitative data. All researchers, regardless of the paradigm they espouse and the particular headings they may adopt to organize their text, need to be able to report on key aspects of their research – and by now we hope it is evident through the structure of this book what we would understand those key aspects to be. On the matter of 'limitations', it is perhaps worth noting that this does not require an apologetic approach. All research is limited by virtue of the way it is constructed conceptually and pragmatically. Our responsibility is simply to be as clear as possible about the partiality and bounded nature of our research – treating our endeavours with due humility.

One approach to presentation (Sarantakos, 2005) is that the reporting should be done with clarity, precision, objectivity, fairness, impersonality, and so on. In other words, from this viewpoint the main criteria for composing the report are that it should be accurate and complete. The report becomes as far as possible a neutral medium which conveys to the reader a true representation of the research processes and outcomes, assuming that all readers will read it in the same way, and as intended by the author.

There is a different viewpoint on writing, however, which attends to the rhetorical and persuasive devices that render it legitimate and plausible to the reader (Potter, 1996). Gilbert (1993) suggests that all forms of report writing involve social acts of communication and persuasion. This approach also treats the reader as an active participant, who interacts with and interprets the text according to his or her own ideological and social positioning (Cranny-Francis et al., 2003: 89–138). The writer deploys linguistic devices and these 'work', or don't, according to the distinctive beliefs and customs at play in constructing truth value within different knowledge communities. D'Cruz et al. (2009b: 237) explore this in relation to differences across professional groupings, and suggest:

> Assumptions and expectations of professional scholarly writing, as [being] representative of trustworthy knowledge, offer opportunities for readers to critically reflect on norms about what valid and trustworthy knowledge is and how it ought to be represented.

Denzin (1994) follows a similar approach in discussing the 'art and politics of interpretation'. Here, the relations between truth, reality and text are presented as highly complex. The writer is seen to be engaged in a practice that is at once expressive and productive, involved in a complicated interchange between meaning, interpretation and representation. The act of writing becomes a political act in the sense that the researcher/writer has a positioned sense of self in order to connect with their text and with their reader, and to make knowledge claims that carry legitimacy and authority in relation to members of diverse interpretive communities.

Others have observed how such perspectives have led to rather more in the way of experimentation with newer forms of writing. Punch (1998: 266) referred to a 'proliferation of forms of writing in qualitative research', and cites Miles and Huberman (1994: 299), who have been proven correct in their forecast that: 'the reporting of qualitative data may be one of the most fertile fields going; there are no fixed formats, and the ways data are being analysed and interpreted are getting more and more various'.

The issues concern written form but go beyond that. There is a different view of the performance of writing: not so much representational as 'a way of learning, a way of knowing, a form of analysis and inquiry' (Punch, 1998: 279). Punch (1998: 280) quotes Coffey and Atkinson (1996: 109):

> The net effect of recent developments is that we cannot approach the task of 'writing up' our research as a straightforward (if demanding) task. We have to approach it as an analytical task, in which the form of our reports and representations is as powerful and significant as their content.

These considerations have moved us into what might be termed the politics of writing, which combines with the politics of knowledge to produce a heady atmosphere of alternative practices in 'reporting'. Choices emerge as conventional ways of approaching and thinking about the writing task are seen as historic and fulfilling certain customs and traditions, ones which need to be critically evaluated and appropriated or not, according to the purpose and obligations of the research. Writing, particularly 'reporting' on qualitative research, can become a creative exercise when the traditional dualisms of fact and fiction, literature and science, no longer hold (Richardson, 1994, 2000; Richardson and St Pierre, 2005), which requires reflexivity on the part of the writer, and especially a continuing engagement with the political aspects of knowledge making.

As noted previously, we need to remain cognizant of the complementary politics of reading. The interpretation of reports in both their content and form is within but also outside the influence of the author, as is control over their exposure and use. Institutions of publishing in many respects act as gatekeepers in the promotion of research, and peer review processes that control what is published are rarely scrutinized for their inherent biases in regulating 'scholarly' knowledge, influencing knowledge communities, and creating hierarchies related to perceived 'expertise' among members of such communities. Hence, it is possible to see how service users' views may be more easily suppressed if they do not pass such gatekeeping tests. Within many organizations, the suppression, burying or reframing of reports that are politically unfavourable remains a stark possibility. At the extreme, too, it is not unknown for legal injunctions to be sought to prevent researchers from speaking out. Reporting, as we saw with dissemination, is more than a technical exercise: it occurs in socio-political contexts, with ethical implications.

'Having an impact': communities of practice

The expectation that research be disseminated assumes a social significance beyond research communities themselves, in that it influences social change and development (Corby, 2006). Indeed, the relationship between social research and social change has long been debated and the interest in dissemination strategies is perhaps the most recent manifestation of this.

Meanwhile, indigenous perspectives in Australia have emphasized how research has been exercised largely within colonizing practices that have opposed the interests of their communities. This has been occurring while Western researchers have been formulating various models regarding the potential for research to have some effect on social issues. The three most notable of these models have been referred to as the engineering, enlightenment and critical models (Hammersley, 1995).

The *engineering model* sees researchers intervening directly in social matters on the basis of their expert knowledge and with institutionalized authority. In the *enlightenment model*, the researcher seeks a much less direct role by taking responsibility to 'impact on the policy climate through processes of intellectual association and influence' (Bloor, 1997: 222). The *critical model* argues for action-oriented research for progressive change 'achieved through emancipation rather than policy influence' (Bloor, 1997: 222).

Bloor, himself a qualitative researcher rather than a practitioner, concludes that what he terms 'practitioner-oriented research' offers a promising model for effecting meaningful social change through research practices.

> The qualitative researcher may become part of his or her local practitioner collectivity and trades on that position as a collectivity member to disseminate research findings. ... There is therefore the opportunity for practitioners to make evaluative judgments about their own practices and experiment with the adoption of new approaches described in the research findings. (Bloor, 1997: 236)

You will have noticed that the possibilities for linking research and change through making connections between researcher and participant or stakeholder *communities* is a recurrent theme in the literature. Theoretically, this theme might be traced to the idea of there being networks of 'communities of practice' (Wenger, 1998), with their distinctive cultures and discourses, and of research activity constituting a particular network(s) of such communities. From this perspective, then, 'having an impact' involves making connections between communities of practice. This might be sought, for example, through the intended merger of researcher and participant, as found in some applications of participatory action research; or through a sense of shared membership as in Bloor's example above; or it might be related more to the positioning of respective members and their reflexive appropriation of certain linguistic or change strategies. Jones (2012) explores the challenges of achieving 'research-minded practice' as in part being a challenge of mutual learning across the distinctive and contrasting cultures to be found in the worlds of practice and research.

A common observation is that, whatever variation is pursued, the matter of achieving 'impact' requires its own analysis and action, and needs early consideration and planning. Wadsworth (2011) offers a framework for developing a plan for action to be taken once the key messages from the research have been determined. Her steps are presented in summary fashion in Box 8.1.

Box 8.1   Developing an action plan for making an impact

Planning for action on key messages from your research:

- Work out what you want to achieve

  - What do you want to happen?
  - What action do you want taken?

- Who would need to know, understand and accept your key messages in order to make these things happen?
- What do you want each of these people to do?
- What would be the best ways to present your key messages to these people for these purposes?

  - What do you want to get over to them?
  - How, where and when is this best done?

Source: Wadsworth (2011: 154, adapted)

Knowledge making in a world of knowledge management

We have argued for social work research that is inclusive of different ways of knowing and different ways of knowledge making, reflexive in its relations with others, critical within its embeddedness in networks of power, and ethical in its pursuit of anti-oppressive, emancipatory and transformative practices. We have emphasized the importance of contextualizing our understandings and actions. We need to ask: What are the prospects for approaching social work research in this way? Is this viable within current and future contexts of practice?

In some respects, one could say that the approach to social work research we are advocating has emerged out of just such considerations. It positions the researcher in the specifics of their local contexts and presents existing knowledge on the concepts and techniques of research as a resource that is there is to be drawn upon in systematic and purposeful ways according to the situation in hand. Yet, there are questions here about the places occupied by social work researchers and the features of their everyday 'communities of practice'. To what extent do they allow for the approach we are supporting?

Systems of governance within human service organizations have been subject to continuing change over recent decades, and this has altered substantially the role and relations of the professionals working within them (Scarborough, 1996). Waves of new public management ideologies have recast work cultures and practices, and in broad terms have established that the professional is there to serve the organization's goals and not vice versa (Jones, 1999). The management of performance occurs through an array of mechanisms and processes, including the increasing use of instructional computer software within the workplace (Hough, 2003) and structured decision-making tools (Gillingham, 2011). Knowledge, including research-based knowledge, is becoming institutionalized through the production of 'best practice' standards and accompanying compliance procedures. Such developments would seem to threaten both the scope for knowledge making by social work researchers, and its alignment with participatory, transformative processes.

Within these developments, there has been some call for the promotion of cultures of learning and research in human services. This would certainly appear consistent with strategic objectives to deliver effective services of high quality, responsive to consumers and communities. As Gregory (1997: 202) says, human service organizations:

> probably require greater capacity for learning and adaptation … otherwise they may continue to categorise and act upon people in the light of inadequately examined, self-validating, organisational (and professional) beliefs.

Yet, as he describes, the working environment 'leaves little time and energy for critical reflection on the assumptions that underpin their work' and 'there may tend to be an inverse correlation between the certainty of task technology and the political sensitivity of that task' (Gregory, 1997: 202).

What would seem to be required is an analysis of the spaces and places created for social work research within the contemporary contexts of its practice. Addressing the policy domain, for example, Muetzelfeldt and Briskman (2000) observe the fragmentation of services that has accompanied the use of (competitively based) contracts, and now the consequences of partnership approaches from centre-left politics still searching for effective forms of collaborative management. They suggest that different channels of connectedness and communication have arisen, formal and informal, to counter fragmentation. This then generates new sets of conflicts and contradictions, and alternative possibilities for the exercise of discretion and for inter-organizational learning processes. Such an analysis points to emergent professional roles that might well hold opportunities for creative research processes.

Addressing the practice domain, Fook (2002: 161–5) offers some helpful suggestions (summarized below) for seizing opportunities for critical practice in 'hostile environments':

- *Reframing our practice as contextual.* This involves breaking the opposition between 'practice' and 'environment' by 'working with the context no matter what that context might be' and 'creating different microclimates within broader contexts'
- *Expropriating and translating the discourse.* This involves 'identifying aspects of the dominant discourse that may be turned to other ends' while 'emphasising the organisational benefits'. The translation, for example, of 'evaluation', 'quality' and 'community consultation' in this way could create possibilities for critical research practices
- *Identifying contradictions, complexities and points of alliance.* The assumption here is that 'contexts are complex' and so there will always be aspects which are 'ambiguous or in conflict', creating the potential for alliances on specific projects or initiatives
- *Contributing to change while being part of the problem?* 'If we understand that each specific context in which we work, and even each specific act within it has the potential to function in a number of ways simultaneously, then this indicates that we need to engage with people or situations in ways which minimise the harmful functions and maximise the empowering ones.'

Echoed here are the messages found throughout this book that analytic, reflexive and creative capabilities fused with an appreciation of power and ethics are central to the emancipatory goals of the critically research-minded practitioner.

What is research? – revisited

In the very first exercise, you were invited to 'exorcise the demons' associated with research. The final exercise invites you to consider what, if anything, has changed in your view of research now that you have reached the end of this book.

Exercise: 'Exorcising the demons' once more

- Recall your responses the first time you completed this exercise.
- How different, if at all, does research look to you now?
- What has changed? Try to be as specific as possible.
- Now what, if anything, do you see as the contribution of research to you, to your practice and to social work?
- What does this tell you about your own ways of knowing, of practising and of researching?

Conclusion

Rather than dissemination of research being an afterthought, we have suggested that this is to be considered from the outset. Such a statement is appropriate for all research, but it is particularly so for social work research that has a purpose focused on contributing to social values and human wellbeing. Understanding and achieving dissemination does require us to develop skills in written presentation, but equally to embrace the multiple ways in which we can engage to achieve desired impact. Ironically, we are brought full circle as we recognize that this is just the very area of intimate concern to the social work profession. Research and practice can be a rich combination.

Overall, in this book we have attempted to cover material that is theoretical, analytical and also technical. The issues are complex ones. Moreover, the political and ethical aspects we have raised throughout do pose both intellectual and personal challenges. As we noted at the outset, the subject of research often seems far removed from the reasons people choose to become social workers. We hope we have been able argue persuasively enough that research should be understood as an integral part of the practice and policy of social work. We take it to be so because we see research as crucial to the mission of social work. At the same time, we are aware that both research and social work have not always behaved well towards the people and communities whose interests they claim to serve. We would like to think that this book makes some contribution to minimizing these aspects and furthering the positive impact that both research and social work can achieve. Research is a demanding but rewarding activity and we hope you decide that it is one worth pursuing.

Further reading

Corby, B. (2006) *Applying Research in Social Work Practice*, Maidenhead, UK: Open University Press (Chapter 9).

Fox, M., Martin, P. and Green, G. (2007) *Doing Practitioner Research*, London: Sage (Chapters 9 and 10).

References

Aarons, G. A. and Palinkas, L. A. (2007) 'Implementation of evidence-based practice in child welfare: Service provider perspectives', *Administration and Policy in Mental Health and Mental Health Services Research*, 34: 411–419, Doi 10.1007/s10488-007-0121-3.

Adams, R., Dominelli, L. and Payne, M. (2005) *Social Work Futures: Crossing Boundaries, Transforming Practice*, Basingstoke, Hampshire: Palgrave Macmillan.

Agger, B. (2007) 'Does postmodernism make you mad? Or, did you flunk statistics?' in W. Outhwaite and S. P. Turner (eds), *The Sage Handbook of Social Science Methodology*, Los Angeles and New York: Sage, pp. 443–456.

Ahmad, W. I. U. and Sheldon, T. (1993) "Race" and statistics', in M. Hammersley (ed.), *Social Research: Philosophy, Politics and Practice*, London: Sage, pp. 124–130.

Alexander, C. (2010) 'Deviant femininities: The everyday making and unmaking of "criminal" youth', in K. Hörschelmann and R. Colls (eds), *Contested Bodies of Childhood and Youth*, Basingstoke, Hampshire: Palgrave Macmillan, pp. 68–83.

Allen-Meares, P. (1984) 'Content analysis: It does have a place in social work research', *Journal of Social Science Research*, 7: 51–68.

Alston, M. and Bowles, W. (2012) *Research for Social Workers* (3rd edition), Crow's Nest, NSW: Allen & Unwin.

American Jewish Community (1993) '1 in 5 polled voices [sic] doubt on Holocaust' *New York Times*, 20 April, p. A12.

Anderson, D. (2004) Health workers' lived experiences of drought in the Mallee, unpublished oral history, Mallee, Victoria: Museum Victoria, Australia.

Anderson, D. (2009) 'Enduring drought then coping with climate change: Lived experience and local resolve in rural mental health', *Rural Society*, 19 (4): 340–352.

Anderson, M. (2007) 'Quantitative history', in W. Outhwaite and S. P. Turner (eds), *The Sage Handbook of Social Science Methodology*, Los Angeles and New York: Sage, pp. 246–263.

Arber, S. and Ginn, J. (1991) *Gender and Later Life: A Sociological Analysis of Resources and Constraints*, London: Sage.

Archard, D. (1993) *Children: Rights and Childhood*, London: Routledge.

Armstrong, D. (2001) *The Voyage of Their Life: The Story of the Derna and its Passengers*, Sydney: Flamingo/HarperCollins.

Atkinson, P. (1990) *The Ethnographic Imagination: Textual Constructions of Reality*, London: Routledge.

Atkinson, P. (2009) 'Illness narratives revisited: The failure of narrative reductionism', *Sociological Research Online*, 14 (5), 16, www.socresonline.org.uk/14/5/16.html, doi:10.5153/sro.2030.

Atwal, A. and Caldwell, K. (2006) 'Nurses' perceptions of multidisciplinary team work in acute health-care', *International Journal of Nursing Practice*, 12 (6): 359–365.

Australian Association of Social Workers (AASW) (2003) *Practice Standards for Social Workers: Achieving Outcomes*, Canberra, Australia: Australian Association of Social Workers.

Australian Association of Social Workers (AASW) (2010) *Code of Ethics*, Canberra, Australia: Australian Association of Social Workers.

Australian Association of Social Workers (AASW) (2012) *Australian Social Work Education and Accreditation Standards*, Canberra, Australia: Australian Association of Social Workers.

Australian Government and Workplace Gender Equality Agency, www.eowa.gov.au/Pay_Equity/Pay_Equity_Information.asp (accessed 13 November 2012).

Australian Institute of Aboriginal and Torres Strait Islander Studies (AIATSIS) (2011) *Guidelines for Ethical Research in Australian Indigenous Studies* (2nd edition), Canberra, Australia: Australian Institute of Aboriginal and Torres Strait Islander Studies.

Babbie, R. (2007) *The Practice of Social Research* (11th edition), Belmont, CA: Thomson Wadsworth.

Bagnoli, A. (2004) 'Researching identities with multi-method autobiographies', *Sociological Research Online*, 9 (2), www.socresonline.org.uk/9/2/bagnoli.html.

Bailey, K.D. (1978) *Methods for Social Research* (3rd edition), New York: The Free Press.

Balen, R., Blyth, E., Calabretto, H., Fraser, C., Horrocks, C. and Manby, M. (2006) 'Involving children in health and social research: "human becomings" or "active beings"?' *Childhood*, 13 (1): 29–48.

Barn, R. (1994) 'Race and ethnicity in social work: Some issues for anti-discriminatory research', in B. Humphries and C. Truman (eds), *Re-thinking Social Research*, Aldershot, UK: Ashgate, pp. 37–58.

Baum, N. (2012) 'Reflective writing assignments to help social work trainees work through poor supervisory relationships', *Social Work Education: The International Journal*, 31 (1): 110–124.

Beale, N. (2010) 'Stigma, health attitudes and the embodiment of youth(ful) identities: Understandings of the self and other', in K. Hörschelmann and R. Colls (eds), *Contested Bodies of Childhood and Youth*, Basingstoke, Hampshire: Palgrave Macmillan, pp. 189–202.

Becker, H. S. (1970) 'Whose side are we on?', in J. D. Douglas (ed.), *The Relevance of Sociology*, New York: Appleton-Century-Crofts, pp. 99–111.

Becker, H. S., Geer, B., Hughes, E. C. and Strauss, A. L. (1961) *Boys in white: Student culture in medical school*, Chicago, IL: University of Chicago Press.

Bell, A. (2007) 'Designing and testing questionnaires for children', *Journal of Research in Nursing*, 12 (5): 461–9, doi: 10.1177/1744987107079616.

Bell, J. (1993) *Doing Your Research Project: A Guide for First-time Researchers in Education and Social Science* (2nd edition), Buckingham, UK: Open University Press.

Beresford, P. (2000) 'Service users' knowledge and social work theory: Conflict or collaboration?', *British Journal of Social Work*, 30 (4): 489–503.

Besserab, D. and Crawford, F. (2010) 'Aboriginal practitioners speak out: Contextualising child protection interventions', *Australian Social Work*, 63 (2): 179–193.

Best, J. (2004) 'Theoretical issues in the study of social problems', in G. Ritzer (ed.), *Handbook of Social Problems: A Comparative International Perspective*, Thousand Oaks, CA: Sage, pp. 14–29.

Bian,Y. (1994) *Work and Inequality in Urban China*. Albany: State University of NewYork Press.

Bigby, C. and Atkinson, D. (2010) 'Written out of history: Invisible women in intellectual disability social work', *Australian Social Work*, 63 (1): 4–17.

Bishop, R. (2005) 'Freeing ourselves from neo-colonial domination in research: A Kaupapa Māori approach to creating knowledge', in N. K. Denzin and Y. S. Lincoln (eds) *The Sage Handbook of Qualitative Research* (3rd edition), Thousand Oaks, CA: Sage, pp. 109–138.

Black, B. (2009) 'Empowering and rights-based approaches to working with older people', in J. Allan, L. Briskman and B. Pease (eds), *Critical Social Work: Theories and Practices for a Socially Just World* (2nd edition), Crow's Nest, NSW: Allen & Unwin, pp. 175–187.

Blaikie, N. (1993) *Approaches to Social Enquiry*, Cambridge, UK: Polity Press.

Blaikie, N. (2000) *Designing Social Work Research: The Logic of Anticipation*, Cambridge, UK: Polity Press.

Blaikie, N. (2009) *Designing Social Research: The Logic of Anticipation* (2nd edition). Cambridge, UK: Polity Press.

Bloor, M. (1997) 'Addressing social problems through qualitative research', in D. Silverman (ed.), *Qualitative Research: Theory, Method and Practice*, London: Sage.

Bloor, M. (2002) 'No longer dying for a living', *Sociology*, 36 (1): 89–104.

Blunt-Williams, K., Meshelemiah, J. C. A. and Venable, V. M. (2011) 'An examination of college students' perceptions of transformative and culturally competent educators: Are social work students unique?', *Social Work Education: The International Journal*, 30 (7): 774–796.

Bogdan, R. and Biklen, S. K. (1982) *Qualitative Research for Education: An Introduction to Theory and Methods*, Boston, MA: Allyn & Bacon.

Bogdan, R. and Biklen, S. K. (1992) *Qualitative Research for Education: An Introduction to Theory and Methods* (2nd edition), Boston, MA: Allyn & Bacon.

Bogdewic, S. (1999) 'Participant observation', in B. F. Crabtree and W. L. Miller (eds), *Doing Qualitative Research* (2nd edition), Thousand Oaks, CA: Sage, pp. 47–69.

Botash, A. S., Babuts, D., Mitchell, N., O'Hara, M., Lynch, L. and Manuel, J. (1994) 'Evaluations of children who have disclosed sexual abuse via facilitated communication', *Archives of Pediatrics and Adolescent Medicine*, 148 (12): 1282–1287.

Boulton, D. (2000) 'Unusual terms: What do you mean by ...?', in B. Humphries (ed.), *Research in Social Care and Social Welfare: Issues and Debates for Practice*, London: Jessica Kingsley, pp. 86–91.

Brannick, T. and Coghlan, D. (2007) 'In defense of being "native": The case for insider academic research', *Organizational Research Methods*, 10 (1): 59–74, doi: 10.1177/1094428106289253.

Bray, A. and Mirfin-Veitch, B. (2003) 'Disabled people and research: Putting families first', in R. Munford and J. Sanders (eds), *Making a Difference in Families: Research that Creates Change*, Crow's Nest, NSW: Allen & Unwin, pp. 74–92.

Braye, S., Preston-Shoot, M. and Thorpe, A. (2008) 'Beyond the classroom: Integrating legal knowledge, practice learning and user experience to prepare students for ethical practice in the human services', *Practical Learning: Achieving Excellence in the Human Services*, proceedings of the 8th International PEPE Conference, Edinburgh, Scotland, 23–25 January.

Briskman, L. (2008) 'Decolonizing social work in Australia: Prospect or illusion', in M. Gray, J. Coates and M. Yellow Bird (eds), *Indigenous Social Work around the World: Towards Culturally Relevant Education and Practice*, Aldershot, UK: Ashgate, pp. 83–93.

Briskman, L., Latham, S. and Goddard, C. (2008) *Human Rights Overboard: Seeking Asylum in Australia*, Melbourne: Scribe.

Briskman, L., Pease, B. and Allan, J. (2009) 'Introducing critical theories for social work in a neo-liberal context', in J. Allan, L. Briskman and B. Pease (eds), *Critical Social Work: Theories and Practices for a Socially Just World* (2nd edition), Crow's Nest, NSW: Allen & Unwin, pp. 3–14.

Brooks, R. (2009) 'Young people and political participation: An analysis of European union policies', *Sociological Research Online*, 14 (1) 7, www.socresonline.org.uk/14/1/7.html>, doi:10.5153/sro.1862.

Brown, S., Lumley, J., Small, R. and Astbury, J. (1994) *Missing Voices: The Experience of Motherhood*, Melbourne: Oxford University Press.

Bruyere, G. (2008) 'Picking up what was left by the trail: The emerging spirit of Aboriginal education in Canada', in M. Gray, J. Coates and M. Yellow Bird (eds), *Indigenous Social Work around the World: Towards Culturally Relevant Education and Practice*, Aldershot, UK: Ashgate, pp. 231–244.

Bryman, A. (1988) *Quantity and Quality in Social Research*, London: Routledge.

Bryman, A. (2001) *Social Research* Methods. Oxford: Oxford University Press.

Bryman, A. (2008) *Social Research Methods* (3rd edition), Oxford: Oxford University Press.

Bryman, A. and Burgess, R. (1994) 'Developments in qualitative data analysis: An introduction', in A. Bryman and R. Burgess (eds), *Analyzing Qualitative Data*, London: Routledge, pp. 1–17.

Bryman, A. and Cramer, D. (2001) *Quantitative Data Analysis with SPSS Release 10 for Windows: A Guide for Social Scientists*. London: Routledge.

Burgen, B. (2010) 'Women with cognitive impairment and unplanned or unwanted pregnancy: A 2-year audit of women contacting the Pregnancy Advisory Service', *Australian Social Work*, 63 (1): 18–34.

Butler, I. and Pugh, R. (2004) 'The politics of social work research', in R. Lovelock, K. Lyons and J. Powell (eds), *Reflecting on Social Work: Discipline and Profession*, Aldershot, UK: Ashgate, pp. 55–71.

Butler, J. (1990) *Gender Trouble: Feminism and the Subversion of Identity*. New York: Routledge.

Byrne-Armstrong, H. (2001) 'Whose show is it? The contradictions of collaboration', in H. Byrne-Armstrong, J. Higgs and D. Horsfall (eds), *Critical Moments in Qualitative Research*, Oxford: Butterworth-Heinemann, pp. 106–114.

Campbell, B. (1988) *Unofficial Secrets: Child Sexual Abuse and the Cleveland Case*, London: Virago.

Carpenter, J. (2005) *Evaluating Outcomes in Social Work Education*, Dundee: Scottish Institute for Excellence in Social Work Education; London: Social Care Institute for Excellence.

Chambers, C. T. and Johnston, C. (2002) 'Developmental differences in children's use of rating scales', *Journal of Pediatric Psychology*, 27 (1): 27–36.

Chandler, J. (1990) 'Researching and the relevance of gender', in R. Burgess (ed.), *Studies in Qualitative Methodology: Reflections of Field Experience*, Greenwich, CT: JAI Press, pp. 119–140.

Chapman, C. (2011) 'Resonance, intersectionality, and reflexivity in critical pedagogy (and research methodology)', *Social Work Research: The International Journal*, 30 (7): 723–744.

Charmaz, K. (2005) 'Grounded theory in the 21st century: Applications for advancing social justice studies', in N. K. Denzin and Y. S. Lincoln (eds), *The Sage Handbook of Qualitative Research* (3rd edition), Thousand Oaks, CA: Sage, pp. 507–535.

Charmaz, K. (2011) 'Grounded theory methods in social justice research', in N. K. Denzin and Y. S. Lincoln (eds), *The Sage Handbook of Qualitative Research* (4th edition), Thousand Oaks, CA: Sage, pp. 359–380.

Cheetham, J. and Kazi, M. A. F (eds) (1998) *The Working of Social Work*, London: Jessica Kingsley.

Cheetham, J., Fuller, R., McIvor, G. and Petch, A. (1992) *Evaluating Social Work Effectiveness*, Buckingham, UK: Open University Press.

Chinell, J. (2011) 'Three voices: Reflections on homophobia and heterosexism in social work education', *Social Work Education: The International Journal*, 30 (7): 759–773.

Cicourel, A. V. (1974) 'Police practices and official records', in R. Turner (ed.), *Ethnomethodology*, Harmondsworth, UK: Penguin, pp. 85–95.

Clacherty, G. (2006) *The Suitcase Stories: Refugee Children Reclaims Their Identities*, Cape Town: Double Storey Books.

Clarke, A. E. (2007) 'Grounded theory: Critiques, debates, and situational analysis', in W. Outhwaite and S. P. Turner (eds), *The Sage Handbook of Social Science Methodology*, Los Angeles and New York: Sage, pp. 423–442.

Clarke, P. (2009) 'Understanding the experience of stroke: A mixed-method research agenda', *The Gerontologist*, 49 (3): 293–302.

Cockburn, T. (2000) 'Case studying organisations: The use of quantitative approaches', in B. Humphries (ed.), *Research in Social Care and Social Welfare: Issues and Debates for Practice*, London: Jessica Kingsley, pp. 59–68.

Coffey, A. and Atkinson, P. (1996) *Making Sense of Qualitative Data: Complementary Research Strategies*, Thousand Oaks, CA: Sage.

Coleman, J. (1966) *Equality of Educational Opportunity*, Washington, DC: US Government Printing Office.

Collins, P. H. (2000) *Black Feminist Thought: Knowledge, Consciousness and the Politics of Empowerment* (2nd edition), New York and London: Routledge.

Colls, R. and Hörschelmann, K. (2010) 'Introduction: Contested bodies of childhood and youth', in K. Hörschelmann and R. Colls (eds), *Contested Bodies of Childhood and Youth*, Basingstoke, Hampshire: Palgrave Macmillan, pp. 1–21.

Coomber, R. (1997) 'Using the internet for survey research', *Sociological Research Online*, 2 (2), www.socresonline.org.uk/socresonline/2/2/2.html.

Corbin Dwyer, S. and Buckle, J. L. (2009) 'The space between: On being an insider–outsider in qualitative research', *International Journal of Qualitative Methods*, 8 (1): 54–63.

Corby, B. (1998) *Managing Child Sexual Abuse Cases*, London: Jessica Kingsley.

Corby, B. (2006) *Applying Research in Social Work Practice*, Maidenhead, UK: Open University Press.

Corner, J. (2003) 'The multidisciplinary team – fact or fiction?' *European Journal of Palliative Care*, 10 (2): 10–13.

Cranny-Francis, A., Waring, W., Stavropoulos, P. and Kirkby, J. (2003) *Gender Studies: Terms and Debates*, New York: Palgrave Macmillan.

Crawford, F. (1997) 'Using self in social work: Doing autoethnography', *Advances in Social Work and Welfare Education*, 2 (1): 75–82.

Crawford, F. (2012) 'Becoming a social worker: Chris's account', *Social Work Education: The International Journal*, 31 (1): 36–46.

Crotty, M. (1998) *The Foundations of Social Research: Meaning and Perspectives in the Research Process*, St Leonards, NSW: Allen & Unwin.

D'Cruz, H. (2000) 'Social work research as knowledge/power in practice', *Sociological Research Online*, May, 5 (1), www.socresonline.org.uk/5/1/dcruz.html.

D'Cruz, H. (2002) 'Constructing the identities of "responsible mothers, invisible men" in child protection practice', *Sociological Research Online*, May, 7 (1), www.socresonline. org.uk/7/1/d'cruz.html.

D'Cruz, H. (2004a) *Constructing Meanings and Identities in Child Protection Practice*, Melbourne: Tertiary Press.

D'Cruz, H. (2004b) 'The social construction of child maltreatment: The role of medical practitioners', *Journal of Social Work*, 4 (1): 99–123.

D'Cruz, H. (2009) 'Social work knowledge-in-practice', in H. D'Cruz, S. Jacobs and A. Schoo (eds), *Knowledge-in-practice in the Caring Professions: Multidisciplinary Perspectives*, Aldershot, UK: Ashgate, pp. 69–92.

D'Cruz, H., Gillingham, P. and Melendez, S. (2007) 'Reflexivity, its meanings and relevance for social work: A critical review of the literature', *British Journal of Social Work*, 37: 73–90, doi:10.1093/bjsw/bc1001.

D'Cruz, H., Gillingham, P. and Melendez, S. (2009) 'Exploring the possibilities of an expanded practice repertoire in child protection: An alternative conceptual approach', *Journal of Social Work*, 9 (1): 61–85.

D'Cruz, H., Jacobs, S. and Schoo, A. (2009a) 'Introduction', in H. D'Cruz, S. Jacobs and A. Schoo (eds), *Knowledge-in-practice in the Caring Professions: Multidisciplinary Perspectives*, Aldershot, UK: Ashgate, pp. 1–12.

D'Cruz, H., Jacobs, S. and Schoo, A. (2009b) 'Conclusions: Knowledge-in-practice in the caring professions: reflections on commonalities and differences', in H. D'Cruz, S. Jacobs and A. Schoo (eds), *Knowledge-in-practice in the Caring Professions: Multidisciplinary Perspectives*, Aldershot, UK: Ashgate, pp. 235–249.

D'Cruz, H. and Jones, M. (2004) *Social Work Research: Ethical and Political Contexts*, London: Sage.

D'Cruz, H., Soothill, K., Francis, B. and Christie, A. (2002) 'Gender, ethics and social work: An international study of students' perceptions at entry into social work education', *International Social Work*, 45 (2): 149–166.

D'Cruz, H. and Stagnitti, K. (2009) 'When parents love and don't love their children: Some children's stories', *Child and Family Social Work*, 15 (2): 216–225, doi: 10.1111/j.1365-2206.2009.00662.x.

Daly, W. (2009) '"Adding their flavour to the mix": Involving children and young people in care in research design', *Australian Social Work*, 62 (4): 460–475.

Davidson, D. (2011) 'Reflections on doing research grounded in my experience of perinatal loss: From auto/biography to autoethnography', *Sociological Research Online*, 16 (1) 6, www.socresonline.org.uk/16/1/6.html, doi: 10.5153/sro.2293.

Davis, J. and Hill, M. (2006) 'Introduction', in E. K. M. Tisdall, J. M. Davis, A. Prout and M. Hill (eds), *Children, Young People and Social Inclusion: Participation for What?* Bristol, UK: Policy Press, pp. 1–19.

Davis, J. E. (2005) *Accounts of Innocence: Sexual Abuse, Trauma and the Self*, Chicago, IL: University of Chicago Press.

Delamont, S. (2009) 'The only honest thing: Autoethnography, reflexivity and small crises in fieldwork', *Ethnography and Education*, 4 (1): 51–63, doi: 10.1080/17457820802703507.

Delaney, C. (1988) 'Participation-observation: The razor's edge', *Dialectical Anthropology* (vol. 13), The Netherlands: Kluwer Academic Publishers, pp. 291–300.

Denzin, N. K. (1994) 'The art and politics of interpretation', in N. K. Denzin and Y. S. Lincoln (eds), *Handbook of Qualitative Research* (2nd edition), Newbury Park, CA: Sage, pp. 500–515.

Denzin, N. K. and Lincoln, Y. S. (eds) (1994) *Handbook of Qualitative Research* (2nd edition), Newbury Park, CA: Sage.

Denzin, N. K. and Lincoln, Y. S. (eds) (2005a) *The Sage Handbook of Qualitative Research* (3rd edition), Thousand Oaks, CA: Sage.

Denzin, N. K. and Lincoln, Y. S. (2005b) 'Introduction: The discipline and practice of qualitative research', in N. K. Denzin and Y. S. Lincoln (eds), *The Sage Handbook of Qualitative Research* (3rd edition), Thousand Oaks, CA: Sage, pp. 1–32.

Denzin, N. K. and Lincoln, Y. S. (2005c) 'Paradigms and perspectives in contention: Part II', in N. K. Denzin and Y. S. Lincoln (eds), *The Sage Handbook of Qualitative Research* (3rd edition), Thousand Oaks, CA: Sage, pp. 183–190.

Denzin, N. K. and Lincoln, Y. S. (2011) 'Introduction: The discipline and practice of qualitative research', in N. K. Denzin and Y. S. Lincoln (eds), *The Sage Handbook of Qualitative Research* (4th edition), Thousand Oaks, CA: Sage, pp. 1–19.

Denzin, N. K., Lincoln, Y. S. and Smith, L. T. (eds) (2008) *Handbook of Critical and Indigenous Methodologies*, Thousand Oaks, CA: Sage.

Denzin, N. K. and Ryan, K. E. (2007) 'Qualitative methodology (including focus groups)', in W. Outhwaite and S. P. Turner (eds), *The Sage Handbook of Social Science Methodology*, Los Angeles and New York: Sage, pp. 578–594.

DeRoos, Y. (2011) 'Analysis of quantitative data', in C. R. Marlow (ed.), *Research Methods for Generalist Social Work* (5th edition), Belmont, CA: Brooks/Cole, pp. 235–278.

do, Anh (2010) *The Happiest Refugee*, Crow's Nest, NSW: Allen & Unwin.

do Mar Castro Varela, M., Dhawan, N. and Engel, A. (eds) (2011) *Hegemony and Heteronormativity: Revisiting 'the Political' in Queer Politics*, Aldershot, UK, and Burlington, VT: Ashgate.

Dodd, S. J. and Epstein, I. (2012) *Practice-based Research in Social Work: A Guide for Reluctant Researchers*, London: Routledge.

Dolgoff, R., Loewenberg, F. M. and Harrington, D. (2005) *Ethical Decisions for Social Work Practice* (7th edition), Belmont, CA: Brooks/Cole.

Dominelli, L. (2005) 'Social work research: Contested knowledge for practice', in R. Adams, L. Dominelli and M. Payne (eds), *Social Work Futures: Crossing Boundaries, Transforming Practice*, Basingstoke, Hampshire: Palgrave Macmillan, pp. 223–236.

Donnelly, J. (2010) 'Maximising participation in international community-level project evaluation: A strength-based approach', *Evaluation Journal of Australasia*, 10 (1): 43–50.

Early Years Foundation Stage Forum, http://eyfs.info/forums/index.php?showtopic= 9750 (accessed 2 February 2012).

Edwards, M., with Howard, C. and Miller, R. (2001) *Social Policy, Public Policy: From Problem to Practice*, St Leonards, NSW: Allen & Unwin.

Ellem, K. A. and Wilson, J. (2010) 'Life story work and social work practice: A case study with ex-prisoners labelled as having an intellectual disability', *Australian Social Work*, 63 (1): 67–82.

Elliott, H. (1997) 'The use of diaries in sociological research on health experience', *Sociological Research Online*, 2 (2), www.socresonline.org.uk/2/2/7.html.

Ellis, C., Adams, T. E. and Bochner, A. P. (2011) 'Autoethnography: An overview', *Forum: Qualitative Social Research Sozialforschung*, 12 (1), Art. 10 – January.

Ellis, C. and Bochner, A. P. (2000) 'Autoethnography, personal narrative, reflectivity: Researcher as subject', in N. K. Denzin and Y. S. Lincoln (eds), *Handbook of Qualitative Rsearch* (2nd edition), Thousand Oaks, CA: Sage, pp. 733–768.

Emerson, R. M. (1995) *Writing Ethnographic Fieldnotes*, Chicago, IL: University of Chicago Press.

Epstein, I. (1987) 'Pedagogy of the perturbed: Teaching research to reluctants', *Journal of Teaching in Social Work*, 1: 71–89.

Erera, P. I. (2002) *Family Diversity: Continuity and Change in the Contemporary Family*, Thousand Oaks, CA: Sage.

Evans, B. C., Coon, D. W. and Ume, E. (2011) 'Use of theoretical frameworks as a pragmatic guide for mixed methods studies: A methodological necessity?', *Journal of Mixed Methods Research*, 5 (4): 276–292.

Everitt, A. (2008) 'Social work research and evaluation: The research-minded practitioner', *Locus SOCI@L*, 1: 24–31.

Everitt, A., Hardiker, P., Littlewood, J. and Mullender, A. (1992) *Applied Research for Better Practice*, London: Macmillan/British Association of Social Workers.

Faith, E. (2008) 'Indigenous social work education: A project for all of us?', in M. Gray, J. Coates and M. Yellow Bird (eds), *Indigenous Social Work around the World: Towards Culturally Relevant Education and Practice*, Aldershot, UK: Ashgate, pp. 245–255.

Farrugia, D. (2011) 'The symbolic burden of homelessness: Towards a theory of youth homelessness as embodied subjectivity', *Journal of Sociology*, 47 (1): 71–87.

Fawcett, B., Goodwin, S., Meagher, G. and Phillips, R. (2010) *Social Policy for Social Change*, South Yarra, Victoria: Palgrave Macmillan.

Feyerabend, P. (1975) *Against Method*, London: New Left Books.

Fielding, N. (2008) 'The role of computer-assisted qualitative data analysis: Impact on emergent methods in qualitative research', in S. N. Hesse-Biber and P. Leavy (eds), *Emergent Methods in Social Research*, Thousand Oaks, CA, and London: Sage, pp. 675–695.

Flick, U. (1998) *An Introduction to Qualitative Research*, London: Sage.

Fook, J. (1996) 'The reflective researcher: Developing a reflective approach to practice', in J. Fook (ed.), *The Reflective Researcher: Social Workers' Theories of Practice Research*, St Leonards, NSW: Allen & Unwin, pp. 1–8.

Fook, J. (1999) 'Critical reflectivity in education and practice', in B. Pease and J. Fook (eds), *Transforming Social Work Practice*, St Leonards, NSW: Allen & Unwin, pp. 195–208.

Fook, J. (2000) 'Theorising from frontline practice: Towards an inclusive approach for social work research', paper presented at the Economic & Social Research Council funded seminar series, 'Theorising Social Work Research', Luton, UK, July.

Fook, J. (2002) *Social Work: Critical Theory and Practice*, London: Sage.

Foucault, M. (1978) 'Politics and the study of discourse', *Ideology and Consciousness*, 3: 7–26.

Foucault, M. (1980) *Power/Knowledge: Selected Interviews and Other Writings 1972–1977* (ed. C. Gordon; trans. C. Gordon, L. Marshall, J. Mepham and K. Soper), London: The Harvester Press.

Fox, J., Craig, M. and Warm, A. (2003) 'Conducting research using web-based questionnaires', *International Journal of Social Research Methodology*, 6 (2): 167–180.

Fox, M., Martin, P. and Green, G. (2007) *Doing Practitioner Research*, London: Sage.

Frankenberg, R. (1993) *The Social Construction of Whiteness: 'White Women, Race Matters'*, St Paul, MN: Routledge/The University of Minnesota Press.

Fraser, H. and Craik, C. (2009) 'Addressing violence and abuse in a gendered world', in J. Allan, L. Briskman and B. Pease (eds), *Critical Social Work: Theories and Practices for a Socially Just World* (2nd edition), Crow's Nest, NSW: Allen & Unwin, pp. 228–239.

Fuchs, S. (1992) 'Relativism and reflexivity in the sociology of scientific knowledge', in G. Ritzer (ed.), *Metatheorizing*, Newbury Park, CA: Sage, pp. 151–167.

Fudge Schormans, A. (2010) 'Epilogues and prefaces: Research and social work and people with intellectual disabilities', *Australian Social Work*, 63 (1): 51–66.

Fuller, R. and Petch, A. (1995) *Practitioner Research: The Reflexive Social Worker*, Buckingham, UK: Open University Press.

Gair, S. (2008) 'Missing the "flight from responsibility": Tales from a non-indigenous educator pursuing spaces for social work education relevant to indigenous Australians', in M. Gray, J. Coates and M. Yellow Bird (eds), *Indigenous Social Work around the World: Towards Culturally Relevant Education and Practice*, Aldershot, UK: Ashgate, pp. 219–230.

Garfinkel, H. (1974) '"Good" organizational reasons for "bad" clinic records', in R. Turner (ed.), *Ethnomethodology*, Harmondsworth, UK: Penguin, pp. 96–101.

Geertz, C. (1973a) 'The impact of the concept of culture on the concept of man', in C. Geertz, *The Interpretation of Cultures: Selected Essays*, New York: Basic Books, pp. 33–54.

Geertz, C. (1973b) 'Thick description: Towards an interpretative theory of culture', in C. Geertz, *The Interpretation of Cultures: Selected Essays*, New York: Basic Books, pp. 3–30.

Gendron, S. (2001) 'Transformative alliance between qualitative and quantitative approaches in health promotion research', in I. Rootman, M. Goodstadt, B. Hyndman, D.V. McQueen, L. Potvin, J. Springett and E. Ziglio (eds), *Evaluation in Health Promotion: Principles and Perspectives. Part 2, Perspectives*, Copenhagen: WHO Regional Publications, European Series 92.

Gibbs, G.R. (2011) *Methodologies*, http://onlineqda.hud.ac.uk/methodologies.php (accessed 27 September 2012).

Gibbs, A. and Stirling, B. (2010) 'Reflections on designing and teaching a social work research course for distance and on-campus students', *Social Work Education: The International Journal*, 29 (4): 441–449.

Gibbs, L. (1991) *Scientific Reasoning for Social Workers: Bridging the Gap between Research and Practice*, New York: Merrill.

Giddens, A. (1984) *The Constitution of Society: Outline of the Theory of Structuration*, Cambridge, UK: Polity Press.

Giffney, N. and O'Rourke, M. (eds) (2009) *The Ashgate Research Companion to Queer Theory*, Aldershot, UK, and Burlington, VT: Ashgate.

Gilbert, N. (1993) 'Writing about social research', in N. Gilbert (ed.), *Researching Social Life*, London: Sage.

Gill, F. and Maclean, C. (2002) 'Knowing your place: Gender and reflexivity in two ethnographies', *Sociological Research Online*, 7 (2), www.socresonline.org.uk/7/2/gill.html>.

Gillingham, P. (2011) 'Decision-making tools and the development of expertise in child protection practitioners: Are we "just breeding workers who are good at ticking boxes"', *Child and Family Social Work*, 16 (4): 412–421.

Glaser, B. (1992) *Basics of Grounded Theory Analysis*, Mill Valley, CA: Sociology Press.

Glaser, B. and Strauss, A (1967) *The Discovery of Grounded* Theory. Chicago, IL: Aline.

Gold, R. (1958) 'Roles in sociological field observation', *Social Forces*, 36 (3): 217–223.

Goodenough, T., Williamson, E., Kent, J. and Ashcroft, R. (2003) 'What did you think about that? Researching children's perceptions of participation in a longitudinal genetic epidemiological study', *Children and Society*, 17: 113–125.

Gould, N. (2004) 'Qualitative research and social work: The methodological repertoire in a practice-oriented discipline', in R. Lovelock, K. Lyons and J. Powell (eds), *Reflecting on Social Work: Discipline and Profession*, Aldershot, UK: Ashgate, pp. 130–144.

Government Statisticians' Collective (1993) 'How official statistics are produced: Views from the inside', in M. Hammersley (ed.), *Social Research: Philosophy, Politics and Practice*, London: Sage, pp. 146–165.

Graham, A. (2008) *Teach Yourself Statistics*, New York: McGraw-Hill.

Graham, A. and Fitzgerald, R. (2010a) 'Children's participation in research: Some possibilities and constraints in the current Australian research environment', *Journal of Sociology*, 46 (2): 133–147.

Graham, A. and Fitzgerald, R. M. (2010b), 'Progressing children's participation: Exploring the potential of a dialogical turn', *Childhood*, 17 (3): 343–359, available at: http://dx.doi.org/10.1177/0907568210369219.

Graham, H. (1993) *Hardship and Health in Women's Lives*, London: Harvester Wheatsheaf.

Grant, S. (2002) *The Tears of Strangers: A Family Memoir*, Sydney: Harper Collins.

Gray, M., Coates, J. and Yellow Bird, M. (eds) (2008) *Indigenous Social Work around the World: Towards Culturally Relevant Education and Practice*, Aldershot, UK: Ashgate.

Grbich, C. (2007) *Qualitative Data Analysis: An Introduction*, London: Sage.

Greenberg, P. (2009) 'Information, knowledge and wisdom in medical practice', in H. D'Cruz, S. Jacobs and A. Schoo (eds), *Knowledge-in-practice in the Caring Professions: Multidisciplinary Perspectives*, Aldershot, UK: Ashgate, pp. 29–49.

Greene, J. (2002) 'Mixed-method evaluation: A way of democratically engaging with difference', *Evaluation Journal of Australasia*, 2 (new series) (2): 23–29.

Greenhill, J., King, D., Lane, A. and MacDougall, C. (2009) 'Understanding resilience in South Australian farm families', *Rural Society*, 19 (4): 318–325.

Gregory, R. (1997) 'The peculiar tasks of public management', in M. Considine and M. Painter (eds), *Managerialism: The Great Debate*, Melbourne: Melbourne University Press.

Grogan, S. (2010) 'Femininity and body image: Promoting positive body image in the "culture of slenderness"', in K. Hörschelmann and R. Colls (eds), *Contested Bodies of Childhood and Youth*, Basingstoke, UK: Palgrave Macmillan, pp. 41–52.

Guba, E. and Lincoln, Y. (1982) 'Epistemological and methodological bases of naturalistic inquiry', *Educational Communication and Technology Journal*, 30 (4): 233–252.

Guba, E. and Lincoln, Y. (1989) *Fourth Generation Evaluation*, Newbury Park, CA: Sage.

Guba, E. (1990) 'The alternative paradigm dialog', in E. Guba (ed.), *The Paradigm Dialog*, Newbury Park, CA: Sage, pp. 17–30.

Hacking, I. (1990) *The Taming of Chance*, Cambridge, UK: Cambridge University Press.

Hacking, I. (1999) *The Social Construction of What?* Boston, MA: Harvard University Press.

Hall, C. (1997) *Social Work as Narrative: Storytelling and Persuasion in Professional Texts*, Aldershot, UK: Ashgate.

Hallahan, L. (2010) 'Legitimising social work disability policy practice: Pain or praxis?', *Australian Social Work*, 63 (1): 117–132.

Hammersley, M. (1995) *The Politics of Social Research*, London: Sage.

Hammersley, M. (1996) 'The relationship between qualitative and quantitative research: Paradigm loyalty versus methodological eclecticism', in J. T. E. Richardson (ed.), *Handbook of Qualitative Research Methods for Psychology and the Social Sciences*, Leicester: PBS Books, pp. 89–107.

Haraway, D. (1991) *Simians, Cyborgs and Women*, London: Free Association Books.

Harding, S. (1987) 'Is there a feminist method?', in S. Harding (ed.), *Feminism and Methodology*, Bloomington, IN: Indiana University Press, pp. 1–14.

Hardy, D. and Smith, B. (2008) 'Decision making in clinical practice', *British Journal of Anaesthetic and Recovery Nursing*, 9 (1): 19–21.

Hare, I. (2004) 'Defining social work for the 21st century: The international federation of social workers' revised definition of social work', *International Social Work*, 47 (3): 407–424.

Harper, D. (2005) 'What's new visually?', in N. K. Denzin and Y. S. Lincoln (eds), *The Sage Handbook of Qualitative Research* (3rd edition), Thousand Oaks, CA: Sage, pp. 747–762.

Harrison, B. (1996) 'Every picture "tells a story"', in S. Lyon and J. Busfield (eds), *Methodological Imaginations*, Basingstoke, Hampshire: Macmillan, pp. 75–95.

Harrison, L. and Cameron-Traub, E. (1994) 'Patients' perspectives on nursing in hospital', in C. Waddell and A. R. Petersen (eds), *Just Health: Inequality in Illness, Care and Prevention*, London: Churchill Livingstone, pp. 147–158.

Hart, E. and Bond, M. (1995) *Action Research for Health and Social Care: A Guide to Practice*, Buckingham, UK: Open University Press.

Hart, M. A. (2008) 'Critical reflections on an Aboriginal approach to helping', in M. Gray, J. Coates and M. Yellow Bird (eds), *Indigenous Social Work around the World: Towards Culturally Relevant Education and Practice*, Aldershot, UK: Ashgate, pp. 129–139.

Hartman, A. (1990) 'Many ways of knowing', *Social Work*, January: 3–4.

Hartman, A. (1992) 'In search of subjugated knowledge', *Social Work*, 37 (6): 483–484.

Harvey, D. (2009) 'Conceptualising the mental health of rural women: A social work and health promotion perspective', *Rural Society*, 19 (4): 353–362.

Hassard, J. and Kelemen, M. (2002) 'Production and consumption in organizational knowledge: The case of the "paradigms debate"', *Organization*, 9 (2): 331–355, doi: 10.1177/1350508402009002911.

Healy, B. (1996) 'In doing you learn: Some reflections on practice research on an advocacy project', in J. Fook (ed.), *The Reflective Practitioner: Social Workers' Theories of Practice Research*, St Leonards, NSW: Allen & Unwin, pp. 70–81.

Healy, K. (2000) *Social Work Practices: Contemporary Perspectives on Change*, London: Sage.

Healy, K. (2001) 'Participatory action research and social work: A critical appraisal', *International Social Work*, 44 (1): 93–105.

Hekman, S. (2007) 'Feminist methodology', in W. Outhwaite and S. P. Turner (eds), *The Sage Handbook of Social Science Methodology*, Los Angeles and New York: Sage, pp. 534–546.

Hellawell, D. (2006) 'Inside–out: Analysis of the insider–outsider concept as a heuristic device to develop reflexivity in students doing qualitative research', *Teaching in Higher Education*, 11 (4): 483–494, doi: 10.1080/13562510600874292.

Herrnstein, R. J. and Murray, C. (1994) *The Bell Curve: Intelligence and Class Structure in American Life*, New York: Free Press.

Hesse-Biber, S. N. and Crofts, C. (2008) 'User-centred perspectives on qualitative data analysis software: Emergent technologies and future trends', in S. N. Hesse-Biber and P. Leavy (eds), *Emergent Methods in Social Research*, Thousand Oaks, CA, and London: Sage, pp. 655–673.

Higgs, J., Richardson, B. and Abrandt Dahlgren, M. (eds) (2004) *Developing Practice Knowledge for Health Professionals*, London: Butterworth-Heinemann.

Hill, M., Turner, K., Walker, M., Stafford, A. and Seaman, P. (2006) 'Children's perspectives on social exclusion and resilience in disadvantaged urban communities', in E. K. M. Tisdall, J. M. Davis, A. Prout and M. Hill (eds), *Children, Young People and Social Inclusion: Participation for What?*, Bristol: Policy Press, pp. 39–56.

Hillier, L., Johnson, K. and Traustadóttir, R. (2007) 'Research with people with intellectual disabilities', in M. Pitts and A. Smith (eds), *Researching the Margins: Strategies for Ethical and Rigorous Research with Marginalised Communities*, Basingstoke, Hampshire: Palgrave Macmillan, pp. 84–95.

Hillier, L., Mitchell, A. and Mallett, S. (2007) 'Duty of care: Researching with vulnerable young people', in M. Pitts and A. Smith (eds), *Researching the Margins: Strategies for Ethical and Rigorous Research with Marginalised Communities*, Basingstoke, Hampshire: Palgrave Macmillan, pp. 114–129.

Hoinville, G., Jowell, R. and Associates (1982) *Survey Research Practice*, London: Heinemann.

Holman Jones, S. (2005) 'Autoethnography: Making the personal political', in N. K. Denzin and Y. S. Lincoln (eds), *The Sage Handbook of Qualitative Research* (3rd edition), Thousand Oaks, CA: Sage, pp. 763–791.

Holmes, A. (2009) 'The practice of the psychiatrist', in H. D'Cruz, S. Jacobs and A. Schoo (eds), *Knowledge-in-practice in the Caring Professions: Multidisciplinary Perspectives*, Aldershot, UK: Ashgate, pp. 51–67.

Holstein, J. and Gubrium, J. (1995) *The Active Interview*, Qualitative Research Methods Series, Newbury Park, CA: Sage.

Holt, L. (2010) 'Embodying and destabilising (dis)ability and childhood', in K. Hörschelmann and R. Colls (eds), *Contested Bodies of Childhood and Youth*, Basingstoke, Hampshire: Palgrave Macmillan, pp. 203–214.

Hopkins, P. and Hill, M. (2010) 'Contested bodies of asylum-seeking children', in K. Hörschelmann and R. Colls (eds), *Contested Bodies of Childhood and Youth*, Basingstoke, Hampshire: Palgrave Macmillan, pp. 136–147.

Horace Miner Response (2006), www.oppapers.com/essays/Horace-Miner-Response/84848 (short commentary about the aims of the Miner article) (accessed 29 February 2012).

Hörschelmann, K. and Colls, R. (eds) (2010) *Contested Bodies of Childhood and Youth*, Basingstoke, Hampshire: Palgrave Macmillan.

Horton, J. and Kraftl, P. (2010) 'Time for bed! Children's bedtime practices, routines and affects [*sic*]', in K. Hörschelmann and R. Colls (eds), *Contested Bodies of Childhood and Youth*, Basingstoke, Hampshire: Palgrave Macmillan, pp. 215–231.

Hough, G. (2003) 'Enacting critical social work in public welfare contexts', in J. Allan, B. Pease and L. Briskman (eds), *Critical Social Work: An Introduction to Theories and Practices*, Crow's Nest, NSW: Allen & Unwin.

Howe, D. (1997) 'Psychosocial and relationship-based theories for child and family social work: Political philosophy, psychology and welfare practice', *Child and Family Social Work*, 2: 161–170.

Huberman, A. M. and Miles, M. B. (1994) 'Data management and analysis methods', in N. K. Denzin and Y. S. Lincoln (eds), *Handbook of Qualitative Research* (2nd edition), Thousand Oaks, CA: Sage, pp. 428–444.

Hudson, W. and McMurtry, S. L. (1997) 'Comprehensive assessment in social work practice: The multi-problem screening inventory', *Research on Social Work Practice*, 7 (1): 79–88.

Hudson, W. W. (1990) *The Clinical Measurement Package*, Homewood, IL: Dorsey Press.

Huggins, J., Saunders, K. and Tarrago, I. (2000) 'Reconciling our mothers' lives', in J. Docker and G. Fischer (eds), *Race, Colour and Identity in Australia and New Zealand*, Sydney: University of New South Wales Press, pp. 39–58.

Hughes, M. (2011) 'Do challenges to social work students' beliefs, values and behaviour within social work education have an impact on their sense of wellbeing?', *Social Work Education: The International Journal*, 30 (6): 686–699.

Human Rights and Equal Opportunity Commission (1997) *Bringing Them Home: National Inquiry into the Separation of Aboriginal and Torres Strait Islander Children from their Families*, Commonwealth of Australia: Sterling Press.

Humphreys, L. (1970) *Tea Room Trade: Impersonal Sex in Public Places*, Chicago, IL: Aldine.

Humphries, B. (1994) 'Empowerment and social research: Elements for an analytic framework', in B. Humphries and C. Truman (eds), *Re-thinking Social Research: Anti-discriminatory Approaches in Research Methodology*, Aldershot, UK: Ashgate, pp. 185–204.

Humphries, B. (2008) *Social Work Research for Social Justice*, Basingstoke, Hampshire: Palgrave Macmillan.

Humphries, B. and Martin, M (2000) 'Disrupting ethics in social research', in B. Humphries (ed.), *Research in Social Care and Social Welfare: Issues and Debates for Practice*, London: Jessica Kingsley, pp. 69–85.

Humphries, B. and Truman, C. (eds) (1994) *Re-thinking Social Research: Anti-discriminatory Approaches in Research Methodology*, Aldershot, UK: Ashgate.

Hurley, M. (2007) 'Who's on whose margins?' in M. Pitts and A. Smith (eds), *Researching the Margins: Strategies for Ethical and Rigorous Research with Marginalised Communities*, Basingstoke, Hampshire: Palgrave Macmillan, pp. 160–189.

Hutchinson, A. and Bucknall, T. (2009) 'Knowledge to action in the practice of nursing', in H. D'Cruz, S. Jacobs and A. Schoo (eds), *Knowledge-in-practice in the Caring Professions: Multidisciplinary Perspectives*, Aldershot, UK: Ashgate, pp. 121–139.

Hyers, L. L., Swim, J. K. and Mallett, R. K. (2006) 'The personal is political: Using daily diaries to examine everyday prejudice-related experiences', in S. N. Hesse-Biber and P. Leavy (eds), *Emergent Methods in Social Research*, Thousand Oaks, CA, and London: Sage, pp. 313–335.

Ife, J. (2001) *Human Rights and Social Work: Towards Rights-based Practice*, Cambridge, UK: Cambridge University Press.

Ife, J. (2002) *Community Development: Community-based Alternatives in an Era of Globalization* (2nd edition), Frenchs Forest, NSW: Pearson Education Australia.

Iganski, P., Payne, G. and Roberts, J. (2001) 'Inclusion or exclusion? Reflections on the evidence of declining of racial disadvantage in the British labour market', *International Journal of Sociology and Social Policy*, 21 (4–6): 184–211.

IKE (1994) *Koorie Research Programme: Ethics, Protocols and Methodologies – A Discussion Paper*, Geelong, Victoria: Institute of Koorie Education, Deakin University.

Institute for Research and Innovation in Social Services (IRISS) (2011–12) 'The Learning Exchange: Evidence-informed practice', http://lx.iriss.org.uk/category/learning-exchange-collections/evidence-informed-practice, (accessed 16 August 2012).

International Association of Schools of Social Work (IASSW) (2001) 'Definition of social work', www.iassw-aiets.org/index.php?option=com_content&task=blogcategory&id=26&Itemid=51, International Association of Schools of Social Work/International Federation of Social Workers, Definition of Social Work, Jointly Agreed 27 June 2001, Copenhagen (accessed 23 August 2012).

International Federation of Social Workers (2010), www.ifsw.org/f38000032.html, (retrieved 13 July 2010).

Iphofen, R. (2009) *Ethical Decision-making in Social Research*, Basingstoke, Hampshire: Palgrave Macmillan.

Irvine, A. (1995) 'The social work role with personality disordered clients', in R. Fuller and A. Petch (eds), *Practitioner Research: The Reflexive Social Worker*, Buckingham, UK: Open University Press.

Irwin, S. (2008) 'Data analysis and interpretation: Emergent issues in linking qualitative and quantitative evidence', in S. N. Hesse-Biber and P. Leavy (eds), *Handbook of Emergent Methods*, New York and London: Guilford Press, pp. 415–435.

Ishido, Y. (2010) 'Living in between: Hybridity and hybridisation', in M. Kumar, H. D'Cruz and N. Weerakkody (eds), *Where Are You From? Voices in Transition*, Altona, Victoria: Common Ground Publishers, pp. 69–78.

Jacobs, S. (2002a) 'The genesis of "scientific community"', *Social Epistemology*, 16 (2): 157–168.

Jacobs, S. (2002b) 'Polyani's presagement of the incommensurability concept', *Studies in the History and Philosophy of Science*, 33: 105–120.

Jayakaran, R. (2002) *Use of the Ten Seed Technique*, World Vision China, People's Republic of China, www.rcpla.org/pdf%20download/Ten%20seed.pdf (accessed 11 October 2011).

Jayaratne, T. E. (1993) 'The value of quantitative methodology for feminist research', in M. Hammersley (ed.), *Social Research: Philosophy, Politics and Practice*, London: Sage, pp. 109–123.

Jenkins, G. D., Nader, D. A., Lawler, E. R. and Cammann, C. (1975) 'Standardised observations: An approach to measuring the nature of jobs', *Journal of Applied Psychology*, 60: 171–181.

Jensen, A. (1969) 'How much can we boost IQ and scholastic achievement?' *Harvard Educational Review*, 39: 273–274.

Jesson, J. K., with Matheson, L. and Lacey, F. M. (2011) *Doing Your Literature Review: Traditional and Systematic Techniques*, London: Sage.

Johnson, K. (2009) 'Disabling discourses and enabling practices in disability politics', in J. Allan, L. Briskman and B. Pease (eds), *Critical Social Work: Theories and Practices for a Socially Just World* (2nd edition), Crow's Nest, NSW: Allen & Unwin, pp. 188–200.

Jones, D. P. H. (1994) 'Editorial: Autism, facilitated communication and allegations of child abuse and neglect', *Child Abuse and Neglect*, 18 (6): 491–494.

Jones, M. (1999) 'Supervisor or superhero: New role strains for front-line supervisors in human services', *Asia Pacific Journal of Social Work*, 9 (1): 79–97.

Jones, M. (2004) 'Supervision, learning and transformative practices', in N. Gould and M. Baldwin (eds), *Social Work, Critical Reflection and the Learning Organization*, Aldershot, UK: Ashgate, pp. 11–22.

Jones, M. (2012) 'Research minded practice in social work', in P. Stepney and D. Ford (eds), *Social Work Models, Methods and Theories* (2nd edition), Lyme Regis, UK: Russell House Publishing, pp. 272–286.

Journal of Multidisciplinary Research, http://jmrpublication.org/.

Jupp, V. and Norris, C. (1993) 'Traditions in documentary analysis', in M. Hammersley (ed.), *Social Research: Philosophy, Politics and Practice*, London: Sage, pp. 37–51.

Kanuha, V. K. (2000) '"Being" native versus "Going native": Conducting social work research as an insider', *Social Work*, 45 (5): 439–447, doi: 10.1093/sw/45.5.439.

Kasof, J. (1993) 'Sex bias in the naming of stimulus persons' *Psychological Bulletin*, 113 (1): 140–163.

Kaufman Hall, V. (2001) 'Playing in the "mud" of government', in H. Byrne-Armstrong, J. Higgs and D. Horsfall (eds), *Critical Moments in Qualitative Research*, Oxford: Butterworth-Heinemann, pp. 115–127.

Kayrooz, C. and Trevitt, C. (2005) *Research in Organizations and Communities: Tales from the Real World*, Crow's Nest, NSW: Allen & Unwin.

Kellehear, A. (1989) 'Ethics and social research', in J. Perry (ed.), *Doing Fieldwork: Eight Personal Accounts of Social Research*, Geelong, Victoria: Deakin University Press.

Kellehear, A. (1993) *The Unobtrusive Researcher: A Guide to Methods*, St Leonards, NSW: Allen & Unwin.

Kemmis, S. and McTaggart, R. (eds) (1988) *The Action Research Planner* (3rd edition), Geelong, Victoria: Deakin University Press.

Kemmis, S. and McTaggart, R. (2005) 'Participatory action research: Communicative action and the public sphere' in N. K. Denzin and Y. S. Lincoln (eds), *The Sage Handbook of Qualitative Research* (3rd edition), London: Sage, pp. 559–604.

King, N. M. P., Henderson, G. E. and Stein, J. (1999) *Beyond Regulations: Ethics in Human Subjects Research*, Chapel Hill, NC: University of North Carolina Press.

Kitzinger, C. and Wilkinson, S. (1993) 'Theorizing heterosexuality', in S. Wilkinson and C. Kitzinger (eds), *Heterosexuality: A Feminism and Psychology Reader*, London: Sage, pp. 1–31.

Klein, J. T. (2007) 'Interdisciplinary approaches in social science research', in W. Outhwaite and S. P. Turner (eds), *The Sage Handbook of Social Science Methodology*, Los Angeles and New York: Sage, pp. 32–49.

Kuhn, T. (1970) *The Structure of Revolutions* (2nd edition). Chicago, IL: University of Chicago Press.

Kumar, M., D'Cruz, H. and Weerakkody, N. (eds) (2010) *Where Are You From? Voices in Transition*, Altona, Victoria: Common Ground Publishers.

Kumar, R. (1996) *Research Methodology: A Step-by-step Guide for Beginners*, Sydney: Longman.

Kumar, R. (1999) *Research Methodology*, London: Sage.

Kumar, R. (2011) *Research Methodology: A Step-by-step Guide for Beginners* (3rd edition), Los Angeles: Sage.

Kumashiro, K. K. (2004) *Restoried Selves: Autobiographies of Queer Asian-Pacific-American Activists*, New York: Harrington Park Press, an imprint of The Haworth Press.

Labaree, R. V. (2002) 'The risk of "going observationalist": Negotiating the hidden dilemmas of being an insider participant observer', *Qualitative Research*, 2 (1): 97–122, doi: 10.1177/1468794102002001641.

Ladino, C. (2002) "You make yourself sound so important": Fieldwork experiences, identity construction, and non-western researchers abroad', *Sociological Research Online*, 7 (4), www.socresonline.org.uk/7/4/ladino.html.

Lansdown, G. (2006) 'International developments in children's participation: Lessons and challenges', in E. K. M. Tisdall, J. M. Davis, A. Prout and M. Hill (eds), *Children, Young People and Social Inclusion: Participation for What?*, Bristol, UK: Policy Press, pp. 139–156.

LaPiere, R. T. (1934), 'Attitudes vs actions', *Social Forces*, 13: 230–237.

Lawn, S. and Battersby, M. (2009) 'Skills for person-centred care: Health professionals supporting chronic condition prevention and self-management', in H. D'Cruz, S. Jacobs and A. Schoo (eds), *Knowledge-in-practice in the Caring Professions: Multidisciplinary Perspectives*, Aldershot, UK: Ashgate, pp. 161–192.

Lee, R. M. (1993) *Doing Research on Sensitive Topics*, London: Sage.

Levine, H. G. (1985) 'Principles of data storage and retrieval for use in qualitative evaluations', *Educational Evaluation and Policy Analysis*, 7 (2): 169–186.

Ling, H. K. (2008) 'The development of culturally appropriate social work practice in Sarawak, Malaysia', in M. Gray, J. Coates and M. Yellow Bird (eds), *Indigenous Social Work around the World: Towards Culturally Relevant Education and Practice*, Aldershot, UK: Ashgate, pp. 97–106.

Lister, R. (2005) 'Investing in the citizen-workers of the future', in H. Hendrick (ed.), *Child Welfare and Social Policy: An Essential Reader*, Bristol: Policy Press, pp. 449–462.

Lofland, J. (1971) *Analyzing Social Settings: A Guide to Qualitative Observation and Analysis*. Belmon, CA: Wadsworth.

London School of Economics (2011) EUKids Online: Questionnaires for children and parents, www2.lse.ac.uk/media@lse/research/EUKidsOnline/EUKidsII%20(2009-11)/Survey/Master%20questionnaires.aspx (accessed 2 February 2012).

Lorde, A. (1982) *Zami: A New Spelling of My Name*, London: Pandora.

Lui, C.-W., Warburton, J., Winterton, R. and Bartlett, H. (2011) 'Critical reflections on a social inclusion approach for an ageing Australia', *Australian Social Work*, 64 (3): 266–282.

Lyons, K. and Taylor, I. (2004) 'Gender and knowledge in social work', in R. Lovelock, K. Lyons and J. Powell (eds), *Reflecting on Social Work: Discipline and profession*, Aldershot, UK: Ashgate, pp. 72–94.

MacDonald, G., Sheldon, B. with Gillespie, J. (1992) 'Contemporary studies of the effectiveness of social work', *British Journal of Social Work*, 22 (6): 615–643.

Macfarlane, S. (2009) 'Opening spaces for alternative understandings in mental health practice', in J. Allan, L. Briskman and B. Pease (eds), *Critical Social Work: Theories and Practices for a Socially Just World* (2nd edition), Crow's Nest, NSW: Allen & Unwin, pp. 201–213.

MacKenzie, D. A. (1981) *Statistics in Britain 1865–1930: The Social Construction of Scientific Knowledge*, Edinburgh: Edinburgh University Press.

MacNaughton, G., Smith, K. and Lawrence, H. (2003) *Hearing Young Children's Voices: Consulting with Children from Birth to Eight Years of Age*, ACT Children's Strategy, Children's Services Branch, ACT Department of Education, Youth and Family Services, Canberra, and Centre for Equity and Innovation in Early Childhood, The University of Melbourne, Australia.

Mafile'o, T. (2008) 'Tongan social work practice', in M. Gray, J. Coates and M. Yellow Bird (eds), *Indigenous Social Work around the World: Towards Culturally Relevant Education and Practice*, Aldershot, UK: Ashgate, pp. 117–127.

Mahler, V. and Jesuit, D. K. (2006) 'Fiscal redistribution in the developed countries: New insights from the Luxembourg Income Study', *Socio-Economic Review*, 4 (3): 483–511.

Manicas, P. (2007) 'The social sciences since World War II: The rise and fall of Scientism', in W. Outhwaite and S. P. Turner (eds), *The Sage Handbook of Social Science Methodology*, Los Angeles and New York: Sage, pp. 7–31.

Marlow, C. and Boone, S. (2005) *Research Methods for Generalist Social Work* (4th edition), Belmont, CA: Brooks/Cole.

Marlow, C. R. (2011) *Research Methods for Generalist Social Work* (5th edition), Belmont, CA: Brooks/Cole.

Martel, Y. (2003) *The Life of Pi*, Edinburgh: Canongate.

Martin, M. (1994) 'Developing a feminist participative research framework: Evaluating the process', in B. Humphries and C. Truman (eds), *Re-thinking Social Research*, Aldershot, UK: Ashgate, pp. 123–145.

Mason, J. (1994) 'Linking qualitative and quantitative data analysis', in A. Bryman and R. G. Burgess (eds), *Analyzing Qualitative Data*, London: Routledge, pp. 89–110.

Massachussetts General Hospital (2010) www2.massgeneral.org/schoolpsychiatry/check-lists_table.asp (accessed 16 August 2012).

Maxwell, J. A. and Miller, B. A. (2008) 'Categorizing and connecting strategies in qualitative data analysis', in S. N. Hesse-Biber and P. Leavy (eds), *Handbook of Emergent Methods*, New York and London: Guilford Press, pp. 461–477.

Mayall, B. (2006) 'Child-adult relations in social space', in E. K. M. Tisdall, J. M. Davis, A. Prout and M. Hill (eds), *Children, Young People and Social Inclusion: Participation for What?*, Bristol, UK: Policy Press, pp. 199–215.

McDonnell, D. (1986) *Theories of Discourse: An Introduction*, Oxford: Basil Blackwell.

MacIntyre, G., Green Lister, P., Orme, J., Crisp, B. R., Manthorpe, J., Hussein, S., Moriarty, J., Stevens, M. and Sharpe, E. (2011) 'Using vignettes to evaluate the outcomes of student learning: Data from the evaluation of the new social work degree in England', *Social Work Education: The International Journal*, 30 (2): 207–222.

McKenzie, J. S. (2009) '"You don't know how lucky you are to be here!": Reflections on covert practices in an overt participant observation study', *Sociological Research Online*, 14 (2) 8, www.socresonline.org.uk/14/2/8.html, doi:10.5153/sro.1925.

McLachlan, G. and Reid, I. (1994) *Framing and Interpretation*, Melbourne: Melbourne University Press.

McLaughlin, H. (2007) *Understanding Social Work Research*, London: Sage.

McLaughlin, H. (2010) '"You've got to be a saint to be a social worker": The (mis)operation of fitness to practise processes for students already registered onto English social work training programmes', *Social Work Education: The International Journal*, 29 (1): 80–95.

McLaughlin, H. (2012) *Understanding Social Work Research* (2nd edition), London: Sage.

McNair, R. P. (2003) 'Lesbian health inequalities: A cultural minority issue for health professionals', *The Medical Journal of Australia*, 178 (12): 643–645.

Melrose, M. (2011) 'Regulating social research: Exploring the implications of extending ethical review procedures in social research', *Sociological Research Online*, 16 (2) 14.

Mertens, D. (2010) 'Social transformation and evaluation', *Evaluation Journal of Australasia*, 10 (2): 3–10.

Mickler, S. (1998) *The Myth of Privilege: Aboriginal Status, Media Visions, Public Ideas*, Fremantle, Western Australia: Fremantle Arts Centre Press.

Miles, M. B. and Huberman, A. M. (1994) *Qualitative Data Analysis: An Expanded Sourcebook* (2nd edition), Thousand Oaks, CA: Sage.

Milgram, S. (1963) 'Behavioural study of obedience', *Journal of Abnormal and Social Psychology*, 67: 371–378.

Millar, J., Thomson, J., Rae, W. and Horne, A. (2008) '"We're here tae make a difference", *Practical learning Achieving Excellence in the Human Services*, Proceedings of the 8th International PEPE Conference, Edinburgh, Scotland, 23–25 January.

Millei, Z. and Lee, L. (2007) '"Smarten up the parents": Whose agendas are we serving? Governing parents and children through the Smart Population Foundation Initiative in Australia', *Contemporary Issues in Early Childhood*, 8 (3): 208–21. Link to published version is available at: http://dx.doi.org/10.2304/ciec.2007.8.3.208 (accessed 1 November 2012).

Miller, P. (2009) 'Using knowledge in the practice of dealing with addiction: An ideal worth aiming for', in H. D'Cruz, S. Jacobs and A. Schoo (eds), *Knowledge-in-practice in the Caring Professions: Multidisciplinary Perspectives*, Aldershot, UK: Ashgate, pp. 213–234.

Miner, H. (1956) 'Body ritual among the Nacirema', *American Anthropologist*, 58 (3): 503–507.

Mitchell, J. P. (2007) 'Ethnography', in W. Outhwaite and S. P. Turner (eds), *The Sage Handbook of Social Science Methodology*, Los Angeles and New York: Sage, pp. 55–66.

Moore, G. T., Sugiyama, T. and O'Donnell, L. (2003) 'Children's *physical* environments rating scale', paper presented at the Early Childhood Education 2003 Conference, Hobart, Tasmania, Australia and the Te Tari Puna Ora o Aotearoa/New Zealand Childcare Association 40th Annual Conference, Wellington, New Zealand, July 2003. Published in R. Cornish (ed.), *Children: The Core of Society, Proceedings of the Australian Early Childhood Association Biennial Conference* [CD-ROM]. Canberra: Australian Early Childhood Association, 2003, paper 73, 9 pgs.

Morgan, S. (2000) 'Documentary and text analysis: Uncovering meaning in a worked example', in B. Humphries (ed.), *Research in Social Care and Social Welfare: Issues and Debates for Practice*, London: Jessica Kingsley, pp. 119–131.

Morgenshtern, M. and Novotna, G. (2012) '(In)(Out)Sider(s): White immigrant PhD students reflecting on their teaching experience', *Social Work Education: The International Journal*, 31 (1): 47–62.

Morison, S. and Greene, E. (1992) 'Juror and expert knowledge of child sexual abuse', *Child Abuse and Neglect*, 16 (4): 595–614.

Morland, I. and Willox, A. (eds) (2005) *Queer Theory*, Basingstoke, Hampshire and New York: Palgrave Macmillan.

Morrow, S. L. (2005) 'Quality and trustworthiness in qualitative research in counseling psychology', *Journal of Counseling Psychology*, 52 (2): 250–260, doi: 10.1037/0022-0167.52.2.250.

Morse, J. M., Barrett, M., Mayan, M., Olson, K. and Spiers, J. (2002) 'Verification strategies for establishing reliability and validity in qualitative research', *International Journal of Qualitative Methods*, 1 (2): 13–22.

Moser, C.A. and Kalton, G. (1989) *Survey Methods in Social Investigation*, London: Gower.

Moss, P. (2006) 'From children's services to children's spaces', in in E. K. M. Tisdall, J. M. Davis, A. Prout and M. Hill (eds), *Children, Young People and Social Inclusion: Participation for What?*, Bristol, UK: Policy Press, pp. 179–198.

Muetzelfeldt, M. and Briskman, L. (2000) 'Market rationality, organisational rationality and professional rationality: Experiences from the "contract state"', paper presented at the conference 'Playing the market game? Governance models in child and youth welfare', University of Bielefeld, Germany, 9–11 March.

Mulder, M. R. and Vrij, A. (1996) 'Explaining conversation rules to children: An intervention study to facilitate children's accurate responses', *Child Abuse and Neglect*, 20 (7): 623–632.

Munford, R. and Sanders, J. (eds) (2003) *Making a Difference in Families: Research that Creates Change*, Crow's Nest, NSW: Allen & Unwin.

Myers, J. E. B. (1993) 'Expert testimony regarding child sexual abuse', *Child Abuse and Neglect*, 17 (1): 175–185.

Nadkarni, V. (2010) 'Editorial: Social work education in Asia: New horizons', *Social Work Education: The International Journal*, 29 (8): 815–817.

Naples, N. A. (2007) 'Feminist methodology and its discontents', in W. Outhwaite and S. P. Turner (eds), *The Sage Handbook of Social Science Methodology*, Los Angeles and New York: Sage, pp. 547–564.

National Committee for the Prevention of Elder Abuse, *Multidisciplinary Teams*, www.preventelderabuse.org/communities/mdt.html (accessed 23 October 2012).

National Resource Center on ADHD, www.help4adhd.org/treatment/scales (accessed 16 August 2012).

Nelson, L. H. (1990) *Who Knows? From Quine to a Feminist Empiricism*, Philadelphia, PA: Temple University Press.

Neuman, W. L. (2006) *Social Research Methods: Qualitative and Quantitative Approaches* (6th edition), Boston, MA: Pearson Education/Allyn & Bacon.

Neuman, W. L. and Kreuger, L. W. (2003) *Social Work Research Methods: Qualitative and Quantitative Approaches*, Boston, MA: Allyn & Bacon.

NHMRC (National Health and Medical Research Council), Australian Research Council and Australian Vice Chancellor's Committee (2007) *National Statement on Ethical Conduct in Human Research*, Canberra: Commonwealth of Australia.

Nimmagadda, J. and Martell, D. R. (2008) 'Home-made social work: The two-way transfer of social work practice knowledge between India and the USA', in M. Gray, J. Coates and M. Yellow Bird (eds), *Indigenous Social Work around the World: Towards Culturally Relevant Education and Practice*, Aldershot, UK: Ashgate, pp. 141–152.

Norton, C. L., Russell, A., Wisner, B. and Uriarte, J. (2011) 'Reflective teaching in social work education: Findings from a participatory action research study', *Social Work Education: The International Journal*, 30 (4): 393–407.

Oakley, A. (1999) 'Interviewing women: A contradiction in terms', in H. Roberts (ed.), *Doing Feminist Research*, London: Routledge & Kegan Paul.

O'Connor, I., Wilson, J., Setterlund, D. and Hughes, M. (2008) *Social Work and Human Service Practice* (5th edition), Frenchs Forest, NSW: Pearson Education Australia.

O'Leary, Z. (2004) *The Essential Guide to Doing Research*, London: Sage.

Oliver, M. (1992) 'Changing the social relations of research production', *Disability, Handicap and Society*, 7 (2): 101–114.

Orme, J. and Shemmings, D. (2010) *Developing Research-based Social Work Practice*. Basingstoke, Hampshire: Palgrave Macmillan.

Osei-Hwedie, K. and Rankopo, M. J. (2008) 'Developing culturally relevant social work education in Africa: The case of Botswana', in M. Gray, J. Coates and M. Yellow Bird (eds), *Indigenous Social Work around the World: Towards Culturally Relevant Education and Practice*, Aldershot, UK: Ashgate, pp. 203–217.

Ostrander, N. and Chapin-Hogue, S. (2011) 'Learning from our mistakes: An autopsy of an unsuccessful university–community collaboration', *Social Work Education: The International Journal*, 30 (4): 454–464.

Ottenberg, S. (1990) 'Thirty years of field notes: Changing relationships to the text', in R. Sanjek (ed.), *Field Notes: The Makings of Anthropology*, Ithaca, NY: Cornell University Press, pp. 139–160.

Packham, C. (2000) 'Community auditing: Appropriate research methods for effective youth and community work interventions', in B. Humphries (ed.), *Research in*

Social Care and Social Welfare: Issues and Debates for Practice, London: Jessica Kingsley, pp. 102–118.

Palinkas, L. A., Schoenwald, S. K., Hoagwood, K., Landsverk, J., Chorpita, B. F. and Weisz, J. R. (2008) 'An ethnographic study of implementation of evidence-based treatments in child mental health: First steps', *Psychiatric Services*, 59 (7): 738–746.

Parton, N. (1991) *Governing the Family: Child Care, Child Protection and the State*, London: Macmillan.

Parton, N., Thorpe, D. and Wattam, C. (1997) *Child Protection: Risk and the Moral Order*, London: Macmillan.

Patton, M. Q. (1987) *How to Use Qualitative Methods in Evaluation*, Newbury Park, CA: Sage.

Patton, M. Q. (1990) *Qualitative Evaluation and Research Methods*, Thousand Oaks, CA: Sage.

Patton, M. Q. (1997) *Utilisation-focused Evaluation: The New Century Text* (3rd edition), London: Sage.

Paulsen, R. (2010) 'Mediated psychopathy: A critical discourse analysis of newspaper representations of aggression', *Kritike*, 4 (2): 60–86.

Payne, G. and Payne, J. (2004) *Key Concepts in Social Research*, London: Sage.

Pease, B. (2010) 'Challenging the dominant paradigm: Social work research, social justice and social change', in I. Shaw, K. Briar-Lawson, J. Orme and R. Ruckdeschel (eds), *The Sage Handbook of Social Work Research*, London: Sage, pp. 98–112.

Pease, B. and Fook, J. (eds) (1999) *Transforming Social Work Practice: Postmodern and Critical Perspectives*, Sydney: Allen & Unwin.

Peile, C., McCouat, M. and Rose-Miller, M. (1995) 'Child abuse paradigms: An analysis of the basic theoretical and epistemological assumptions underlying child abuse literature', unpublished paper, Department of Social Work and Social Policy, University of Queensland, Brisbane.

Percy-Smith, B. and Thomas, N. (eds) (2010) *A Handbook of Children and Young People's Participation: Perspectives from Theory and Practice*, London and New York: Routledge (e-book).

Petr, C. G. and Barney, D. D. (1993) 'Reasonable efforts for children with disabilities: The parents' perspective', *Social Work*, 38 (3): 247–254.

Pithouse, A. (1987) *Social Work: The Social Organisation of an Invisible Trade*, Aldershot, UK: Ashgate.

Pitts, M. and Smith, A. (eds) (2007) *Researching the Margins: Strategies for Ethical and Rigorous Research with Marginalised Communities*, Basingstoke, Hampshire: Palgrave Macmillan.

Plano Clark, V. L., Cresswell, J. W., O'Neil Green, D. and Shope, R. J. (2008) 'Mixing quantitative and qualitative approaches: An introduction to mixed methods research', in S. N. Hesse-Biber and P. Leavy (eds), *Handbook of Emergent Methods*, New York and London: Guilford Press, pp. 363–387.

Plath, D. (2012) 'Implementing evidence-based practice: An organisational perspective', *British Journal of Social Work*, doi:10.1093/bjsw/bcs169.

Platt, J. (1986) 'Functionalism and the survey: The relation of theory and method', *Sociological Review*, 34 (3): 501–536.

Pockett, R., Walker, E. and Dave, K. (2010) '"Last orders": Dying in a hospital setting', *Australian Social Work*, 63 (3): 250–265.

Potter, J. (1996) *Representing Reality*. London: Sage.

Powell, J., Lovelock, R. and Lyons, K. (2004) 'Introduction', in R. Lovelock, K. Lyons and J. Powell (eds), *Reflecting on Social Work: Discipline and Profession*, Aldershot, UK: Ashgate, pp. 1–19.

Prout, A. and Tisdall, E. K. M. (2006) 'Conclusion: Social inclusion, the welfare state and understanding children's participation', in E. K. M. Tisdall, J. M. Davis, A. Prout and M. Hill (eds), *Children, Young People and Social Inclusion: Participation for What?*, Bristol, UK: Policy Press, pp. 235–246.

Punch, M. (1986) *The Politics and Ethics of Fieldwork*, Qualitative Research Methods Series, Newbury Park, CA: Sage.

Punch, M. (1993) 'Observation and the police: The research experience', in M. Hammersley (ed.), *Social Research: Philosophy, Politics and Practice*, London: Sage, pp. 181–199.

Punch, K. (1998) *Introduction to Social Research: Quantitative and Qualitative Approaches*, London: Sage.

Pung, A. (2006) *Unpolished Gem*, Melbourne: Black Inc.

Quine, S. and Browning, C. (2007) 'Methodological and ethical issues in conducting research with older people', in M. Pitts and A. Smith (eds), *Researching the Margins: Strategies for Ethical and Rigorous Research with Marginalised Communities*, Basingstoke, Hampshire: Palgrave Macmillan, pp. 130–142.

Rabbitts, E. and Fook, J. (1996) 'Empowering practitioners to publish: A writer's and a publisher's perspectives', in J. Fook (ed.), *The Reflective Researcher: Social Workers' Theories of Practice Research*, St Leonards, NSW: Allen & Unwin.

Rapp, C. A., Etzel-Wise, D., Marty, D., Coffman, M., Carlson, L., Asher, D., Callaghan, J. and Holter M. (2010) 'Barriers to evidence-based practice implementation: Results of a qualitative study', *Community Mental Health Journal*, 46 (2): 112–118 (E-Pub. 2009, doi:10.1007/s10597-009-9238-z).

Rasinski, K. A. (1989) 'The effect of question wording on public support for government spending', *Public Opinion*, 53: 388–94.

Reason, P. and Bradbury, H. (eds) (2008a) *The Sage Handbook of Action Research: Participative Inquiry and Practice* (2nd edition), London: Sage.

Reason, P. and Bradbury, H. (2008b) 'Introduction', in P. Reason and H. Bradbury (eds), *The Sage Handbook of Action Research: Participative Inquiry and Practice* (2nd edition), London: Sage, pp. 1–13.

Reason, P. and Bradbury, H. (eds) (2008c) 'Exemplars: Part III', in P. Reason and H. Bradbury (eds), *The Sage Handbook of Action Research: Participative Inquiry and Practice* (2nd edition), London: Sage.

Reinharz, S. (1992) *Feminist Methods in Social Research*, New York: Oxford University Press.

Renzetti, C. (1992) *Violent Betrayal: Partner Abuse in Lesbian Relationships*, Newbury Park, CA: Sage.

Renzetti, C. and Lee, M. (eds) (1993) *Researching Sensitive Topics*, Thousand Oaks, CA: Sage.

Reynolds, H. (2000) 'Indigenous social welfare: From a low priority to recognition and reconciliation', in A. McMahon, J. Thomson and C. Williams (eds), *Understanding the Australian Welfare State: Key Documents and Themes* (2nd edition), Croydon, Victoria: Macmillan Education Australia, pp. 97–109.

Richardson, B. (2011) 'A matter of choice: A critical discourse analysis of ECEC policy in Canada's 2006 federal election', *Occasional Paper No. 25*, Toronto, Canada: Childcare Resource and Research Unit.

Richardson, L. (1994) 'Writing: A method of inquiry', in N. K. Denzin and Y. S. Lincoln (eds), *Handbook of Qualitative Research*, Newbury Park, CA: Sage, pp. 516–529.

Richardson, L. (2000) 'Writing: A method of inquiry' in N. K. Denzin and Y. S. Lincoln (eds), *Handbook of Qualitative Research* (2nd edition), Thousand Oaks, CA: Sage, pp. 923–948.

Richardson, L. and St Pierre, E. A. (2005) 'Writing: A method of inquiry', in N. K. Denzin and Y. S. Lincoln (eds), *The Sage Handbook of Qualitative Research* (3rd edition), Thousand Oaks, CA: Sage, pp. 959–978.

Ridge, T. (2006) 'Childhood poverty: A barrier to social participation and inclusion', in E. K. M. Tisdall, J. M. Davis, A. Prout and M. Hill (eds), *Children, Young People and Social Inclusion: Participation for What?*, Bristol, UK: Policy Press, pp. 23–38.

Riessman, C. K. (1993) *Narrative Analysis*, Qualitative Research Methods Series, Newbury Park, CA: Sage.

Riessman, C. K. (1994a) 'Subjectivity matters: The positioned investigator', in C. K. Riessman (ed.), *Qualitative Studies in Social Work Research*, Newbury Park, CA: Sage, pp. 133–138.

Riessman, C. K. (1994b) 'Narrative approaches to trauma', in C. K. Riessman (ed.), *Qualitative Studies in Social Work Research*, Thousand Oaks, CA: Sage, pp. 67–71.

Rintoul, S. (1993) *The Wailing: A National Black Oral History*, Port Melbourne, Victoria: William Heinemann Australia.

Robson, E. (2010) 'Children's bodies: Working and caring in sub-Saharan Africa', in K. Hörschelmann and R. Colls (eds), *Contested Bodies of Childhood and Youth*, Basingstoke, Hampshire: Palgrave Macmillan, pp. 148–162.

Rojek, C., Peacock, G. and Collins, S. (1988) *Social Work and Received Ideas*, London: Routledge.

Rose, G. (2001) *Visual Methodologies*, London: Sage.

Rose, N. (1998) *Inventing Our Selves: Psychology, Power, and Personhood*, Cambridge, UK: Cambridge University Press.

Rose, N. (1999a) *Governing the Soul: The Shaping of the Private Self* (2nd edition), London and New York: Free Association Books.

Rose, N. (1999b) *Powers of Freedom: Reframing Political Thought*, Cambridge, UK: Cambridge University Press.

Rowntree, D. (2004) *Statistics without Tears: An Introduction for Non-Mathematicians*, Boston, MA: Pearson.

Royse, D. (1999) *Research Methods in Social Work*, Chicago, IL: Nelson-Hall.

Royse, D. and Thyer, B. (1996) *Program Evaluation* (2nd edition), Chicago, IL: Nelson-Hall.

Royse, D., Thyer, B., Padgett, D. and Logan, T. K. (2001) *Program Evaluation: An Introduction* (3rd edition), Belmont, CA: Brooks/Cole.

Rubin, A. and Babbie, E. (2007) *Essential Research Methods for Social Work*, Belmont, CA: Brooks/Cole.

Rubin, A. and Babbie, E. (2008) *Research Methods for Social Work* (6th edition), Belmont, CA: Thomson/Brooks Cole.

Rubin, A. and Babbie, E. (2011) *Research Methods for Social Work* (7th edition), Belmont, CA: Brooks/Cole.

Russell, R. and Tyler, M. (2002) 'Thank heaven for little girls', *Sociology*, 36 (3): 619–637.

Ryan, M. and Martyn, R. (1996) 'Writing about social work education: A content analysis of Australian journal articles 1983–1993', *Australian Social Work*, 49 (4): 19–23.

Ryan, M. and Martyn, R. (1997) 'Women writing on social work education: Findings from a study of the content analysis of Australian journal articles 1983–1993', *Australian Social Work*, 50 (2): 13–18.

Ryan, M. and Sheehan, R. (2009) 'Research articles in *Australian Social Work* from 1998–2007: A content analysis', *Australian Social Work*, 62 (4): 525–542.

Said, E. (1978) *Orientalism*, Harmondsworth: Penguin.

Salmon, G. (1994) 'Personal view: Working in a multidisciplinary team: Need it be so difficult?', *British Medical Journal*, 309: 1520.

Samuel, W. W. E. (2002) *German Boy: A Child in War*, London: Sceptre/Hodder & Stoughton.

Sanders, J. and Munford, R. (2003) 'Strengthening practice through research: Research in organisations', in R. Munford and J. Sanders (eds), *Making a Difference in Families: Research that Creates Change*, Crow's Nest, NSW: Allen & Unwin.

Sarantakos, S. (2005) *Social Research* (3rd edition), Basingstoke, Hampshire: Palgrave Macmillan.

Sardar, Z. (2011) 'The boy with no identity', *New Internationalist*, 445 (September), pp. 20–21.

Saunders, P. (2002) *The Ends and Means of Welfare: Coping with Economic and Social Change in Australia*, Cambridge, UK: Cambridge University Press.

Savvakis, M. and Tzanakis, M. (2004) 'The researcher, the field and the issue of entry: Two cases of ethnographic research concerning asylums in Greece', *Sociological Research Online*, 9 (2), www.socresonline.org.uk/9/2/savvakis.html.

Scanlon, J. (1993) 'Challenging the imbalance of power in feminist oral history – developing a take-and-give methodology, *Women's Studies International Forum*, 16 (6), 639–645.

Scarborough, H. (ed.) (1996) *The Management of Expertise*, London: Macmillan.

Schiele, J. H. (ed.) (2011) *Social Welfare Policy: Regulation and Resistance among People of Color*, Los Angeles, CA: Sage.

Schofield, J. W. (1993) 'Increasing the generalizability of qualitative research', in M. Hammersley (ed.), *Social Research: Philosophy, Politics and Practice*, London: Sage, pp. 200–225.

Schön, D. (1983) *The Reflective Practitioner: How Professionals Think in Action*, New York: Basic Books.

Schratz, M. and Steiner-Löffler, U. (1998) 'Pupils using photographs in school self-evaluation', in J. Prosser (ed.), *Image-based Research: A Sourcebook for Qualitative Researchers*, London: Falmer Press, pp. 235–251.

Schutt, R. (1999) *Investigating the Social World* (2nd edition), Thousand Oaks, CA: Pine Forge Press.

Seale, C. (2002) 'Quality issues in qualitative inquiry', *Qualitative Social Work*, 1 (1): 97–110.

Sevenhuijsen, S. (1998) *Citizenship and the Ethics of Care: Feminist Considerations on Justice, Morality and Politics*, London: Routledge.

Shaw, I. (2005) 'Practitioner research: Evidence or critique?, *British Journal of Social Work* 35 (8): 1231–1248, doi: 10.1093/bjsw/bch223.

Shaw, I. (2007) 'Is social work research distinctive?', *Social Work Education: The International Journal*, 27 (7): 659–669.

Shaw, I. (2011) *Evaluating in Practice* (2nd edition), Aldershot, UK: Ashgate.

Shaw, I. and Norton, M. (2007) *The Kinds and Quality of Social Work Research in UK Universities*, London: Social Care Institute of Excellence.

Sheean, F. and Cameron, J. M. (2009) 'The risky business of birth', in H. D'Cruz, S. Jacobs and A. Schoo (eds), *Knowledge-in-practice in the Caring Professions: Multidisciplinary Perspectives*, Aldershot, UK: Ashgate, pp. 141–160.

Sheldon, B. (1998) 'Social work practice in the 21st century', *Research on Social Work Practice*, 8 (5): 577–588.

Sheldon, B. (2000) *Evidence-based Practice*, Lyme Regis, UK: Russell House.

Sheldon, B. (2001) 'The validity of evidence-based practice in social work: A reply to Stephen Webb', *British Journal of Social Work*, 31 (5): 801–809.

Sheldon, B. and Chilvers, R. (2000) *Evidence-based Social Care: A Study of Prospects and Problems*, Lyme Regis, UK: Russell House.

Shenton, A. K. (2004) 'Strategies for ensuring trustworthiness in qualitative research projects', *Education for Information*, 22: 63–75.

Shlonsky, A. and Wagner, D. (2005) 'The next step: Integrating actuarial risk assessment and clinical judgment into an evidence-based practice framework in CPS case management', *Children & Youth Services Review*, 27 (4): 409–427.

Silverman, D. (1998) 'Qualitative/quantitative', in C. Jenks (ed.), *Core Sociological Dichotomies*, London: Sage, pp. 78–95.

Sim, J. and Wright, C. (2000) *Research in Health Care: Concepts, Designs and Methods*, Cheltenham, UK: Stanley Thorne.

Sin, R. (2008) 'Reconfiguring "Chineseness" in the international discourse on social work in China', in M. Gray, J. Coates and M. Yellow Bird (eds), *Indigenous Social Work around the World: Towards Culturally Relevant Education and Practice*, Aldershot, UK: Ashgate, pp. 165–176.

Skeggs, B. (1994) 'Situating the production of feminist ethnography', in M. Maynard and J. Purvis (eds), *Researching Women's Lives from a Feminist Perspective*, London: Taylor and Francis, pp. 72–92.

Slattery, D. (2010) 'The political inherency of evaluation: The impact of politics on the outcome of 10 years of evaluative scrutiny of Australia's mandatory detention policy', *Evaluation Journal of Australasia*, 10 (1): 17–27.

Smith, A. and Pitts, M. (2007) 'Researching the margins: An introduction', in M. Pitts and A. Smith (eds), *Researching the Margins: Strategies for Ethical and Rigorous Research with Marginalised Communities*, Basingstoke, Hampshire: Palgrave Macmillan, pp. 3–41.

Smith, A. D. (1993) *Fires in the Mirror: Crown Heights, Brooklyn, and other Identities*, New York: Anchor.

Smith, L. T. (1999) *Decolonizing Methodologies: Research and Indigenous Peoples*, London: Zed Books.

Smith, L. T. (2005) 'On tricky ground: Researching the native in the age of uncertainty', in N. K. Denzin and Y. S. Lincoln (eds), *The Sage Handbook of Qualitative Research* (3rd edition), Thousand Oaks, CA: Sage, pp. 85–107.

Smith, M., Meyer, S., Stagnitti, K. and Schoo, A. (2009) 'Knowledge and reasoning in practice: An example from physiotherapy and occupational therapy', in H. D'Cruz, S. Jacobs and A. Schoo (eds), *Knowledge-in-practice in the Caring Professions: Multidisciplinary Perspectives*, Aldershot, UK: Ashgate, pp. 193–212.

Smith, R. (2009) *Doing Social Work Research*, Maidenhead, UK: Open University Press.

Snizek, W. E. (1976) 'An empirical assessment of "sociology: a multiple paradigm science"', *American Sociologist*, 11 (4): 217–219.

Stanley, L. and Wise, S. (1993) *Breaking Out Again: Feminist Ontology and Epistemology* (2nd edition), London: Routledge.

Stevenson, M. (2010) 'Flexible and responsive research: Developing rights-based emancipatory disability research methodology in collaboration with young adults', *Australian Social Work*, 63 (1): 35–50.

Stivers, C. (1993) 'Reflections on the role of personal narrative in social science', *Signs: Journal of Women in Culture and Society*, 18 (2): 408–425.

Strauss, B. and Corbin, J. (1990) *Basics of Qualitative Research*, Newbury Park, CA: Sage.

Strauss, A. and Corbin, J. (1998) *Basics of Qualitative Research* (2nd edition), Thousand Oaks, CA: Sage. [Also cited in Denzin and Ryan (2007) as Strauss, A. and Corbin, J. (1999) *Basics of Qualitative Research* (2nd edition), Thousand Oaks, CA: Sage.]

Tadajewski, M. (2008) 'Incommensurable paradigms, cognitive bias and the politics of marketing theory', *Marketing Theory*, 8 (3): 273–297, doi: 10.1177/1470593108093557.

Tadajewski, M. (2009) 'The debate that won't die? Values incommensurability, antagonism and theory choice', *Organization*, 16 (4): 467–485, doi: 10.1177/1350508409104504.

Takahashi, R. (2011) 'Japanese American resistance to World War II: Executive, legislative, and judicial policies', in J. H. Schiele (ed.), *Social Welfare Policy: Regulation and Resistance among People of Color*, Los Angeles, CA: Sage, pp. 135–163.

Taylor, B. (1993) 'Phenomenological method in nursing: Theory versus reality', in D. Colquhoun and A. Kellehear (eds), *Health Research in Practice: Political, Ethical and Methodological Issues*, London: Chapman & Hall, pp. 112–125.

Taylor, C. and White, S. (2000) *Practising Reflexivity in Health and Welfare*, Buckingham, UK: Open University Press.

Taylor, C. and White, S. (2001) 'Knowledge, truth and reflexivity: The problem of judgement in social work', *Journal of Social Work*, 1 (1): 37–59.

Taylor, J. (2011) 'The intimate insider: Negotiating the ethics of friendship when doing insider research', *Qualitative Research*, 11 (1): 3–22, doi: 10.1177/1468794110384447.

Teare, J. F., Peterson, R. W., Authier, K., Schroeder, L. and Daly, D. L. (1998) 'Maternal satisfaction following post-shelter family reunification', *Child and Family Forum*, 27 (2): 125–138.

Teddlie, C., Tashakkori, A. and Johnson, B. (2008) 'Emergent techniques in the gathering and analysis of mixed methods data', in S. N. Hesse-Biber and P. Leavy (eds), *Handbook of Emergent Methods*, New York and London: Guilford Press, pp. 389–413.

Teo, P. (2000) 'Racism in the news: A critical discourse analysis of news reporting in two Australian newspapers', *Discourse Society*, 11 (1): 7–49.

The College of Social Work (England) (2012), Professional Capabilities Framework (PCF), www.collegeofsocialwork.org/pcf.aspx (accessed 23 August 2012).

Thomas, R. (1996) 'Statistics as organizational products', *Sociological Research Online*, 1 (3), www.socresonline.org.uk/socresonline/1/3/5.html.

Thompson, E. H. (Jr.) (1994) 'Older men as invisible men in contemporary society', in E. H. Thompson (Jr.) (ed.), *Older Men's Lives*, Thousand Oaks, CA: Sage, pp. 1–21.

Thomson, A. (1996) *Critical Reasoning: A Practical Introduction*, London: Routledge.

Thorpe, D. (1994) *Evaluating Child Protection*, Buckingham, UK: Open University Press.

Tilbury, C., Buys, N. and Creed, P. (2009) 'Perspectives of young people in care about their school-to-work transition', *Australian Social Work*, 62 (4): 476–490.

Tomass, M. (2001) 'Incommensurability of economic paradigms: A case study of the monetary theories of Mises and Marx', *Review of Political Economy*, 13 (2): 221–243.

Trials of Galileo, Compass, ABC TV, Sunday, 9 May 2010, 10.10–11.10 pm, www.abc.net.au/compass/pastepisodes.htm.

Tronto, J. (1993) *Moral Boundaries: A Political Argument for the Ethics of Care*, London: Routledge.

Truman, C. (2000) 'New social movements and social research', in C. Truman, D. M. Mertens and B. Humphries (eds), *Research and Inequality*, London: UCL Press, pp. 24–36.

Truman, C. and Humphries, B. (1994) 'Re-thinking social research: Research in an unequal world', in B. Humphries and C. Truman (eds), *Re-thinking Social Research: Anti-discriminatory Approaches in Research Methodology*, Aldershot, UK: Ashgate, pp. 1–20.

van Blerk, L. (2010) 'AIDS, mobility and commercial sex in Ethiopia', in K. Hörschelmann and R. Colls (eds), *Contested Bodies of Childhood and Youth*, Basingstoke, Hampshire: Palgrave Macmillan, pp. 232–246.

van Maanen, J. (1988) 'Field work culture and ethnography', *Tales of the Field*, Chicago, IL: University of Chicago Press, pp. 1–12.

van Norman, G. (1998) 'Interdisciplinary team issues', *Ethical Topics in Medicine*, Washinton, DC: University of Washington. Available at: http://depts.washington.edu/bioethx/topics/team.html (accessed 23 October 2012; date last modified 11 April 2008).

van Rooyen, C. C. (2011) 'Analysis of qualitative data', in C. R. Marlow (ed.), *Research Methods for Generalist Social Work* (5th edition), Belmont, CA: Brooks/Cole, pp. 213–234.

Verolme, H. E. (2000) *The Children's House of Belsen*, Fremantle, Western Australia: Fremantle Arts Centre Press.

Wadsworth, Y. (2011) *Do It Yourself Social Research* (3rd edition), Walnut Creek, CA: Left Coast Press.

Walsh-Tapiata, W. (2008) 'The past, the present and the future: The New Zealand Indigenous experience of social work', in M. Gray, J. Coates and M. Yellow Bird (eds), *Indigenous Social Work around the World: Towards Culturally Relevant Education and Practice*, Aldershot, UK: Ashgate, pp. 107–115.

Ward, P. R., Thompson, J., Barber, R., Armitage, C. J., Boote, J. D., Cooper, C. L. and Jones, G. L. (2010) 'Critical perspectives on "consumer involvement" in health research: Epistemological dissonance and the know-do gap', *Journal of Sociology*, 46 (1): 63–82.

Weaver, H. N. (2008) 'Indigenous social work in the United States: Reflections on Indian tacos, Trojan Horses and canoes filled with indigenous revolutionaries', in M. Gray, J. Coates and M. Yellow Bird (eds), *Indigenous Social Work around the World: Towards Culturally Relevant Education and Practice*, Aldershot, UK: Ashgate, pp. 71–81.

Webb, E. J., Campbell, D. T., Schwartz, R. D. and Sechrest, L. (1966) *Unobtrusive Measures in the Social Sciences*, Chicago, IL: Rand McNally.

Webb, S. (2001) 'Some considerations on the validity of evidence-based practice in social work', *British Journal of Social Work*, 31: 57–79.

Wendt, S. and Seymour, S. (2010) 'Applying post-structuralist ideas to empowerment: Implications for social work education', *Social Work Education: The International Journal*, 29 (6): 670–682.

Wenger, E. (1998) *Communities of Practice: Learning, Meaning and Identity*, Cambridge, UK: Cambridge University Press.

Wetherell, M. (1994) 'Commentary: The knots of power and negotiation, blank and complex subjectivities', *Journal of Community and Applied Social Psychology*, 4 (4): 305–308.

Wetton, N. and McWhirter, J. (1998) 'Images and curriculum development in health education', in J. Prosser (ed.), *Image-based Research: A Sourcebook for Qualitative Researchers*, London: Falmer Press, pp. 263–283.

Wilensky, H. (2002) *Rich Democracies: Political Economy, Public Policy, and Performance*, Los Angeles: University of California Press.

Williams, M., Tutty, L.M. and Grinnell, R.M. Jr. (1995) *Research in Social Work: An Introduction*, Itasca, IL: F. E. Peacock.

Williamson, E., Goodenough, T., Kent, J. and Ashcroft, R. (2005) 'Conducting research with children: The limits of confidentiality and child protection protocols', *Children and Society*, 19: 397–409, doi: 10.1002/CHI.852.

Witkin, S. L. (1992) 'Should empirically-based practice be taught in BSW and MSW programs? No!', *Journal of Social Work Education*, 28 (3): 265–268.

Witkin, S. L. (1995) 'Whither social work research? An essay review', *Social Work*, 40: 424–428.

Wolf, M. A. (1992) *A Thrice-told Tale: Feminism, Post-modernism, and Ethnographic Responsibility*, Stanford, CA: Stanford University Press.

Wolf, M.A. (1996) 'Afterword: Musing from an old gray wolf', in D. L. Wolf (ed.), *Feminist Dilemmas in Fieldwork*, Boulder, CO: Westview Press, pp. 215–222.

Wolfe, R. (1992) 'Data management', in M. C. Alkin (ed.), *Encyclopaedia of Educational Research* (6th edition), New York: Macmillan, pp. 293–299.

Wood, L. and Kroger, R. O. (2000) *Doing Discourse Analysis: Methods for Studying Action in Talk and Text*, Thousand Oaks, CA, and London: Sage.

Woodyer, T. (2008) 'The body as research tool: Embodied practice and children's geographies', *Children's Geographies*, 6 (4): 349–362.

Woolnough, S. and Arkell, E., with Tobias, J. (2010) *Improving Cancer Outcomes: An Analysis of the Implementation of the UK's Cancer Strategies 2006–2010*, London: Cancer Research UK.

Xu, Q. (2011) 'The impact of deportation on Chinese Americans: A family's pain, a community's struggle', in J. H. Schiele (ed.), *Social Welfare Policy: Regulation and Resistance among People of Color*, Los Angeles, CA: Sage, pp. 185–211.

Yan, M. C. and Tsang, A. K. T. (2008) 'Re-envisioning indigenization: When *Bentuhuade* and *Bentude* social work intersect in China', in M. Gray, J. Coates and M. Yellow Bird (eds), *Indigenous Social Work around the World: Towards Culturally Relevant Education and Practice*, Aldershot, UK: Ashgate, pp. 191–202.

Yellow Bird, M. (2008) 'Postscript: Terms of endearment. A brief dictionary for decolonizing social work with Indigenous Peoples', in M. Gray, J. Coates and M. Yellow Bird (eds), *Indigenous Social Work around the World: Towards Culturally Relevant Education and Practice*, Aldershot, UK: Ashgate, pp. 275–291.

Yellow Bird, M. and Gray, M. (2008) 'Indigenous people and the language of social work', in M. Gray, J. Coates and M. Yellow Bird (eds), *Indigenous Social Work around the World: Towards Culturally Relevant Education and Practice*, Aldershot, UK: Ashgate, pp. 59–69.

Yin, R. K. (1994) *Case Study Research: Design and Methods* (2nd edition), Thousand Oaks, CA: Sage.

Yuen-Tsang, A. and Ku, B. (2008) 'A journey of a thousand miles begins with one step: The development of culturally relevant social work education and fieldwork practice in China', in M. Gray, J. Coates and M. Yellow Bird (eds), *Indigenous Social Work around the World: Towards Culturally Relevant Education and Practice*, Aldershot, UK: Ashgate, pp. 177–190.

Index

NOTE: Page numbers in *italic type* refer to figures and tables.